WordPress 3 Complete

Create your own complete website or blog from scratch with WordPress

April Hodge Silver

[PACKT] open source *
PUBLISHING   community experience distilled

BIRMINGHAM - MUMBAI

WordPress 3 Complete

First published: January 2010

Production Reference: 1180111

Published by Packt Publishing Ltd.
32 Lincoln Road
Olton
Birmingham, B27 6PA, UK.

ISBN 978-1-849514-10-1

www.packtpub.com

Cover Image by Charwak A (charwak86@gmail.com)

Credits

Authors
April Hodge Silver

Reviewers
Grigore Alexandru
Srikanth AD
Natalie MacLees

Acquisition Editor
Usha Iyer

Development Editor
Susmita Panda

Technical Editor
Kavita Iyer

Copy Editor
Neha Shetty

Editorial Team Leader
Akshara Aware

Project Team Leader
Ashwin Shetty

Project Coordinator
Poorvi Nair

Proofreader
Clyde Jenkins

Indexer
Tejal Daruwale

Production Coordinator
Aparna Bhagat

Cover Work
Aparna Bhagat

About the Author

April Hodge Silver has been designing and developing new websites from scratch since 1999, just before her graduation from Columbia University. Early in her career, she worked for several web companies and startups, including DoubleClick and About.com. Since 2004, she has been self-employed through her company, Springthistle Design, and has worked with a staggering variety of companies, non-profits, and individuals to realize their website dreams. In her professional work, April's focus is always on usability, efficiency, flexibility, clean design, and client happiness. WordPress is the best solution for many of Springthistle's Clients, though April also develops custom web applications using PHP and MySQL. More about April's professional work at `http://springthistle.com`.

In her free time, April enjoys creating recipes in the kitchen, reading books, and creating artwork, which she displays at `http://artistapril.com`.

I am so grateful to everyone at Packt who worked with me to make this book possible. Also, many thanks go to my wife Tessa, who supported me in so many ways while I was working on this book. Finally, thanks go to Ruth and Hazel, who provided key guidance on commas.

About the Reviewers

Grigore Alexandru is a XHTML/CSS/JAVASCRIPT programmer, with major WordPress knowledge and coding skills, currently working at OSF-Global Services in Romania. He is currently studying at the FEAA College in the A.I Cuza University in Iasi, Romania, learning economical sciences.

Alex perfected his skills during the work at OSF-Global services, learning in depth about CSS/XHTML coding skills, as well as jQuery programming and other web based tech. Currently, Alex is developing for the company at which he currently works and also for ThemeForest WordPress and HTML sections.

> First of all, I would like to thank my company for letting me advance on my skills, and also I would like to thank PACKT Publishing for allowing me to review the second WordPress book so far. I hope that we will work together again in the future.

Srikanth AD is a web developer, SEO consultant, and tech blogger. He is passionate about web development and optimizing websites for better search engine visibility and ranking.

He contributes articles and reviews pertaining to web design trends, web applications, and other resources across multiple blogs. He has written articles for some of the popular blogs, such as MakeUseOf, TheNextWeb, QuickOnlineTips, and 1stWebDesigner.

Portfolio: `http://www.srikanth.techonaut.com`.

Natalie MacLees is the founder of Purple Pen Productions (`purplepen.com`), an interactive agency based in Los Angeles, California. She has been designing websites since 1997 and is a passionate advocate of both accessibility and usability. She loves teaching and sharing her knowledge, both in seminars and workshops and also with her clients. She discovered WordPress a few years ago as a flexible, extendable, and quick way to build robust websites that clients could manage on their own. She is the organizer of the Southern California WordPress Meetup Group.

www.PacktPub.com

Support files, eBooks, discount offers and more

You might want to visit www.PacktPub.com for support files and downloads related to your book.

Did you know that Packt offers eBook versions of every book published, with PDF and ePub files available? You can upgrade to the eBook version at www.PacktPub. com and as a print book customer, you are entitled to a discount on the eBook copy. Get in touch with us at service@packtpub.com for more details.

At www.PacktPub.com, you can also read a collection of free technical articles, sign up for a range of free newsletters and receive exclusive discounts and offers on Packt books and eBooks.

http://PacktLib.PacktPub.com

Do you need instant solutions to your IT questions? PacktLib is Packt's online digital book library. Here, you can access, read and search across Packt's entire library of books.

Why Subscribe?

- Fully searchable across every book published by Packt
- Copy and paste, print and bookmark content
- On demand and accessible via web browser

Free Access for Packt account holders

If you have an account with Packt at www.PacktPub.com, you can use this to access PacktLib today and view nine entirely free books. Simply use your login credentials for immediate access.

Table of Contents

Preface

WordPress 3 Complete begins from scratch, starting with how to install WordPress, all the way to the most advanced topics such as creating your own themes, writing plugins, and including custom post types in your website. Starting with downloading and installing the core WordPress software, you will take a detailed look at WordPress settings and also choose the settings that will work best for your website or blog. After that, the book will teach you all about content management functionality for your site from posts and pages to categories and tags, all the way to links, media, menus, images, galleries and more. Finally, you'll learn how to create your own themes and plugins to enhance the overall functionality of your website. Once you're done with WordPress 3 Complete, you'll be an expert in everything WordPress, from content management through technical steps such as backing up your site.

What this book covers

Chapter 1, Introduction to WordPress, explains how WordPress is an excellent software that can run your website (blog or not). It's packed with excellent features, and is so flexible that it can really do anything you want, and it has a wealth of online resources. Additionally, it's super easy-to-use, and you need no special skills or prior experience to use it. Last but not least, it is free!

Chapter 2, Getting Started, explains how to install WordPress on a remote server, change the basic default settings of your blog, write posts, and comment on those posts.

Chapter 3, Creating Blog Content, teaches everything you need to know to add content to your blog and manage that content, be it about posts, categories and comments, or tags, spam, and excerpts.

Chapter 4, Pages, Plugins, Image Galleries Menus, and More, explores all of the content WordPress can manage that's not directly about blogging. You can also learn about static pages, menus, bookmark links, the media library, image galleries, plugins, and more.

Chapter 5, Choosing and Installing Themes, describes how to manage the basic look of your WordPress website. You also learn where to find themes, why they are useful, and how to implement new themes on your WordPress website.

Chapter 6, Developing Your Own Theme, explains how to make your own theme. With just the most basic HTML and CSS abilities, you can create a design and turn it into a fully functional WordPress theme.

Chapter 7, Feeds and Podcasting, explains what an RSS feed is and how to make feeds available for our WordPress blog. It also explores how to syndicate a whole blog or just posts within a certain category, and how to create your own podcast with or without the help of plugins.

Chapter 8, Developing Plugins and Widgets, teaches everything you need to know about creating basic plugins and widgets, how to structure the PHP file, where to put your functions, and how to use hooks. It also teaches about adding management pages and adding a widget that is related to a plugin.

Chapter 9, Community Blogging, explains how to manage a group of users working with a single blog, which is a community of users. Community blogging can play an important role in a user group, or a news website. It also explains how to manage the different levels of privileges for users in a community.

Chapter 10, Creating a Non-Blog Website, explores designing and building a basic theme that focuses primarily on non-blog content. It also creates multiple widget areas, multiple menu areas, and a smooth slider to the homepage.

Chapter 11, Administrator's Reference, covers many of the common administrative tasks you may face when you're managing a WordPress-driven website. This includes backing up your database and files, moving your WordPress installation from one server or folder to another, and doing general problem-solving and troubleshooting.

What you need for this book

- A Computer
- A Web browser
- A text editor
- FTP software

Users may like a text editor that highlights code (such as Coda, TextMate, HTMLKit, and so on), but a simple text editor is all that's required.

Users may like to run a local copy of WordPress on their computer, in which case they need a server like Apache and MySQL installed (though WAMP and MAMP would take care of all that for them), but it's also not necessary as they could do the entire thing remotely.

Who this book is for

This book is a guide to WordPress for both beginners and those who have slightly more advanced knowledge of WordPress. If you are new to blogging and want to create your own blog or website in a simple and straightforward manner, then this book is for you. It is also for people who want to learn to customize and expand the capabilities of a WordPress website. You do not require any detailed knowledge of programming or web development, and any IT-confident user will be able to use the book to produce an impressive website.

Conventions

In this book, you will find a number of styles of text that distinguish between different kinds of information. Here are some examples of these styles, and an explanation of their meaning.

Code words in text are shown as follows: "We can include other contexts through the use of the include directive."

A block of code is set as follows:

```
<!DOCTYPE html>
<html dir="ltr" lang="en-US">
<head>
    <meta charset="UTF-8" />
    <title>Blog title</title>
    <style type="text/css">@import url("style.css");</style>
```

When we wish to draw your attention to a particular part of a code block, the relevant lines or items are set in bold:

```
function ahs_doctypes_regex($text) {
    $types = get_option('ahs_supportedtypes');
    $types = ereg_replace(',[ ]*',',|',$types);
    $text =
```

New terms and **important words** are shown in bold. Words that you see on the screen, in menus or dialog boxes for example, appear in the text like this: " To add a new page, go to your WP Admin and navigate to **Pages | Add New** ".

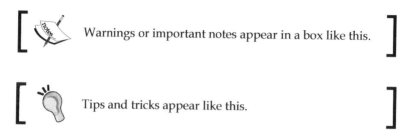

Warnings or important notes appear in a box like this.

Tips and tricks appear like this.

Reader feedback

Feedback from our readers is always welcome. Let us know what you think about this book—what you liked or may have disliked. Reader feedback is important for us to develop titles that you really get the most out of.

To send us general feedback, simply send an e-mail to feedback@packtpub.com, and mention the book title via the subject of your message.

If there is a book that you need and would like to see us publish, please send us a note in the **SUGGEST A TITLE** form on www.packtpub.com or e-mail suggest@packtpub.com.

If there is a topic that you have expertise in and you are interested in either writing or contributing to a book, see our author guide on www.packtpub.com/authors.

Customer support

Now that you are the proud owner of a Packt book, we have a number of things to help you to get the most from your purchase.

Downloading the example code for the book

You can download the example code files for all Packt books you have purchased from your account at http://www.PacktPub.com. If you purchased this book elsewhere, you can visit http://www.PacktPub.com/support and register to have the files e-mailed directly to you.

Errata

Although we have taken every care to ensure the accuracy of our content, mistakes do happen. If you find a mistake in one of our books—maybe a mistake in the text or the code—we would be grateful if you would report this to us. By doing so, you can save other readers from frustration and help us improve subsequent versions of this book. If you find any errata, please report them by visiting http://www.packtpub.com/support, selecting your book, clicking on the **errata submission form** link, and entering the details of your errata. Once your errata are verified, your submission will be accepted and the errata will be uploaded on our website, or added to any list of existing errata, under the Errata section of that title. Any existing errata can be viewed by selecting your title from http://www.packtpub.com/support.

Piracy

Piracy of copyright material on the Internet is an ongoing problem across all media. At Packt, we take the protection of our copyright and licenses very seriously. If you come across any illegal copies of our works, in any form, on the Internet, please provide us with the location address or website name immediately so that we can pursue a remedy.

Please contact us at copyright@packtpub.com with a link to the suspected pirated material.

We appreciate your help in protecting our authors, and our ability to bring you valuable content.

Questions

You can contact us at questions@packtpub.com if you are having a problem with any aspect of the book, and we will do our best to address it.

1
Introduction to WordPress

These days, everyone has a good reason to have a website. It's not just large companies anymore. Individuals, families, and small or independent businesses all need to have one. Some individuals and small businesses don't have the financial resources to hire a website development company or a freelance web developer to create a website for them. This is where WordPress comes in very handy. WordPress is an open source web software application that you can use to create and maintain an online website, even if you have a minimum of technical expertise.

Since it is a web application, WordPress does not need to be installed on your home computer. It can live on the server (a kind of computer) that belongs to your website hosting company. It is also free, easy to use, and packed with excellent features. Originally, WordPress was an application meant to run a blog website, but it has now evolved into a fully-featured **Content Management System (CMS)**.

In this chapter, we'll explore:

- The reasons that will make you choose WordPress to run your website
- The greatest advantages of WordPress
- Online resources for WordPress

What is WordPress?

WordPress is an open source blog engine. **Open source** means that nobody owns it, everybody works on it, and anyone can contribute to it. **Blog engine** means a software application that can run a blog. It's a piece of software that lives on the web server and makes it easy for you to add and edit posts, themes, comments, and all of your other content. More expansively, WordPress can be called a *publishing platform* because it is by no means restricted to blogging.

WordPress was originally a fork of an older piece of software named *b2/cafelog*. WordPress was developed by Matt Mullenweg and Mike Little, but is now maintained and developed by a team of developers that includes Mullenweg.

Use it for a blog or a website

There are generally two popular types of websites for which WordPress is meant to be used.

- Normal website with relatively static content—pages, subpages, and so on.
- Blog website—chronologically organized, frequently updated, categorized, tagged, and archived.

For those of you unfamiliar with blog websites and blogging terminology, let's take a look at the basics.

Blog: Definition and common terms

A **blog**, which is short for **weblog**, is a website that usually contains regular entries like any other kind of log. These entries can be of various types such as commentary, descriptions of events, photos, videos, personal remarks, or political ideas. They are usually displayed in reverse chronological order, with the most recent additions on the top. These entries can be organized in a variety of ways—by date, by topic, by subject, and so on.

A blog is a special type of website that gets updated regularly. Unlike a site where the content is static, a blog behaves more like an online diary, wherein the blogger posts regular updates. Hence, blogs are dynamic with ever-changing content. A blog can be updated with new content and the old content can be changed or deleted at any time.

Most blogs focus their content on a particular subject—for example current events, hobbies, technical expertise—or else they are more like personal online diaries.

According to Wikipedia, the term *weblog* was first used in 1997, and people started using blogs globally in 1999. The terms *weblog*, *weblogging*, and *weblogger* were added to the Oxford Dictionary in 2003, though these days most people leave off the "we" part.

Common terms

If you are new to the world of blogging, you may want to familiarize yourself with the following common terms.

Post

Each entry in the blog is called a **post**. Every post usually has a number of different parts. Of course, the two most obvious parts are title and content. The **content** is text, images, links, and so on. Posts can even contain multimedia. Every post also has a publication timestamp, and most also have one or more categories, tags, comments, and so on. It is these posts, or entries, that are displayed in reverse chronological order on the main page of the blog. The latest post is displayed first in order to give the viewer the latest news on the subject.

Categories and tags

Categories and **tags** are ways to organize and find posts within a blog and even across blogs. Categories are like topics, whereas tags are more like keywords. For example, for a blog about food and cooking, there might be a category called **Recipes**, but every post in that category would have different tags (for example, soup, baked, vegetarian, dairy-free, and so on).

Comments

Most blogs allow visitors to post comments about the posts. This gives readers the opportunity to interact with the writer of the blog, thus making the whole enterprise interactive. Often, the writer of the blog will respond to comments by posting additional comments with the single click of a reply button, which makes for a continuous public online conversation or dialogue.

Theme

The **theme** for a blog is the design and layout that you choose for your blog. In most blogs, the content (for example, posts) is separate from the visual layout. This means you can change the visual layout of your blog at any time without having to worry about the content being affected. One of the best things about themes is that it takes only seconds to install and start using a new one. Plus, there are thousands of free or low-cost themes available online so you can take your pick (or make your own!).

RSS

RSS is an acronym for **Really Simple Syndication**, and *Chapter 7* addresses the topic of feeds in detail. For now, understand that RSS and feeds are a way to syndicate the content of your blog so that people can subscribe to it. This means people do not actually have to visit your blog regularly to see what you've added. Instead, they can subscribe and have new content delivered to them via e-mail or through a feed reader such as Google Reader.

Page

It's important to understand the difference between a page and a post. Unlike posts, pages do not depend on having timestamps and are not displayed in chronological order. They also do not have categories or tags. A **page** is a piece of content with only a title and content (an example would be **About Me** or **Contact Us**). It is likely that the number of pages on your site remains relatively static, whereas new posts are added every day or so. Thus pages have static content, while posts have dynamic content.

Why choose WordPress?

WordPress is not the only publishing platform out there, but it has an awful lot to recommend it. In the following sections, I've called attention to WordPress's most outstanding features.

A long time in refining

In web years, WordPress has been around for quite a while and was in development the whole time, getting better constantly. WordPress's very first release, Version 0.70, was released in May, 2003. Since then, it has had ten major releases, with a number of minor ones in between. Each release came with more features and better security.

Active in development

WordPress is a constantly evolving application. It's never left alone to stagnate. The developers are working continually to keep it ahead of spammers and hackers, and also to evolve the application based on the evolving needs of its users.

Large community of contributors

WordPress is not being developed by a lonely programmer in a dark basement room. On the contrary, there is a large community of people working on it collaboratively by developing, troubleshooting, making suggestions, and testing the application. With such a large group of people involved, the application is likely to continue to evolve and improve without pause.

Amazingly extendable

In addition to having an extremely strong core, WordPress is also quite extendable. This means that once you get started with it, the possibilities are nearly limitless. Any additional functionality that you can dream of can be added by means of a plugin that you or your programmer friends can write.

Detailed feature list

Here is a detailed list of many features of WordPress:

- Compliant with W3C standards
- Unlimited categories and subcategories
- Automatic syndication (RSS and Atom)
- Uses XML RPC interface for trackbacks and remote posting
- Allows posting via e-mail and mobile devices
- Supports plugins and themes
- Imports data from other blogs (Moveable Type, Textpattern, Greymatter, b2evolution, and blogger)
- Easy to administer and blog without any previous experience
- Convenient, fully functional, built-in search
- Instant and fast publishing of content — no re-building of pages required
- Multilanguage capable
- Link manager, also known as a blogroll or link list
- Allows password-protected content
- Comments manager and spam protection
- Built-in workflow (write, draft, review, and publish)
- Intelligent text formatting via a WYSIWYG editor

New feature list since 2.7

Since the last edition of this book was published, quite a staggering number of new features have been added to the WordPress software. If you're new to WordPress, this list may not mean a whole lot to you, but if you're familiar with WordPress and have been using it for a long time, you'll find this list quite enlightening.

- Scrolling back to the same location after saving a file in the Plugin and Theme editors
- Adding support for "include" and "exclude" to [gallery]
- Showing "Draft updated" instead of "Post updated" when saving draft
- Renaming various menu items, for example **Posts | Edit** becomes **Posts | Posts**, and **Links | Edit** becomes **Links | Links**, and so on

- Moving **Tools | Upgrade** menu option to **Dashboard | Updates** and overhauling of user interface so themes, plugins, and core upgrade under one panel

- Improved revision comparison user interface

- Lots of new template files for custom taxonomies and custom post types, among others

- Not asking for confirmation when marking a comment as spam

- Not notifying post to author of his/her own comments

- Showing absolute date instead of relative date for scheduled posts

- Addition toggle all button to the **Gallery** tab in the uploader

- Browsing the theme directory and installing themes from the admin

- Allowing the dashboard widgets to be arranged in up to four columns

- Allowing "No role for this blog" to be chosen in **Users | Add New panel**

- Choosing username and password during installation rather than using "admin"

- Multisite now built in

- Supporting time zones and automatic daylight savings time adjustment

- Supporting IIS 7.0 URL Rewrite Module

- Faster loading of admin pages via script compression and concatenation

- Lots of arguments added to template functions

- Addition of password strength meter to **Add User** and **Edit User**

- New default theme "Twenty Ten" takes full advantage of the current features of WordPress

- Custom header and background APIs

- Support for shortlinks (though you need a plugin to realize this fully)

- A lighter admin color scheme to increase accessibility and put the focus more squarely on your content.

- Contextual help text accessed under the **Help** tab of every screen in the WordPress administration

- Changes **Remove** link on widgets to **Delete** because it doesn't just remove it, it deletes the settings for that widget instance

- Syntax highlighting and function lookup built into plugin and theme editors

Learning more

If you'd like to see detailed complete lists of all new features added since WordPress version 2.7, take a look at these links:

- `http://codex.wordpress.org/Version_2.8`
- `http://codex.wordpress.org/Version_2.9`
- `http://codex.wordpress.org/Version_3.0`

Also, you can read a fully explained feature list at `http://wordpress.org/about/features/`.

Online WordPress resources

One very useful characteristic of WordPress is that it has a large, active online community. Everything you will ever need for your WordPress website can likely be found online, and probably for free.

WordPress news

As WordPress is always actively developed, it's important to keep yourself up-to-date with the software community about their latest activities.

If you visit the Dashboard of your own WordPress site regularly, you'll be able to stay up-to-date with WordPress news and software releases. There are widgets on the dashboard that display latest news and announcements, and an alert always appears when there is a new version of WordPress available for download and installation.

If you prefer to visit the website, then the most important spot to visit or subscribe to is WordPress Releases. Whenever there is a new release—be it a major release, or an interim bug fix, or an upgrade—it will be here: `http://wordpress.org/development/category/releases/`.

Also, be sure to stay tuned to the main WordPress blog at `http://wordpress.org/development/`.

The Codex

The WordPress **Codex** is the central repository of all the information the official WordPress team has published to help people work with WordPress.

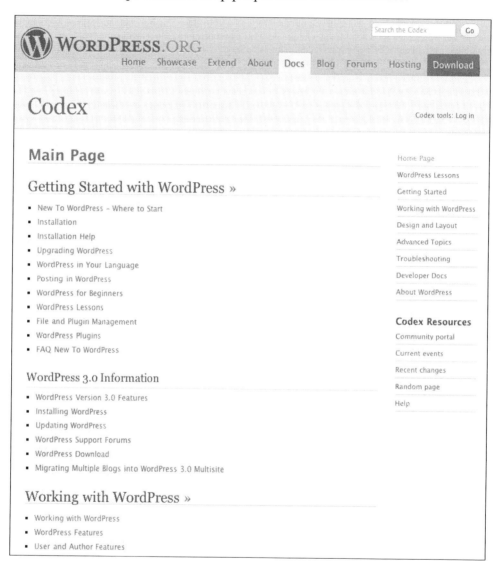

The Codex has some basic tutorials for getting started with WordPress, such as a detailed step-by-step discussion of installation, lists of every template tag and hook, and a lot more. Throughout this book, I'll be providing links to specific pages within the Codex, which will provide more or advanced information on the topics in this book.

Support from other users

The online WordPress community asks questions and responds with solutions on the WordPress forum: http://support.wordpress.org. That's an excellent place to go if you can't find the answer to a problem in the codex. If you have the question, then probably someone else has had it as well, and WordPress experts spend time in the forum answering questions and giving solutions. There's also an IRC channel where you can get additional support.

Theme and plugin directories

There are official directories for themes and for plugins on wordpress.org. Though not every theme and plugin is available here, the ones that are here have been vetted by the community to some extent. Anything you download from these directories is likely to be relatively bug-free. Plugins and themes that you get from other sources can have malicious code, so be careful. You can also see what the community thinks of these downloads by looking at ratings, comments, and popularity.

Additionally, plugins in the **Plugin Directory** are automatically upgradable from within your WordPress Administration Panel, whereas other plugins have to be upgraded manually. We'll cover this in more detail in a later chapter. You can find the **Theme Directory** at http://wordpress.org/extend/themes/ and the **Plugin Directory** at http://wordpress.org/extend/plugins/.

WordPress.com

You'll notice that all of the URLs above belong to wordpress.org. There is another website, Wordpress.com, which is actually a free blog-hosting service. Anyone can open an account on WordPress.com and instantly have his or her own WordPress-driven website. According to WordPress.com, there were over 16 million blogs on WordPress.com and over 25 million active installations of the WordPress.org software as of December 2010.

In *Chapter 2*, we will discuss all of the differences between having your blog on WordPress.com versus downloading the software from WordPress.org and hosting it yourself, but the basic difference is the level of control. If your blog is on WordPress.com, you have less control over plugins, themes, and other details of the blog because everything is managed and made worry-free by the WordPress.com service.

Summary

Having a website of your own is essential these days, whether you are an individual, a small business, or some other group. It is whether you are blogging regularly, or just want some accurate static content up on the Internet. In this chapter, we reviewed basic information about blogging and common blog terms for those of you who are new to the concept.

WordPress is excellent software application that can run your website (blog or not). It's packed with excellent features, is so flexible that it can really do anything you want, and it has a wealth of online resources. Additionally, it's super easy-to-use, and you need no special skills or prior experience to use it. Last, but not least, it is free!

In the next chapter, we will explore the choices and steps involved in installing WordPress and getting started.

2
Getting Started

This chapter will guide you through the process of setting up WordPress and customizing its basic features. You can choose between a couple of options regarding where your WordPress installation will live. Keep in mind that WordPress is relatively small (under 10 MB), easy to install, and easy to administer.

WordPress is available in easily downloadable formats from its website, `http://wordpress.org/download/`. WordPress is a free, open source application, and is released under GNU **General Public License (GPL)**. This means that anyone who produces a modified version of software released under the GPL is required to keep those same freedoms, that people buying or using the software may also modify and redistribute, attached to his or her modified version. This way, WordPress and other software released under GPL are kept open source.

In this chapter, you will learn how to:

- Create a free blog on WordPress.com
- Install WordPress manually on your web host
- Perform basic setup tasks in the WordPress Admin panel

Where to build your WordPress website

The first decision you have to make is where your blog is going to live. You have two basic options for the location where you will create your site. You can:

- Use WordPress.com
- Install on a server (hosted or your own)

Let's look at some of the advantages and disadvantages of each of these two choices.

The advantage of using WordPress.com is that **they take care of all of the technical details for you**. The software is already installed; they'll upgrade it for you whenever there's an upgrade; and you're not responsible for anything else. Just manage your content! The big disadvantage is that **you lose almost all of the theme and plugin control** you'd have otherwise. WordPress.com will not let you upload or edit your own theme, though it will let you (for a fee) edit the CSS of any theme you use. WordPress.com will not let you upload or manage plugins at all. Some plugins are installed by default (most notably **Akismet**, for spam blocking, and a fancy statistics plugin), but you can neither uninstall them nor install others. Additional features are available for a fee as well. This chapter will cover creating a blog on WordPress. com, and you can learn about navigating around the WP Admin in the next chapter. However, much of what this book covers will be impossible on WordPress.com.

The huge advantage of installing WordPress on another server (which means either a server that belongs to the web host with which you signed up, or a server you set up on your own computer) is that **you have control over everything**. You can add and edit themes, add and remove plugins, and even edit the WordPress application files yourself if you want. You'll have to keep your own WordPress software up-to-date, but that's relatively simple, and we'll cover it in this chapter. The only disadvantage is that you have to do the installation and maintenance yourself, which, as you'll see, shouldn't be too intimidating. Plus, some web hosts provide a one-click or easy-to-use installer, which lets you skip over some of the nitty-gritty steps involved in manual installation.

As I said, we'll discuss using WordPress.com in this chapter. However, you will have to install WordPress on your own server if you want to accomplish any of the more advanced topics from this book.

The following table is a brief overview of the essential differences between using WordPress.com versus installing WordPress on your own server:

	WordPress.com	Your own server
Installation	You don't have to install anything, just sign up	Install WordPress yourself, either manually or via your host's control panel (if offered)
Themes	Use any theme made available by WordPress.com	Use any theme available anywhere, written by anyone (including yourself)
Plugins	No ability to choose or add plugins	Use any plugin available anywhere, written by anyone (including yourself)
Upgrades	WordPress.com provides automatic upgrades	You have to upgrade it yourself when upgrades are available
Widgets	Widget availability depends on available themes	You can widgetize any theme yourself

	WordPress.com	Your own server
Maintenance	You don't have to do any maintenance	You're responsible for the maintenance of your site
Advertising	No advertising allowed	Advertise anything and in any amount you like

Using WordPress.com

WordPress.com (`http://wordpress.com`) is a free service provided by the WordPress developers, where you can register a blog or non-blog website easily and quickly with no hassle. However, because it is a hosted service, your control over some things will be more limited than it would be if you hosted your own WordPress website. As mentioned before, WordPress.com will not let you edit or upload your own themes or plugins. Aside from this, WordPress.com is a great place to maintain your personal site if you don't need to do anything fancy with a theme. To get started, go to `http://wordpress.com`, which will look something like the following:

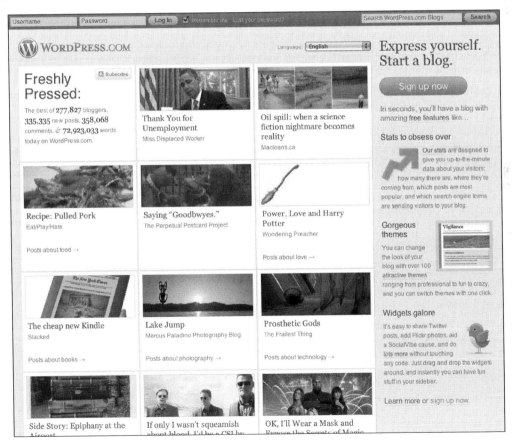

To register your free website, click on the loud orange-and-white **Sign up now** button. You will be taken to the signup page. In the following screenshot, I've entered my username (what I'll sign in with) and a password (note that the password measurement tool will tell you if your password is strong or weak), as well as my e-mail address. Be sure to check the **Legal flotsam** box and leave the **Gimme a blog!** radio button checked. Without it, you won't get a website.

After providing this information and clicking on the **Next** button, WordPress will ask for other choices (**Blog Domain**, **Blog Title**, **Language**, and **Privacy**), as shown in following screenshot. You can also check if it's a private blog or not. Note that you cannot change the blog domain later! So be sure it's right.

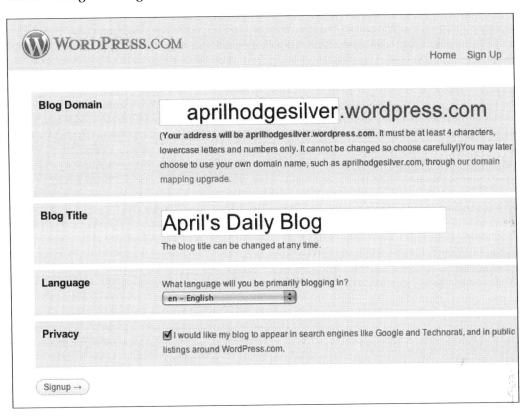

After providing this information and clicking on **Signup**, you will be sent to a page where you can enter some basic profile information. This page will also tell you that your account is set up, but your e-mail ID needs to be verified. Be sure to check your inbox for the e-mail with the link, and click on it. Then, you'll be truly done with the installation.

Now, you can skip the next section of this chapter, which is about installing WordPress manually. You can go directly to the section on the WP Admin panel to start learning about it.

Installing WordPress manually

The WordPress application files can be downloaded for free if you want to do a manual installation. If you've got a website host, this process is extremely easy and requires no previous programming skills or advanced blog user experience.

Some web hosts offer automatic installation through the host's online control panel. However, be a little wary of this because some hosts offer automatic installation, but they do it in a way that makes updating your WordPress difficult or awkward, or restricts your ability to have free rein with your installation in the future.

Preparing the environment

A good first step is to make sure you have an environment setup that is ready for WordPress. This means two things: making sure that you verify that the server meets the minimum requirements, and making sure that your database is ready.

For WordPress to work, your web host must provide you with a server that does the following two things:

- Support PHP, which must be at least Version 4.3.
- Provide you with write access to a MySQL database. MySQL has to be at least Version 4.1.2.

You can find out if your host meets these two requirements by contacting your web host. If your web server meets these two basic requirements, you're ready to move on to the next step.

As far as web servers go, Apache is the best. However, WordPress will also run on a server running the Microsoft IIS server (though using **permalinks** will be difficult, if possible at all).

Enabling mod_rewrite to use pretty permalinks

If you want to use **permalinks**, your server must be running Unix, and Apache's mod_rewrite option must be enabled. Apache's mod_rewrite is enabled by default in most web hosting accounts. If you are hosting your own account, you can enable mod_rewrite by modifying the Apache web server configuration file. You can check the URL http://www.tutorio.com/tutorial/enable-mod-rewrite-on-apache to learn how to enable mod_rewrite on your web server. If you are running on shared hosting, then ask your system administrator to install it for you. However, it is more likely that you already have it installed on your hosting account.

Downloading WordPress

Once you have checked out your environment, you need to download WordPress from `http://wordpress.org/download/`. Take a look at the following screenshot in which the download links are available on the right side:

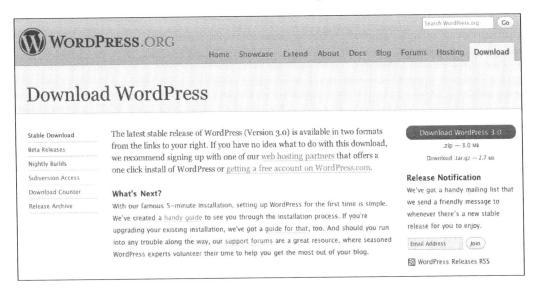

The `.zip` file is shown as a big blue button because that'll be the most useful format for the most people. If you are using Windows, Mac, or Linux operating systems, your computer will be able to unzip that downloaded file automatically. (The `.tar.gz` file is provided because some Unix users prefer it.)

A further note on location

We're going to cover installing WordPress remotely. However, if you plan to develop themes or plugins, I suggest that you also install WordPress locally on your own computer's server. Testing and deploying themes and plugins directly to the remote server will be much more time-consuming than working locally. If you look at the screenshots I will be taking of my own WordPress installation throughout the book, you'll notice that I'm working locally (for example, `http://wpbook:8888/` is a local URL).

After you download the WordPress `.zip` file, extract the files, and you'll get a folder called `wordpress`. It will look like the following screenshot:

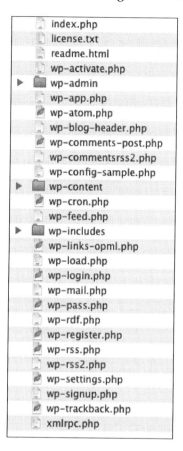

Upgrading from an earlier version of WordPress

If you are upgrading an existing installation of WordPress, you should probably leave this chapter and instead read the section on *Upgrading WordPress* in *Chapter 11* of this book.

Uploading the files

Now, we need to upload all these files to our web server using any FTP client (or simply put them in our local server directory on our local computer). FTP stands for File Transfer Protocol. There are several FTP clients available on the Internet, which are either freeware (no cost) or as shareware (a small fee). If you don't already have an FTP client, try one of these:

- Filezilla—`http://filezilla-project.org/download.php?type=client` (for Mac or Windows)
- Fetch—`http://fetchsoftworks.com/` (for Mac only)
- SmartFTP—`http://www.smartftp.com/` (for Windows only)

You can also use the popular web-based FTP application net2ftp at `http://www.net2ftp.com`. These services are useful if you don't want to install a desktop application on your computer. You can also check if your host provides browser-based FTP software.

In my screenshots you'll see that I'm using Transmit, which is the professional FTP software I use on my Mac. It works the same way as the examples above.

 A note about security: whenever possible, you should use Secure FTP (called sFTP) rather than regular FTP. If you're using sFTP, all of the data sent and received are encrypted, whereas with FTP, data are sent in plain text and can be easily nabbed by hackers. Check both your FTP software and your hosting options, and select sFTP if it's available.

Using your FTP client or service, connect to your FTP server using the server address, username, and password provided to you by your host. Next, open the folder where you want WordPress to live. You may want to install WordPress in your root folder, which will mean that visitors will see your WordPress website's home page when they go to your main URL—for example, `http://yoursite.com`. Alternatively, you may want to install WordPress in a subfolder; for example: `http://yoursite.com/blog/`.

On the left side, you will see the files from your local folder, and on the right side you will see your remote folder. (Note: the FTP client you are using may have a slightly different layout, but this is the general idea):

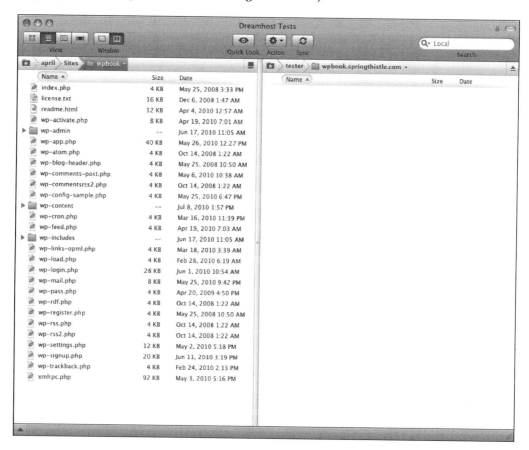

Now select all of the WordPress files on your local machine from the left pane, and drag all of them to the right pane. You can watch as your FTP client uploads the files one at a time and they appear in the right panel. This could take a few minutes, so be patient!

If you're installing WordPress on your local server, just be sure to place the WordPress files in the correct webroot directory on your computer.

Once all of the files are done uploading, you're ready to do the installation.

Installing WordPress

Now it's time to install WordPress. For example, I will be working on my local server and just put brand-new WordPress files at `http://wpbook:8888/`. So, this is going to be the URL of my WordPress website. If you access your WordPress URL via your browser, it will look like the following:

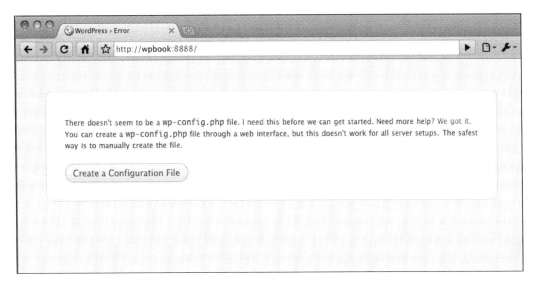

It says that you need to create a file named `wp-config.php` before proceeding further. WordPress (and I) recommend that you do this manually, rather than using the **Create a Configuration File** link. If you do choose to use the config creator, you'll need the information below as well (though there will be no opportunity for the security phrases).

Open the `wordpress` folder and find the file named `wp-config-sample.php`. Make a copy of this file and name it `wp-config.php`. We'll modify this file together. Don't worry; you need not be a PHP programmer. Just open this file with a simple editor such as Notepad. The following is the copied text from the original `wp-config.php` file. Note that I've removed most of the comments, so that we can focus on the items we need to change.

```php
<?php
/** The name of the database for WordPress */
define('DB_NAME', 'database_name_here');

/** MySQL database username */
define('DB_USER', 'username_here');
```

```
/** MySQL database password */
define('DB_PASSWORD', 'password_here');

/** MySQL hostname */
define('DB_HOST', 'localhost');

/** Database Charset to use in creating database tables. */
define('DB_CHARSET', 'utf8');

/** The Database Collate type. Don't change this if in doubt. */
define('DB_COLLATE', '');

define('AUTH_KEY',         'put your unique phrase here');
define('SECURE_AUTH_KEY',  'put your unique phrase here');
define('LOGGED_IN_KEY',    'put your unique phrase here');
define('NONCE_KEY',        'put your unique phrase here');
define('AUTH_SALT',        'put your unique phrase here');
define('SECURE_AUTH_SALT', 'put your unique phrase here');
define('LOGGED_IN_SALT',   'put your unique phrase here');
define('NONCE_SALT',       'put your unique phrase here');

$table_prefix  = 'wp_';
?>
```

 One thing to know about PHP is that any text that comes after a double slash (//), or between a slash-star and star-slash (/*   */), is a comment. It's not actual PHP code. Its purpose is to inform you what that line or that section is about.

As you can see from the previous code, there are a number of settings that you can insert here. Let's walk through the most important ones.

As I mentioned in an earlier section, you need to have write access to a database. Most large web hosts offer you a way to create your own databases, with usernames and passwords, via an online control panel. If you're not sure how to do this, just e-mail or call your hosting provider for this information. You'll need four pieces of information about your database for the WordPress configuration file. They are:

- Database server—for example, localhost
- Username—for example, localdbuser
- Password—for example, 62dcx0hnm
- Database name—for example, wpbookdb

Your database server might not be localhost. If it's not, you can ask your hosting provider, or take a look at this handy cheat sheet: `http://codex.wordpress.org/ Editing_wp-config.php#Possible_DB_HOST_values`.

Once you have those four things, you can fill them into your `wp-config.php` file. For example, see how mine is filled out here:

```
// ** MySQL settings ** //
define('DB_NAME', 'wpbookdb');
define('DB_USER', 'localdbuser');
define('DB_PASSWORD', '62dcx0hnm');
define('DB_HOST', 'localhost');
```

Next, for security purposes, you really should put some unique phrases into the unique keys. The secret keys are used by WordPress to add random elements to your passwords and are also used in some other situations. This will help to keep your WordPress installation uniquely protected. No one else is likely to choose the same unique keys that you chose, and therefore, breaking or hacking into your site will be more difficult. You can get some secret keys generated by going to `https://api. wordpress.org/secret-key/1.1/salt/`. Once I did that, I got the following, which I can paste directly over the default code in `wp-config.php`:

```
define('AUTH_KEY', 'uu|6#00Pc/3h?Pg5:Zc#:S=;<3mdw-ai');
define('SECURE_AUTH_KEY', 'vy1.@Nr@Zb^G|0Vfz-|TH5&W');
define('LOGGED_IN_KEY', 'sryMVd`jVpiMWWQqx~!v XE5@fJMTt2[Z');
define('NONCE_KEY', 'i,+UPpMR>Mj3o}(B**^<T:/md,YFF76d]Kf');
define('AUTH_SALT', 'n.8Li=9OjV+_p|}e5yN2k<s{!KJs|[S&Zh');
define('SECURE_AUTH_SALT', 'I#2vPT^u[5vLX|`MzPg/J*y]RTfr');
define('LOGGED_IN_SALT', 'gR%QP^c*jfFUy,iQ}-0g_%;%H)pN0B5');
define('NONCE_SALT', '&L);.IH`v{]zYLO2:h_t#J0D-p)cvyc');
```

The only other thing you may want to consider is the table prefix. I strongly recommend using a prefix. If you want to install WordPress more than once, you'll need to use different prefixes in your different installations. If you are using this same database for other things, it'll be handy if the tables are grouped based on what they're being used for. So either leave the following line as it is, or choose another prefix:

```
$table_prefix  = 'wpbook_';
```

Learning more: The WordPress codex has a long and detailed page that describes everything about editing your wp-config.php file: `http:// codex.wordpress.org/Editing_wp-config.php`.

Now, go back to your browser and reload the page that's pointing to your WordPress installation. If your configuration file makes sense to WordPress, you'll be taken directly to the installation page.

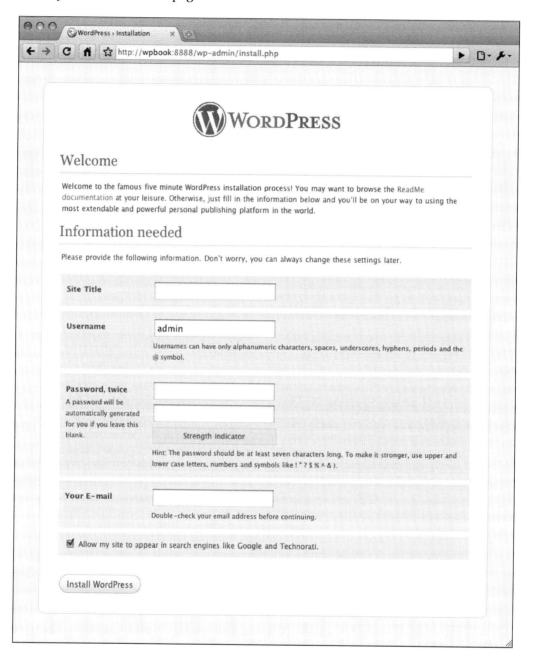

(If you've ever installed an earlier version of WordPress, you'll notice some differences, like the ability to choose your first username and password!) Now, fill out the installation form (you will be able to change all of these later, so don't be too worried about getting locked into your choices):

- **Site title:** Fill in the name of your blog (in my case it's 'Daily Cooking').

- **Username:** Note that the default username is 'admin', but for security purposes, you're better off picking another username. If someone ever tries to hack your blog, they will be halfway there if they already know your username. I've chosen 'ahsilver'.

- **Password:** Choose a secure password, one that has both upper and lowercase letters, a number or two, and even a few punctuation marks.

- **Your E-Mail:** Double-check that this is correct, because this is the e-mail address WordPress will use to contact you about the blog, comments, and so on. If you do not get an e-mail from your WordPress site shortly after installing, check your spam folder.

Now, click on **Install WordPress**. You're done with the install!

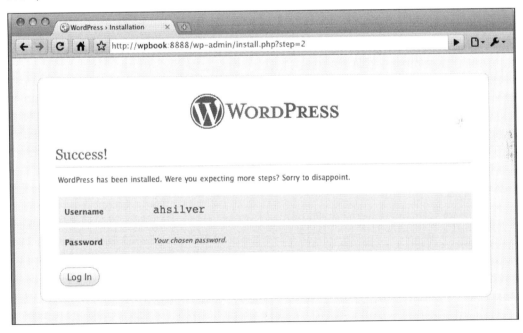

You can click on **Log In** to get to the login page. Or you can always enter your WordPress Admin panel (also known as the WP Admin) by pointing your browser to `http://yoursite.com/wp-admin`. If you're not already logged in, this URL will redirect you to the login page.

Learning more

If you'd like to see an even more detailed step-by-step guide for manual installation, take a look at this page in the WordPress Codex: `http://codex.wordpress.org/Installing_WordPress`.

Also, you can find more detailed installation instructions—as well as specifics on changing file permissions, using FTP, using languages, importing from other blogging engines, and more—in the WordPress Codex here: `http://codex.wordpress.org/Getting_Started_with_WordPress#Installation`.

The WP Admin panel

WordPress installs a powerful and flexible administration area where you can manage all of your website content, and do much more. Throughout the book, I'll be referring to this in shorthand as the **WP Admin**.

Now that you've successfully installed WordPress, it's time for our first look at the WP Admin. There are some immediate basic changes that I recommend doing right away to make sure your installation is set up properly.

You can always get to the WP Admin by going to this URL: `http://yoursite.com/wp-admin/`. Your first time here, you'll be re-directed to the login page. In the future, WordPress will check to see if you're already logged in and, if so, you'll skip the login page. Following is the login page:

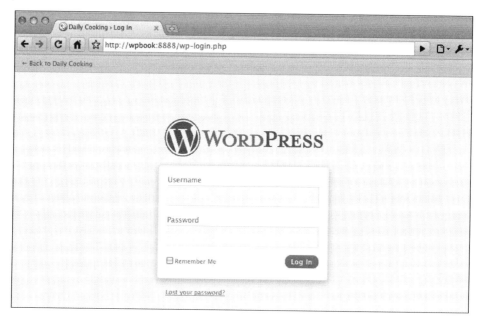

To log in, just enter the username and password you chose during the installation. Then click on **Log In**. Note for the future that on this page there is a link you can use to retrieve your lost password.

Whenever you log in, you'll be taken directly to the **Dashboard** of the WP Admin. Following is a screenshot of the WP Admin that you will see immediately after you log into the blog you just installed:

You'll see a lot of information and options here, which we will explore throughout this book. For now, we will focus on the items that we need to touch upon right after a successful installation. First, let's take a brief look at the top of the WP Admin and the **Dashboard**.

The very top bar, which I'll refer to as the **top bar**, is mostly a medium grey and contains:

- A link to the front page of your WordPress website
- A rollover drop-down menu with handy links to **New Post**, **Drafts**, **New Page**, **Upload**, and **Comments**
- Your username linked to your profile
- A link to log out

You'll also notice the **Screen Options** tab, which appears on many screens within the WP Admin. If you click on it, it will slide down a checklist of items on the page to show or hide. It will be different on each page. I encourage you to play around with that by checking and unchecking items, as you find you need them or don't need them.

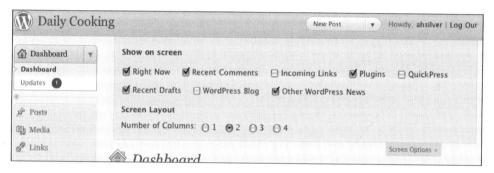

On the left, of course, is the **main menu**:

You can click on any word in the main menu to be taken to the main page for that section, or you can click on the rollover arrow to slide down the subpages for that section. For example, if you click on the arrow next to **Settings**, you'll see the subpages for the **Settings** section:

In this book, when describing to you which page within the WP Admin to go to, I'll write things such as "navigate to **Settings | Privacy**" or "navigate to **Posts | Add New**". This always describes the path you should take to get there via the main menu.

The top menu and the main menu exist on every page within the WP Admin. The main section on the right contains information for the current page you're on. In this case, we're on the **Dashboard**. It contains boxes that have a variety of information about your blog, and about WordPress in general.

Before WordPress 3, the first thing you'd have to do would be to change the password to something easier to remember. However, now that you can choose your password during installation, this is no longer necessary. Let's jump right to general site settings.

Changing general blog information

You may need to change and add some general blog information (such as blog title, one-sentence description, and so on) after a successful installation to get your website set up with the correct information. To get started with this, navigate to **Settings** in the main menu.

There are many options you can set here, most of which are pretty self-explanatory. We'll look at the most important ones, and you can explore the rest on your own. Obviously, you can change your blog's title. You can see from my screenshots that I've called mine **Daily Cooking**:

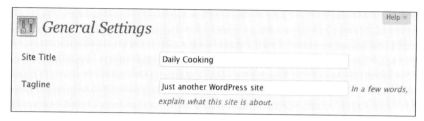

You can also change the blog description, which is used in most themes as a subtitle for the blog, like the subtitle of a book. The default description is **Just another WordPress site**. You'll probably want to change that! I'll change mine to 'Exploring cooking every day of the week'.

The only other thing you probably want to take a look at on this page is the **Timezone**:

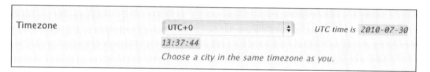

Whether you have a blog (with timestamps on every post) or not, it's important that WordPress knows what timezone you're in, in case you want to schedule a page or post for the future, show users accurate timestamps, or even just make sure that e-mail notifications are correctly time-stamped.

The pull-down menu will show you different UTC settings, along with cities. Just choose a city in your timezone. After you save the changes you made, the time that shows further down the page (next to **Time Format**) will change to the time you chose, so that you can check and make sure it's correct.

When you're done making changes to this page, be sure to click on the **Save Changes** button at the bottom of the page.

Your first post

For this chapter, and the next few chapters, we'll be focusing on using WordPress to run a blog website. In a later chapter, we'll talk more specifically about using WordPress for a non-blog website.

So, with that in mind, let's add the first piece of content to your new blog—a blog post. (This won't be the very first post on the blog itself, because WordPress created a post, a comment, and a page for you when it installed. It will be YOUR first post, however!). To create a post, just click on **New Post** on the top menu. You'll be taken to the following page:

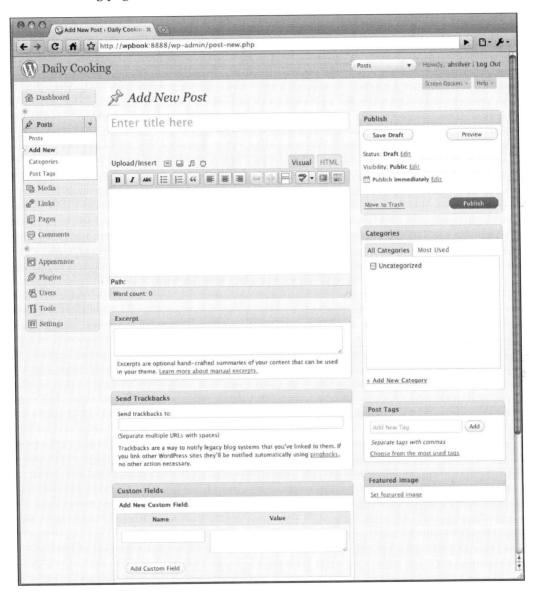

As you can see, there are a lot of options for your post (which we'll explore in more detail in *Chapter 3*). For now, just worry about the basics. Every post should have, at minimum, a title and some content. So go ahead and write in some text for those two things. When you are happy with it, click on the **Publish** button.

You'll get a yellow note telling you that the post is published. Take a look at the front page of your site by clicking on the name of your site in the top bar. You'll see the following:

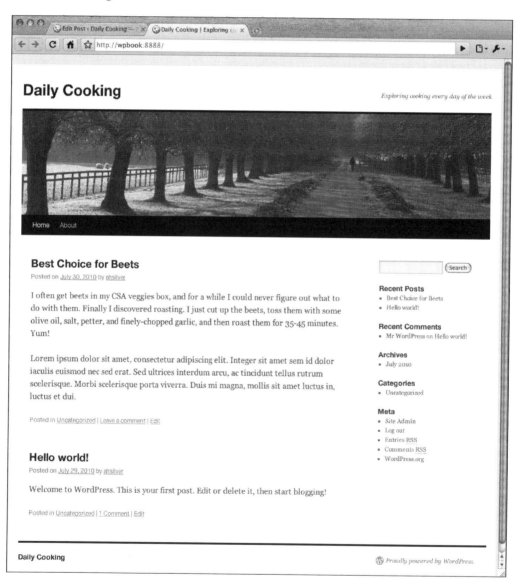

Your first comment

Now let's see what it's like to post a comment. One of the great things about blogs is that they give you, the writer, the opportunity to spark a conversation with your readers. WordPress comes with a fantastic commenting system that allows visitors to add comments to your blog. To add your own comment to your first post, click on the **Leave a comment** link underneath your first post. You'll be taken to the post's individual page at the bottom, where you can find a comment form like the following:

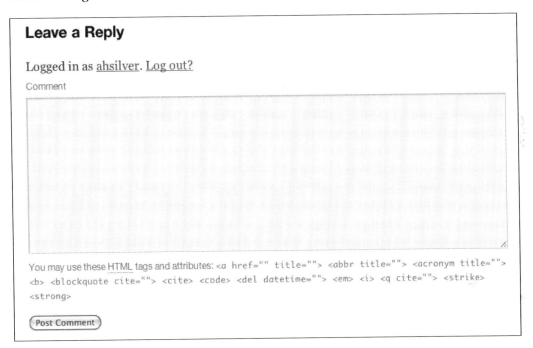

Your visitors, who won't already be logged into the WP Admin, will see a form that looks like the following instead:

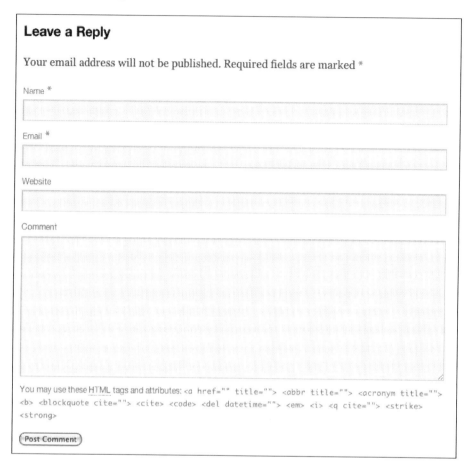

As you're already logged in, all you have to do is write something in the text area and click on **Submit Comment**. Then, you'll see your comment show up under the post, and that's it. Later, we'll explore how you can control which comments show up right away, and which comments have to wait for you to verify them as valid, as well as which fields are required for visitors.

Retrieving a lost password

If you have lost your password and can't get into your WP Admin panel, you can easily retrieve your password by clicking on the **Lost your password?** link on the login page. A newly generated password will be e-mailed to you at the e-mail address you gave during the WordPress installation. This is why you need to be sure that you enter a valid e-mail address. Otherwise, you will not be able to retrieve your password.

Summary

You have learned a lot of things from this chapter. Now you are able to install WordPress on a remote server, change the basic default settings of your blog, write posts, and comment on those posts.

In the next chapter, we will learn about all the other aspects of a blog post that you can control and additional ways to add posts, as well as the intricacies of managing and controlling commenting and discussion on your blog.

3
Creating Blog Content

Now that your WordPress installation is up and running, you are ready to start creating content. In this chapter, you will first become familiar with the WP Admin's display and editing features and conventions. Then, you'll learn how to control all of the information associated with a post, not just the title and content. You will also learn about comments—what they are for and how to manage them. Additionally, we will explore how to keep your content organized and searchable using tags and categories.

WP Admin conventions

In the WP Admin, you have the ability to manage a number of different types of things (objects)—this includes posts, categories, pages, links, media uploads, and more. WordPress uses a similar format for the various screens. Let's explore them below.

Lists of items

For every object in WordPress you might want to manage, there will be a page listing them. For example, let's have a look at what a list of posts might look like:

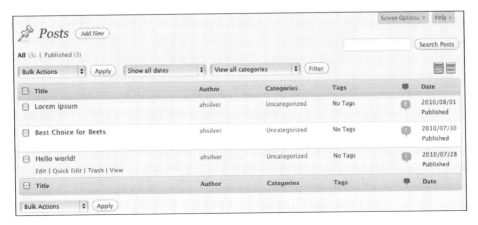

As you can see, the name of the object is at the top, and the list of items has columns. Let's take a look at the important elements:

- Each item in the list shows its **Title**. You can always click on an item title to edit it.

- If you hover your mouse over an item's row, as I hovered over "Hello World" in the preceding screenshot, you will see **four additional links**. Three are self-explanatory (**Edit**, **Trash**, **View**). You can use **Quick Edit** to edit most of the basic information about a post (other than the content, custom fields and most plugin-added items). If you click on **Quick Edit**, you'll quickly see what's available:

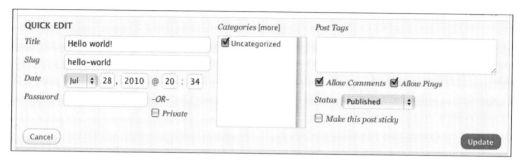

- You can make changes, and then click on **Update**, or click on **Cancel** if you've changed your mind.

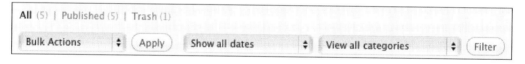

- The area above the list of posts lets you choose whether to view **All posts**, **Published Posts**, **Drafts**, or **Trash**.

- Just below those links is the **Bulk Actions** menu and its **Apply** button. Choose one or more posts by clicking on their checkboxes (or check the top checkbox to check every item) and click **Apply**. Then choose **Edit** or **Trash** from the **Bulk Actions** menu, and you'll be able to bulk delete or bulk edit posts.

- The **filter menu** lets you choose options from the **Dates** and **Categories** pull-down lists, and then click on the **Filter** button to only show items that meet those qualifications.

- At the very top is **Screen Options**. This tab, which appears on every screen will allow you (on list pages like this one) to hide or show particular columns and choose the number of items to show per page.

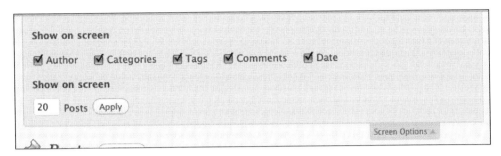

Posting on your blog

The central activity you'll be doing with your blog is adding posts. A **post** is like an article in a magazine; it's got a title, content, and an author (in this case, you, though WordPress allows multiple authors to contribute to a blog). If a blog is like an online diary, then every post is an entry in that diary. A blog post also has a lot of other information attached to it, such as a date, excerpt, tags, and categories. In this section, you will learn how to create a new post and what kind of information to attach to it.

Adding a simple post

Let's review the process of adding a simple post to your blog, which we carried out in the previous chapter. Whenever you want to add content or carry out a maintenance process on your WordPress website, you have to start by logging into the **WP Admin (WordPress Administration panel)** of your site. To get to the admin panel, just point your web browser to `http://yoursite.com/wp-admin`.

 Remember that if you have installed WordPress in a subfolder (for example, `blog`), then your URL has to include the subfolder (that is, `http://yoursite.com/blog/wp-admin`).

When you first log in to the WP Admin, you'll be at the **Dashboard**. The **Dashboard** has a lot of information on it don't worry about that right now. We'll discuss the **Dashboard** in detail later in the book.

The quickest way to get to the **Add New Post** page at any time is to click on the **New Post** link at the top of the page in the top bar.

This is the **Add New Post** page:

To add a new post to your site quickly, all you have to do is:

1. Type in a title into the text field under **Add New Post** (for example, **Making Lasagne**).

2. Type the text of your post in the content box. Note that the default view is **Visual**, but you actually have a choice of the **HTML** view as well.

3. Click on the **Publish** button, which is at the far right. Note that you can choose to save a draft or preview your post.

In the following image, the title field, the content box, and the **Publish** button of the **Add New Post** page are highlighted:

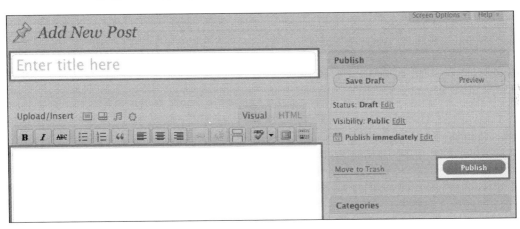

Once you click on the **Publish** button, you have to wait while WordPress performs its magic. You'll see yourself still on the **Edit Post** screen, but now the following message would have appeared telling you that your post was published, and giving you a link to **View post**:

If you view the front page of your site, you'll see that your new post has been added at the top (newest posts are always at the top):

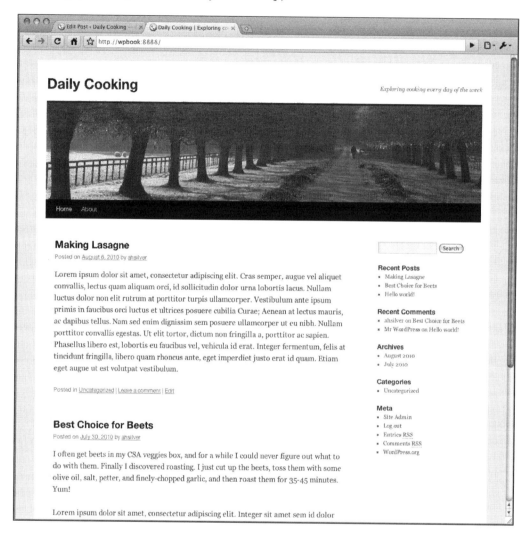

Common post options

Now that we've reviewed the basics of adding a post, let's investigate some of the other options on the **Add New Post** and **Edit Post** pages. In this section we'll look at the most commonly used options, and in the next section we'll look at the more advanced options.

Categories and tags

Categories and tags are two types of information that you can add to a blog post. We use them to organize the information in your blog by topic and content (rather than just by, say, date), and to help visitors find what they are looking for on your blog.

Categories are primarily used for structural organizing. They can be hierarchical, meaning a category can be a parent of another category. A relatively busy blog will probably have at least 10 categories, but probably not more than 15 or 20. Each post in such a blog is likely to have from one up to, maybe four categories assigned to it. For example, a blog about food and cooking might have these categories: **Cooking Adventures**, **In The Media**, **Ingredients**, **Opinion**, **Recipes Found**, **Recipes Invented**, and **Restaurants**. Of course, these numbers are just suggestions; you can create and assign as many categories as you like.

Tags are primarily used as shorthand for describing the topics covered in a particular blog post. A relatively busy blog will have anywhere from 15 to 60 tags in use. Each post in this blog is likely have three to ten tags assigned to it. For example, a post on the food blog about a recipe for butternut squash soup may have these tags: **soup**, **vegetarian**, **autumn**, **hot**, **easy**. Again, you can create and assign as many tags as you like.

Let's add a new post to the blog. After you give it a title and content, let's add tags and categories. When adding tags, just type your list of tags into the **Tags** box on the right, separated by commas:

Then click on the **Add** button. The tags you just typed in will appear below the text field with little **xs** next to them. You can click on an **x** to delete a tag. Once you've used some tags in your blog, you'll be able to click on the **Choose from the most popular tags** link in this box so that you can easily re-use tags.

Categories work a bit differently than tags. Once you get your blog going, you'll usually just check the boxes next to existing categories in the **Categories** box. In this case, as we don't have any existing categories, we'll have to add one or two.

In the **Categories** box on the right, click on the **+ Add New Category** link. Type your category into the text field, and click on the **Add** button. Your new category will show up in the list, already checked. Look at the following screenshot:

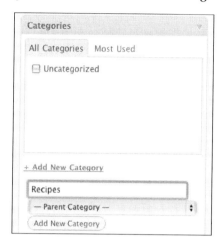

If in the future you want to add a category that needs a parent category, select **Parent category** from the pull-down menu before clicking on the **Add** button. If you want to manage more details about your categories, move them around, rename them, assign parent categories, and assign descriptive text, you can do so on the **Categories** page, which we'll see in detail later in this chapter.

Click on the **Publish** button, and you're done (you can instead choose to schedule a post; we'll explore that in detail in a few pages). When you look at the front page of your site, you'll see your new post on the top, your new category in the sidebar, and the tags and category (that you chose for your post) listed under the post itself.

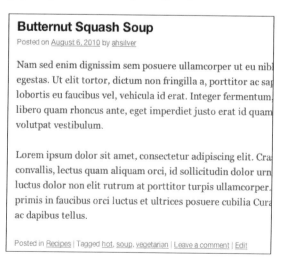

Images in your posts

Almost every good blog post needs an image! An image will give the reader an instant idea of what the post is about, and the image will draw people's attention in as well. WordPress makes it easy to add an image to your post, control default image sizes, make minor edits to that image, and designate a featured image for your post.

Adding an image to a post

Luckily, WordPress makes adding images to your content very easy. Let's add an image to the post we just created. You can click on **Edit** underneath your post on the front page of your site to get there quickly. Alternatively, go back to the WP Admin, open **Posts** in the main menu, and then click on the post's title.

To add an image to a post, first you'll need to have that image on your computer. Before you get ready to upload an image, make sure that your image is optimized for the Web. Huge files will be uploaded slowly and slow down the process of viewing your site. You can re-size and optimize images using software such as GIMP or Photoshop. For the example in this chapter, I have used a photo of butternut squash soup that I took from the website where I got the recipe, and I know it's on the desktop of my computer. Once you have a picture on your computer and know where it is, carry out the following steps to add the photo to your blog post:

1. Click on the little photo icon, which is next to the word **Upload/Insert** and below the box for the title:

2. In the box that appears, click on the **Select Files** button, and browse to your image.

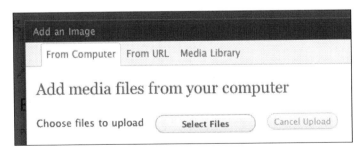

3. Then, click on **Open** and watch the uploader bar. When it's done, you'll have a number of fields you can fill in:

The only fields that are important right now are **Title**, **Alignment**, and **Size**. **Title** is a description for the image, **Alignment** will tell the image whether to have text wrap around it, and **Size** is the size of the image. As you can see, I've chosen the **Left** alignment and the **Medium** size.

4. Now, click on **Insert into Post**. This box will disappear, and your image will show up in the post on the edit page itself (in the Visual editor, that is. If you're using the HTML editor, then the image code HTML will be displayed):

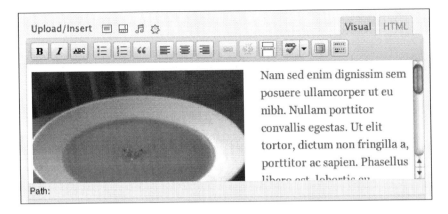

5. Now, click on the **Update Post** button, and go look at the front page of your site again. There's your image!

Controlling default image sizes

You may be wondering about those image sizes. What if you want bigger or smaller thumbnails? Whenever you upload an image, WordPress creates three versions of that image for you. You can set the pixel dimensions of those three versions by opening **Settings** in the main menu, and then clicking on **Media**. This takes you to the **Media Settings** page:

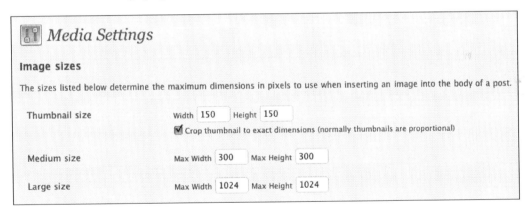

Here you can specify the size of the uploaded images for:

- **Thumbnail size**
- **Medium size**
- **Large size**

If you change the dimensions on this page, and click on the **Save Changes** button, only images you upload in the future will be affected. Images you've already uploaded to the site will have had their thumbnail, medium, and large versions created already using the old settings. It's a good idea to decide what you want your three media sizes to be early on in your blog, so you can set them and have them applied to all images, right from the start.

 Media Settings Tip: Be sure to set the width of the "large" size to the width of your content column on your site. That way, those images will always fit nicely without being too large.

Editing an uploaded image

As of WordPress 2.9, you can now make minor edits on images you've uploaded. I often find that the default thumbnail cropping doesn't suit me. For example, following is a photo of a person on a mountaintop, and right next to it is the thumbnail version WordPress created:

You can't see the person on the mountaintop! So I want to edit the thumbnail image. Just after you've uploaded an image, or after you pull it up in the "add media" screen, you'll see a button that says **Edit Image**, just underneath the thumbnail in the image above. Click it and you'll get a little editing screen:

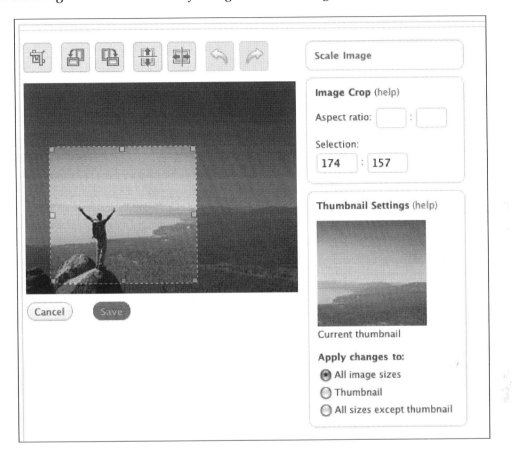

Use your mouse to draw a box as I have done in the preceding image. On the right, in the box marked **Image Crop**, you'll see the pixel dimensions of your selection. Click the crop icon (top left), then the **Thumbnail** radio button (bottom right), and then **Save** (just below your photo). You now have a new thumbnail!

You can also use this screen to rotate and resize your images. Play around a little and you can become familiar with the details.

Designating a post thumbnail or featured image

As of WordPress 2.9, you can designate a single image that represents your post. This is referred to as the **post thumbnail** or **featured image**. Some themes will make use of this, and some will not. The default theme, the one we've been using, is named **TwentyTen**, and it uses the featured image in the header of the site. If a post doesn't have a featured image, it will use a default.

For this particular theme, TwentyTen, the featured image has to be 948 pixels wide and 198 pixels tall. Note that this may be different for other themes. Many themes do not have any particular requirement for a post thumbnail, and only use them, in their thumbnail form, in search results and other post listings.

Let's designate a featured image for the post we just created. I've found a butternut squash image that will work well for my soup post. First, follow the steps above to upload the image. Then, instead of clicking **Insert into post**, click **Use as featured image**:

After doing that, you don't even have to update the post! Just clicking that link takes care of it. When you go to the post page, you'll see your featured image in the header:

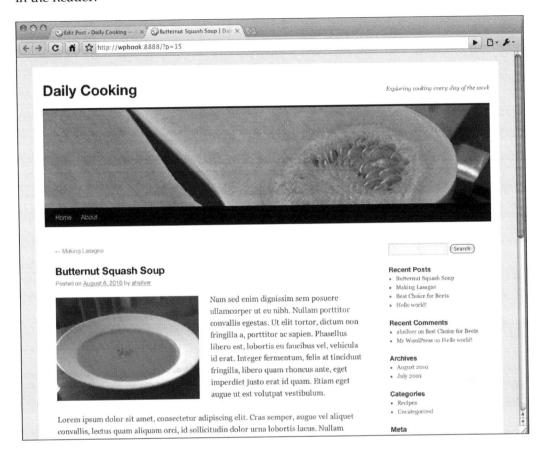

Using the Visual editor versus the HTML editor

WordPress comes with a Visual editor, otherwise known as a **WYSIWYG** editor (pronounced wissy-wig, and stands for **What You See Is What You Get**). This is the default editor for typing and editing your posts. If you're comfortable with HTML, you may prefer to write and edit your posts using the HTML editor—particularly useful if you want to add special content or styling.

To switch from the rich text editor to the HTML editor, click on the **HTML** tab next to the **Visual** tab at the top of the content box:

You'll see your post in all its raw HTML glory, and you'll get a new set of buttons that lets you quickly bold and italicize text, as well as add link code, image code, and so on.

You can make changes and swap back and forth between the tabs to see the result.

Drafts, timestamps, and managing posts

There are three additional, simple but common, items I'd like to cover in this section: drafts, timestamps, and managing posts.

Drafts

WordPress gives you the option to save a draft of your post so that you don't have to publish it right away but can still save your work. If you've started writing a post and want to save a draft, just click on the **Save Draft** button at the right (in the **Publish** box), instead of the **Publish** button. Even if you don't click on the **Save Draft** button, WordPress will attempt to save a draft of your post for you, about once a minute. You'll see this in the area just below the content box. The text will say **Saving Draft...** and then show the time of the last draft saved:

At this point, after a manual save or an auto-save, you can leave the **Edit Post** page and do other things. You'll be able to access all of your draft posts from the **Dashboard** or from the **Edit Posts** page.

Timestamps

WordPress will also let you alter the timestamp of your post. This is useful if you are writing a post today that you wish you'd published yesterday, or if you're writing a post in advance and don't want it to show up until the right day. By default, the timestamp will be set to the moment you publish your post. To change it, just find the **Publish** box, and click on the **Edit** link (next to the calendar icon and **Publish immediately**), and fields will show up with the current date and time for you to change:

Change the details, click on the **OK** button, and then click on **Publish** to publish your post (or save a draft).

Managing posts

If you want to see a list of your posts so that you can easily skim and manage them, you just need to go to the **Edit Posts** page in the WP Admin by navigating to **Posts** in the main menu. You'll see a detailed list of your posts, as seen in the following screenshot:

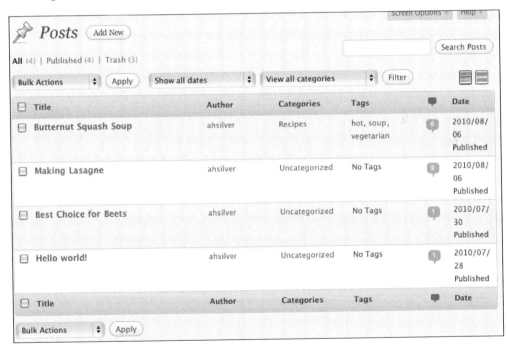

There are are many things you can do on this page, as with every management page in the WP Admin, as we discussed at the beginning of this chapter.

Advanced post options

By now, you have a handle on the most common and simple options for posts, and you may be wondering about some of the other options on the **Edit Post** page. We'll cover them all in this section.

A quick display tip:

When you first visit the **Edit Post** page, all of the four advanced options (**Excerpt**, **Send Trackbacks**, **Custom Fields**, and **Discussion**) are "open" below the post content. If you never use them and want to clean up the look of this page, you can single-click each bar and they'll collapse. You can also rearrange them by dragging them to form a new order.

You can also use **Screen Options** (top right of the page) to uncheck certain boxes, and thus not display them at all.

Excerpt and the MORE tag

WordPress offers theme designers the option to show a post's **excerpt** (instead of its full content) on pages within the theme.

> **Excerpt**
>
> Excerpts are optional hand-crafted summaries of your content that can be used in your theme. Learn more about manual excerpts.

This is how the excerpt works:

- If you enter some text into the excerpt box on the **Edit Post** page, that text will be used as the post's excerpt on theme pages that call for it.
- If you do not enter any text into the excerpt box, WordPress will use the first 55 words of the post's content (which is stripped of HTML tags) followed by [...] (which is not a link).
- If you do not enter any text into the excerpt box, and the theme you are using does something special, the number of words and the final text could be different. For example, the TwentyTen theme replaces the [...] with a link to **Continue Reading**.

You never are required to enter excerpt text. You'll only want to do it if your content's default excerpt doesn't suit you (and if the theme you are using makes use of the excerpt at all).

The **MORE tag** (`<!-- more -->`) should not be confused with the excerpt. This is different from the excerpt because you, not the theme designer, control its use. Text before this tag, for any post that has it, will be the only thing that's shown on all blog pages (for example homepage, category page, search results page, and so on). The full post text will *only* show up on the single post page. All you have to do is put the `<!-- more -->` link at the spot in your post where you'd like the cut-off to be. WordPress will automatically cut off the post there and replace it with a **Read the rest of this post** link.

To add this tag to a post, first place your cursor on the spot where you'd like the post to be split up. Then click on the **more** tag button in the editor. If you're using the Visual editor, the button you want to click looks like the following:

If you're using the HTML editor, the button looks like this:

Trackbacks

Trackbacks are useful if you write a blog post that is a response to an old post on someone else's blog and you want them to know about it.

 Be aware that this is not necessary for current up-to-date WordPress sites, which use an automated system called "pingbacks".

If you want to notify an older blog via trackback, just copy the trackback URL from that person's blog post and paste it into this box. An excerpt of your blog post will show up as a comment on their blog post.

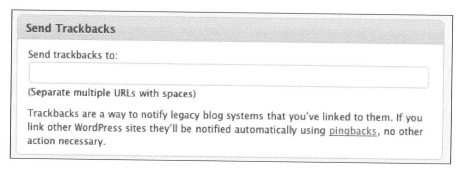

Trackbacks are becoming somewhat out-of-date with the advent of pinging. In fact, many WordPress themes are written to essentially disable trackbacks. **Pinging** is WordPress' way of notifying popular update services, such as Ping-o-Matic!, which other people use to keep up-to-date with your blog and other people's blogs. We will explain more about pinging in the following section.

Discussion

The **Discussion** box has two checkboxes in it: one for allowing comments, and the other for trackbacks and pingbacks. When you first install WordPress, both these checkboxes will be checked by default. You have to uncheck them if you want to turn off the comments or trackbacks and pingbacks for the post.

Pingbacks are essentially the same as trackbacks, but differ in two important ways:

- The notification from your blog to the blog of the person you're commenting on happens automatically—you don't have to enter a special URL into a special field. All you have to do is link your blog post to their blog post.

- Pingbacks don't send any content.

If you uncheck the **Allow comments** box, visitors will not be able to comment on this blog post.

If you uncheck the **Allow trackbacks and pingbacks on this page** box, when other people mention your blog post and link to it on their own websites, your blog post won't notice and won't care. So, if you are using WordPress to run a non-blog website, this is the best option for you.

If the box stays checked, other people's pingbacks about this post will show up under your post along with comments, if any. If you're using WordPress to run a blog website, you'll want pingback to stay checked—especially if you want sites such as Technorati and other rating/authority sites to stay alerted.

If you want either or both of these boxes to be unchecked by default, go to **Settings** and then **Discussion** in the main menu. You can uncheck either or both of the boxes labeled **Allow link notifications from other blogs (pingbacks and trackbacks)** and **Allow people to post comments on the article**:

Learning more:

To learn more about trackbacks and pingbacks you can visit the following sites:

`http://www.tamba2.org.uk/wordpress/ping.`

`http://codex.wordpress.org/Introduction_to_Blogging#Trackbacks.`

`http://codex.wordpress.org/Introduction_to_Blogging#Pingbacks.`

Custom Fields

Custom Fields is a way for you to add additional information about your blog posts that are not part of WordPress by default. By default, every WordPress post has many pieces of information (fields) such as title, content, date, categories, and so on. If there is a field you want all or many of your posts to have, you can add it here (in the Custom Field).

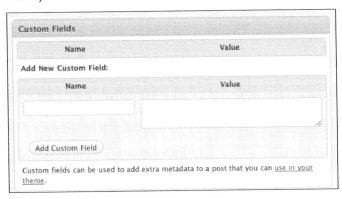

For example, let's say you are a gadget reviewer and every blog post is a review of some new gadget. Every time you write a review, you're writing it about a product made by some company, and you'd like to have that company's logo associated with the blog post. You can make a custom field called **company_logo** and the value can be the path to the logo image.

To display or make use of this custom field information, you either have to modify your theme files manually, or use a plugin.

Learning more

Read more about custom fields in the WordPress codex at `http://codex.wordpress.org/Using_Custom_Fields`.

Protecting content

WordPress gives you the option to hide posts. You can hide a post from everyone but yourself by marking it **Private**, or you can hide it from everyone but the people with whom you share a password by marking it as **Password protected**. To implement this, look at the **Publish** box at the upper right of the **Edit Post** page. If you click on the **Edit** link next to **Visibility: Public**, a few options will appear:

If you click on the **Password protected** radio button, you'll get a box where you can type a password. Visitors to your blog will see the post title along with a note that they have to type in a password to read the post.

If you click on the **Private** radio button, the post will not show up on the blog at all to any viewers, unless you are the viewer and you are logged in.

If you leave the post **Public** and check the **Stick this post to the front page** checkbox, this post will be the first post on the front page, regardless of its publication date.

Be sure to click on the **OK** button if you make any changes.

Pretty permalinks

Permalinks are the permanent links to a particular post; a URL that will never change. For example, right now, the URL for my **Butternut Squash soup** post is `http://wpbook:8888/?p=15` and that won't ever change. WordPress gives you a way to prettify your URLs. If I modify the permalinks settings for this website, the URL would instead be `http://packt:8888/2008/11/butternut-squash-soup/`. The very last part of the URL, `butternut-squash-soup`, is called the post's **slug**. WordPress chooses the slug by taking my post title, making it all lowercase, removing all punctuation, and replacing spaces with dashes. If I'd prefer it to be something else, such as `squash-soup`, I can change it in the area just below the post's title:

Just click on **Edit** to change the slug. Readable URLs are something that Google search loves, so using them helps to optimize your site for search engines. It also helps users figure out what a post is about before clicking on the URL.

By default, pretty permalinks will not be turned on for your WordPress installation. To turn them on, navigate to **Settings | Permalinks**. Click on one of the radio buttons, for example **Month and name**, and click on **Save Changes** at the bottom of the page:

Common settings

○ Default	`http://wpbook:8888/?p=123`
○ Day and name	`http://wpbook:8888/2010/08/11/sample-post/`
● Month and name	`http://wpbook:8888/2010/08/sample-post/`
○ Numeric	`http://wpbook:8888/archives/123`
○ Custom Structure	`/%year%/%monthnum%/%postname%/`

Optional

If you like, you may enter custom structures for your category and tag URLs here. For exam links like `http://example.org/topics/uncategorized/`. If you leave these blank the def

Category base	
Tag base	

Save Changes

As mentioned in *Chapter 2*, your server environment has to be friendly to pretty permalinks (that is running Apache, with `mod_rewrite` turned on). If you have trouble getting pretty permalinks to work on your blog, send the error WordPress gives you to your hosting company, and they can usually help you understand what you can do to fix the problem with your server.

If the Permalinks page has a permissions problem and can't edit your .htaccess file, WordPress will give you some lines of code that you can copy and paste into a blank file. You can then upload that file via FTP, name it `.htaccess`, and thus create it yourself.

Additional writing options

In addition to simply logging into the WP Admin, you have two other choices of ways for adding posts to your blog.

Press This

WordPress offers a neat bookmark called **Press This**. You can put it into your browser's bookmarks or favorites, which will let you quickly write a blog post about the website you're visiting. (This used to be named the **bookmarklet**.) You may have encountered this same feature as offered by Facebook, Del.ico.us, and other social networking sites.

You just have to add **Press This** to your browser once, and then you can use it anytime. To add the **Press This** link to your browser in the WP Admin, go to the **Tools** page. On the bottom of the **Tools** page is a **Press This** link. Just use your mouse, and drag it up to your browser's bookmark bar.

Now you can use it! For example, if you're reading a newspaper website and you read an article you'd like to mention in a blog post, just click the **Press This** bookmark (or favorite). A window will pop up with the **Edit Post** page in it and the URL of the site at which you're looking already written in as a link:

You can then write whatever additional text you want, add tags and categories, and then either save it as a draft or publish it right away.

Posting via e-mail

If you want to add a post to your blog without having to open the WP Admin and log in, you can set up your WordPress installation to accept posts sent via e-mail. First, you have to set up a special secret e-mail address that is accessible via POP. WordPress will check that e-mail address and turn any e-mails in it into posts. If you decide to set up this feature, you will have to be sure not to use this e-mail address for any other purpose!

Once you have the e-mail address set up at your mail server, go to your WP Admin and navigate to **Settings | Writing**. Scroll down a bit to **Post via e-mail**:

Post via e-mail

To post to WordPress by e-mail you must set up a secret e-mail account with POP3 access. Any mail received at this address will be posted, so it's a good idea to keep this address very secret. Here are three random strings you could use: `a7OMJato`, `d4kT4avK`, `FbA6ZxYE`.

Mail Server	mail.example.com	Port	110
Login Name	login@example.com		
Password	password		
Default Mail Category	Uncategorized		

Now just enter the server, login name, and password into the **Writing Settings** page and be sure to click on the **Save Changes** button. Note that on this page, WordPress provides you with three random strings you could use for the e-mail address, so you might want to visit this page first to get one, then set up your POP account, and then return to this page to set up Post via e-mail.

Discussion on your blog—comments

Comments are an important part of most of the blogs. While you are the only person who can write blog posts, the visitors to your blog can add comments to your posts. This can fuel a sense of community within a blog, allow people to give you feedback on your writing, and give your visitors a way to help or talk to other visitors. The only downside of commenting is that unscrupulous people will try to misuse your blog's ability to accept comments, and will try to post spam or advertisements in your blog instead of relevant comments. Luckily, the WordPress community is always developing more ways of fighting spam.

Adding a comment

If you look at the front page of your blog, you'll see that every post has a link that says **Leave a comment** at the bottom. Clicking on that link will take you to the bottom of the post page, which is where comments can be added, as we saw in *Chapter 2*.

Leave a Reply

Your email address will not be published. Required fields are marked *

Name *

Email *

Website

Comment

You may use these HTML tags and attributes: `<a href="" title=""> <abbr title=""> <acronym title="">` `<b> <blockquote cite=""> <cite> <code> <del datetime=""> <em> <i> <q cite=""> <strike>` `<strong>`

(Post Comment)

If you're logged into the WP Admin, you'll see your name and a space to write your comment. If you're not logged in, you'll see a comment form that any other visitor will see (as above). This form includes fields to fill in name, e-mail, and website, along with the commenting text area.

Once you type in the required information and click on the **Post Comment** button, the comment will be entered into the WordPress database along with all of your other blog information. How soon it shows up on the site depends on your discussion settings.

Discussion settings

In the preceding screenshot, notice that **Name** and **Mail** are both marked required (*). As the owner of this blog, you can change the requirements for comments. First, log into the WP Admin and navigate to **Settings | Discussion**. We explored the first box (**Default article settings**) earlier in this chapter.

Submission, notification, and moderation settings

Let's focus on the checkboxes on this page that relate only to **submission**, **notification**, and **moderation**. The boxes that are checked on this page will determine how much moderation and checking a comment has to go through before it gets posted on the blog.

The default settings are relatively strict. The only way to make a more strictly controlled discussion on your blog is to check **An administrator must always approve the comment**. This option means that no matter what, all comments go into the moderation queue and do not show up on the site until you manually approve them.

Let's look at the settings having to do with *submission*. These two options control what the user has to do before he or she is even able to type in a comment:

- **Comment author must fill out name and e-mail**

  As you noticed in the screenshot in the *Adding a comment* section, **Name** and **Mail** are required. If you leave this checked, then anyone posting a comment will encounter an error if they try to leave either of the fields blank. This doesn't add a huge amount of security because robots know how to fill out a name and an e-mail, and because anyone can put fake information in there. However, it does help your blog readers to keep a track of who is who if a long discussion develops, and it can slightly discourage utterly impulsive commenting.

- **Users must be registered and logged in to comment**

  Most bloggers do not check this box because it means that only visitors who register for the blog can comment. Most bloggers don't want random people registering, and most visitors don't want to be compelled to register for your blog. If you check this box, there's a good chance you'll get no comments (which may be what you want). Alternatively, if you're setting up a blog for a closed community of people, this setting might be useful.

Now let's look at the settings that have to do with *moderation*. These two options have to do with the circumstances that allow comments to appear on the site. They are by the **Before a comment appears** header:

- **An administrator must always approve the comment**

  As I mentioned before, if this box is checked, every comment has to be manually approved by you before it appears on the site.

- **Comment author must have a previously approved comment**

  If you uncheck the box above this, but check this one, then you've relaxed your settings a little bit. This means that if the person commenting has commented before and had his or her comment approved, then the person's future comments don't have to be verified by you; they'll just appear on the website immediately. The person just has to enter the same name and e-mail as the one in the previously approved comment.

  Now let's look at the settings that have to do with *notification*. These two options are under the **Email me whenever** header. These options are related to the circumstances of receiving an e-mail notification about the comment activity.

- **Anyone posts a comment**

  This is generally a good setting to keep. You'll get an e-mail whenever anyone posts a comment—whether or not it needs to be moderated. This will make it easier for you to follow the discussion on your blog, and to be aware of a comment that is not moderated and requires deletion quickly.

- **A comment is held for moderation**

  If you're not particularly interested in following every comment on your blog, you can uncheck the **Anyone posts a comment** checkbox and only leave this one checked. You will only get an e-mail about legitimate-looking comments that appear to need moderation and need your approval.

  The remaining settings, which are all by the **Other comment settings** header, have to do with *comment display* and are pretty self-explanatory. You won't be able to see many of these settings in action until you have lots of comments.

When to moderate or blacklist a comment

If you scroll down the page a bit, you'll see the **Comment Moderation** area:

```
Comment Moderation

          Hold a comment in the queue if it contains  2      or more links. (A common
          characteristic of comment spam is a large number of hyperlinks.)

          When a comment contains any of these words in its content, name, URL, e-mail, or IP,
          it will be held in the moderation queue. One word or IP per line. It will match inside
          words, so "press" will match "WordPress".
```

This is an extension of the moderation settings from the top of the page. Note that if you've checked the **An administrator must approve the comment** checkbox, you can safely ignore this **Comment Moderation** box. Otherwise, you can use this box to help WordPress figure out which comments are probably ok and which might be spam or inappropriate for your blog. You can tell WordPress to suspect a comment if it has more than a certain number of links, as spam comments often are just a list of URLs.

The larger box is for you to enter suspect words and IP addresses:

- Here you can type words that are commonly found in spam (you can figure this out by looking in your junk mail in your e-mail!), or just uncouth words in general.

- The IP addresses you will enter into this box would be those of any comments you've gotten in the past from someone who comments inappropriately or adds actual spam. Whenever WordPress receives a comment on your blog, it captures the IP address for you so that you'll have them handy.

Scroll down a bit more, and you'll see the **Comment Blacklist** box:

```
Comment Blacklist

          When a comment contains any of these words in its content, name, URL, e-mail, or IP,
          it will be marked as spam. One word or IP per line. It will match inside words, so
          "press" will match "WordPress".
```

Unlike the **Comment Moderation** box we just saw, which tells WordPress how to identify the comments to suspect, the **Comment Blacklist** box tells WordPress how to identify comments that are almost definitely bad. These comments won't be added to the moderation queue and you won't get an e-mail about them; they'll be marked right away as spam.

Avatar display settings

The final box on this page is the **Avatars** box:

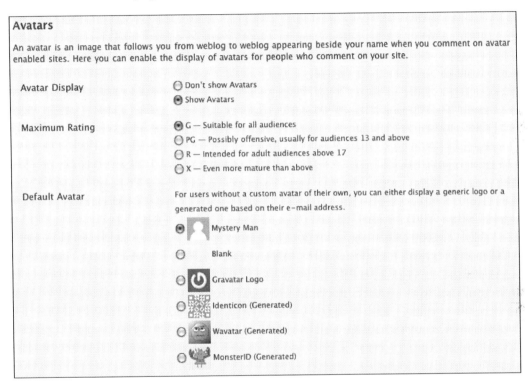

An **avatar** is an image that is a person's personal icon. Visitors who are very active on the Internet and comment frequently may have set up an avatar that they like to use. If so, it will show up on your blog if you leave the **Show Avatars** radio button checked.

The second box, **Maximum Rating**, will tell WordPress if it should not show avatars that have been rated too highly.

The third box, **Default Avatar**, tells WordPress what avatar to use for visitors who do not come with their own avatar. When you installed WordPress, it created a comment for you on the first post, and also created a default avatar for you. You can see the default avatar, **Mystery Man**, in use on the **Hello World!** post:

Hello world!

Posted on July 28, 2010 by ahsilver

Welcome to WordPress. This is your first post. Edit or delete it, then start blogging!

This entry was posted in Uncategorized. Bookmark the permalink. Edit

Best Choice for Beets →

One Response to *Hello world!*

Mr WordPress *says:*

July 29, 2010 at 8:34 pm (Edit)

Hi, this is a comment.
To delete a comment, just log in and view the post's comments. There you will have the option to edit or delete them.

Reply

If you want to create your own avatar that will follow you around the Internet, I suggest you sign up for a **Gravatar** (Globally Recognized **Avatar**). This service was started by the WordPress people; if you have registered for WordPress.com, you can login with those same credentials and set up your Gravatar at http://gravatar.com.

Moderating comments

Now that we've thoroughly explored the settings for which comments need to be moderated, let's discuss what you actually need to do to moderate comments. Moderating means that you look over a comment that is in limbo and decide whether it's good or bad. If it's good, it gets to appear on the website; and if it is bad, it's either marked as spam or is deleted and is never seen by anyone but you and the poster who wrote it.

To view comments waiting for moderation, log in to your WP Admin and navigate to **Comments** in the main menu.

If you have any comments waiting for moderation, there will be a little number in the main menu telling you how many comments await moderation.

This main **Comments** page is fully featured, just like the **Posts** page. For each comment, you see the following information from left to right:

- Comment text, along with links to **Approve** it so that it shows up on the site, you can also mark it as **Spam**, **Delete** it, **Edit** it, **Quick Edit** it, or **Reply** to it
- Commenter name, avatar, e-mail address, and IP
- Comment submission time and date

- The title of the post on which the comment was made (which is also a link to edit that post), a number in parentheses indicating how many approved comments are already there on that post (which is also a link that will filter the comments list so that it shows only comments on this page), and a link to the post itself (indicated with a hash **#**)

Comments that are awaiting moderation have a yellow background, like the first comment in the preceding screenshot (you can also see my Gravatar, which shows up for the second comment).

You can click on the **Quick Edit** link for any post to open form fields right within this list. This will allow you to edit the text of the post and the commenter's name, e-mail, and URL.

You can use the links at the top—**All**, **Pending**, **Approved**, and **Spam**—to filter the list based on those statuses. You can also filter either pings or comments with the **Show all comment types** pull-down filter menu. You can check one or more comments to apply any of the bulk actions available in the **Bulk Actions** menus at the top and bottom of the list.

Another quick way to get to this page, or to apply an action to a comment, is to use the links in the e-mail that WordPress sends you when a comment is held for moderation.

How to eliminate comment spam

Comment spam are comments that get posted on your blog that have spam content, just like spam e-mail. If you've set up your moderation settings to be relatively secure, then these comments won't appear on your blog. However, you may get dozens of e-mail a day from WordPress asking you to moderate comments that it knows need moderation, but doesn't know are spam.

The best tool available for eliminating comment spam from your blog is the **Akismet** plugin. This plugin, which comes (though inactive) with your WordPress installation, utilizes the Akismet spam-fighting service. We'll be discussing plugins in more detail later in this book. For now, we'll review how to get Akismet working on your blog. If your blog is built on WordPress.com, then Akismet is already activated by default on your blog.

Learning more

You can learn more about the Akismet spam-fighting service at http://akismet.com/.

Getting a WordPress.com API key

The Akismet plugin requires that you have a `WordPress.com` API key. To get one, you have to create an account at `WordPress.com`, even if you don't have a blog there. Follow the instructions in *Chapter 2* to create an account at `WordPress.com`. Once your account is active, log in to `WordPress.com` and use the menu at the very top to go to your **My Account**, and then **Personal Settings**. Once there, you'll see your **WordPress.com API key** right at the top:

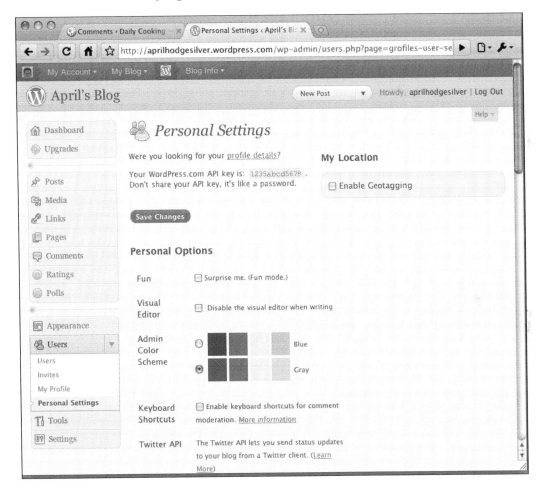

Select and copy that text. You may want to paste it into a text file to be sure you have it.

Activating Akismet

Now go back to your WordPress installation and navigate to **Plugins** in the main menu:

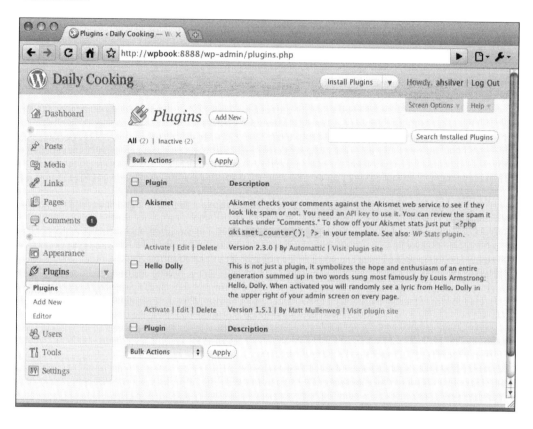

You'll see Akismet listed as the first plugin. Click on the **Activate** link. A yellow message bar will appear at the top of the page that says **Akismet is almost ready. You must enter your WordPress.com API key for it to work.** Click on that link and you'll be taken to a page where you can enter your API key you copied from WordPress.com:

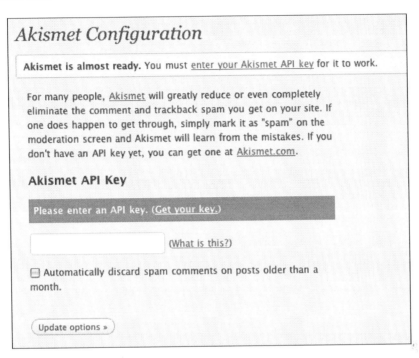

Paste your API key into the box. I suggest you also check the box below it to discard spam comments automatically. Akismet is very good at identifying which comment is actually spam, and checking this box will make those comments disappear. However, if you're concerned about Akismet misidentifying comments, leave this unchecked.

Now click on **Update options>>** and your blog is protected from comment spam!

Adding and managing categories

Earlier in this chapter, you learned how to add a category quickly when adding a post. Now let's talk about how to manage your categories in a bigger way. First, navigate to **Posts | Categories** in your WP Admin. You'll see the **Categories** page:

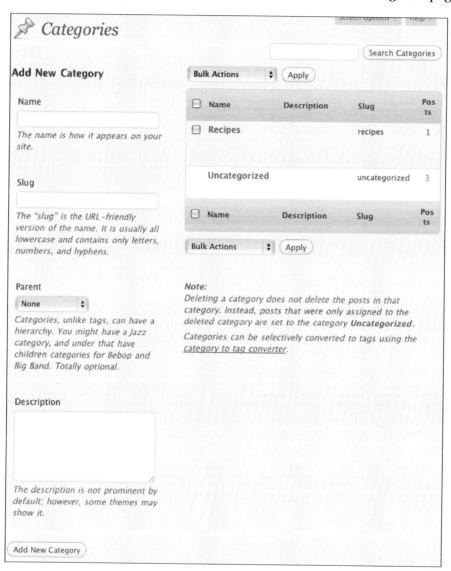

This is a useful page that combines the ability to add, edit, and review all of your categories. As you can see, any category that you've added via the **Edit Post** page is listed. You can **Edit**, **Quick Edit**, or **Delete** any category by clicking on the appropriate link in the list.

If you add a category on this page, you can also choose its slug. The **slug** is the short bit of text that shows up in the URL of your site if you have pretty permalinks enabled. If you don't choose a slug, WordPress will create one for you by taking the category name, reducing it to all lowercase, replacing spaces with dashes, and removing any other punctuation mark.

Another thing you can do on this page is choose a parent category for any category. If you choose to use parent categories, your categories will be displayed hierarchically.

Summary

In this chapter, you learned everything you need to know to add content to your blog and manage that content. You learned about posts, categories, and comments. You discovered tags, spam, and excerpts. You also learned about adding and editing images, using the rich text editor, changing timestamps, customizing excerpts, and the different ways of posting.

Your control of your blog content is complete, and you are well equipped to set your blog on fire!

In the next chapter, you'll learn about all the other types of content that you can manage on your website with WordPress.

4
Pages, Plugins, Image Galleries Menus, and More

You now have the blog part of your website fully under control. By now, you've probably noticed that WordPress offers you a lot more than simply posts, comments, and categories.

In this chapter, we will explore and control all of the other content types that WordPress already has. You'll be able to create static pages that aren't a part of your ongoing blog, bookmark links that will drive visitors to other websites, and add and manage built-in image galleries to display photos and other images. You'll also learn how to manage navigation menus and also add plugins, which will enhance the capabilities of your entire website.

Pages

At first glance, pages look very similar to posts. Both pages and posts have a title and a content area in which we can write extended text. However, pages are handled quite differently from posts. Pages don't have a timestamp, categories, or tags. Posts belong to your blog, which are meant to be a part of an ongoing expanding section of your website, and are added regularly. Pages are more static and aren't generally expected to change that much.

When you installed WordPress, a page was automatically created for you (along with the first post and first comment). You can see it by clicking on the **About** link in the main navigation menu at the top of your site:

Adding a page

To add a new page, go to your WP Admin, and navigate to **Pages | Add New**, or use the drop-down menu in the top grey menu by clicking on the arrow next to **New Post** and choosing **New Page**. This will take you to the **Add New Page** screen:

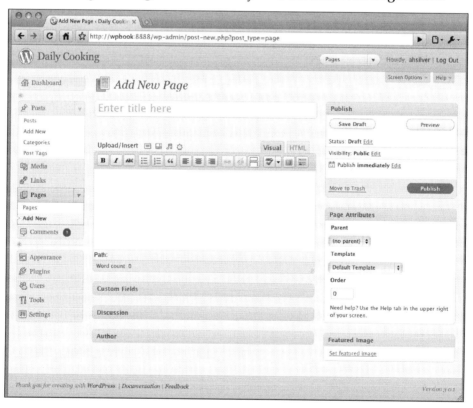

The minimum you need to do to create a new page is type in a title and some content. Then, click on the blue **Publish** button, just as you would for a post, and your new page will appear linked in the main navigation of your website, next to **About**.

You'll recognize most of the fields on this page from the **Add New Post** page, and they work the same for pages as they do for posts. Let's talk about the one new section, the box called **Attributes**.

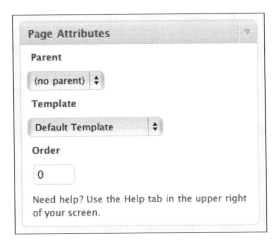

Parent

WordPress allows you to structure your pages hierarchically. This way, you can organize your website's pages into main pages and subpages, which is useful if you're going to have a lot of pages on your site. For example, if I were writing this blog along with three other authors, we would each have one page about us on the site, but they'd be subpages of the main **About** page. If I were adding one of these pages, I'd choose **About** as the parent page for this new page.

Template

Theme designers often offer alternate templates that can be used for special pages. The TwentyTen WordPress theme comes with one additional templates: **One Column, No Sidebar**. Let's try using that template.

Just give your new page a title (for example, **History**) and some content. Then, choose **One Column, No Sidebar** from the **Template** pull-down menu, and publish your page. When you go to your site and click on the **History** link in the main navigation, you'll see the following:

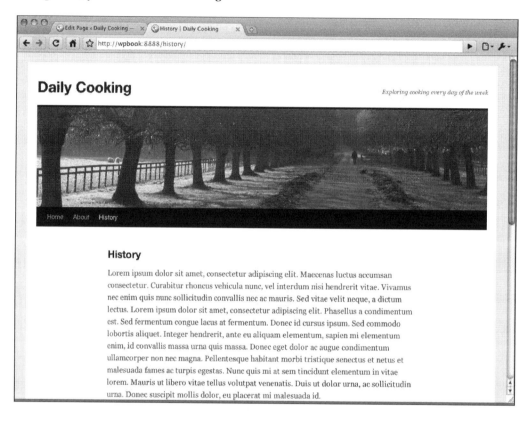

As you can see, the sidebar doesn't appear at all, which makes this different from pages that use the default template (such as the **About** page that we looked at earlier). All that appears is your content.

This particular template can be useful if you want to have a page that removes the distraction of the sidebar. Other themes may come with a variety of templates, depending on what the theme designer thought you'd find useful. If you're creating your own WordPress theme, you can create any number of templates that have different layouts or have special content.

Order

By default, the pages in your page list on the sidebar or main navigation of your blog will be in alphabetical order by page title. If you want them in some other order, you can specify it by entering numbers in the **Order** box for all of your pages. Pages with lower numbers (**0**) will be listed before pages with higher numbers (**5**).

As you can see, this method of ordering pages is quite clunky, especially if you want to rearrange a bunch of pages in relation to each other. Luckily, there is a plugin named pageMash that makes ordering pages much easier. pageMash creates an additional management page in the WP Admin that displays all of your pages in draggable divs:

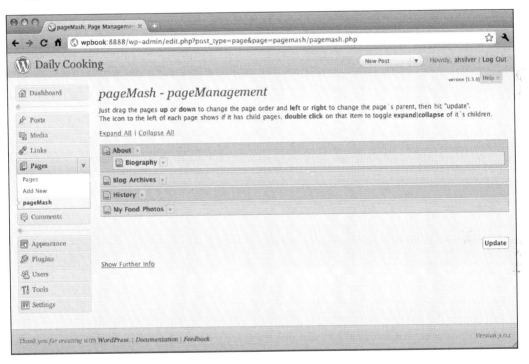

Simply rearrange the blue and green divs, and then click on the **Update** button.

You can download pageMash from `http://wordpress.org/extend/plugins/pagemash/`. Later in this chapter, we'll look in more detail at adding and using plugins.

Managing pages

To see a list of all the pages on your website in the WP Admin, navigate to **Pages | Edit** in the main menu. You'll see the **Pages** screen:

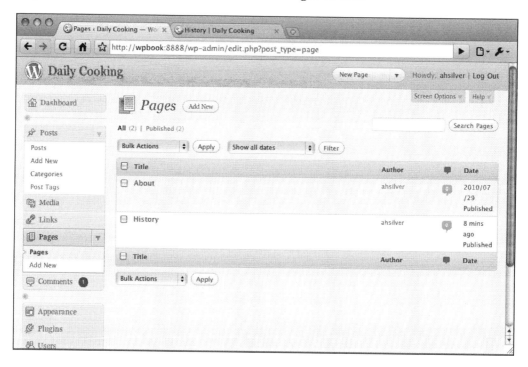

By now this list format should begin to look familiar to you. You've got your list of pages, and in each row are a number of useful links allowing you to **Edit**, **Quick Edit**, **Delete**, or **View** the page. You can click on an author's name to filter the list by that author. You can use the two links at the top, **All** and **Published**, to filter the pages by status. You can check boxes and mass-edit pages by using the **Bulk Actions** menu at the top and bottom of the list. You can also search your pages with the search box at the top.

Menus

As of WordPress 3.0, there are now **Menus** available within the WP Admin. Not all themes will support menus, but luckily for us, TwentyTen does.

The Menus feature lets you create custom menus with links to pages, category or tag archives, and even arbitrary links to any URL. Then you can place your custom menu into your theme.

Adding a Menu

Let's take a look at the Menus management screen. To get there, just navigate to
Appearance | Menus:

To create your first menu, enter a title where it says **Enter menu name here**, and then click on the **Create Menu** button. Your new menu will be created, with nothing in it, and all of the grayed-out areas of the page will become available. You can select a checkbox next to a page, and click on **Add to Menu**:

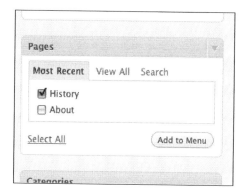

You can enter a URL in the **Custom Links** box, and click on **Add to Menu**:

You can click checkboxes next to one or more categories, and click on **Add to Menu**:

Then, be sure to click on **Save Menu** in the upper-right corner. Following is what my new menu looks like now:

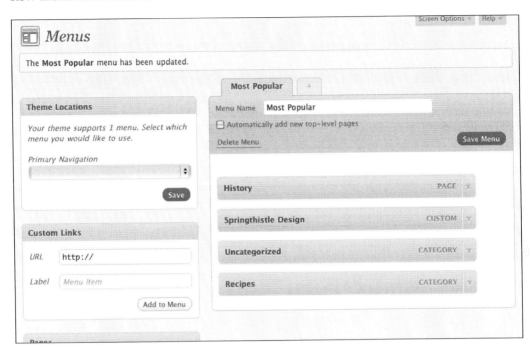

You can also drag items to the right to make them subitems of the item above. For example, I'll add my **About** page to the menu and make sure **History** is a subitem. Now, my menu looks like the following:

You can make more menus by using the + tab at the top to repeat the process above. Now you might ask: I created my new menu, but how do I make it show up on my site? Read on...

Displaying a Menu

If you have a menu-enabled theme, then once you have one menu, a new box will appear on the Menus page showing you the menu locations. TwentyTen has just one menu location, and it's named **Primary Navigation**:

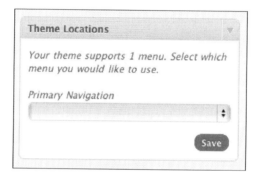

In that pull-down menu, you'll see a list of all the menus you created. You can choose to have one of them displayed in the **Primary Navigation**. If I choose the menu I just created to show there (and click on **Save** in that box), then my primary navigation on the website will look like the following:

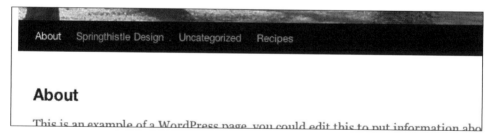

As you can see, TwentyTen displays subitems in a rollover menu activated by the location of your mouse cursor. The other place that your menus can be used is in an instance of the Custom Menu widget.

Widgets

A **widget** is a small box of content, dynamic or not, that shows up somewhere on a widget-enabled site. Often, that location is in the sidebar of a blog, but that's not a rule. A widget area can be anywhere a theme developer wants it to be. Common widgets contain:

- A monthly archive of blog posts
- Recent comments posted on the blog
- A clickable list of categories
- A tag cloud
- A search box, and so on

Most themes these days are widget-enabled, with one or more widget areas (they work like locations for menus) available on your blog. To control the widgets on your new TwentyTen-themed website, navigate to **Appearance | Widgets**:

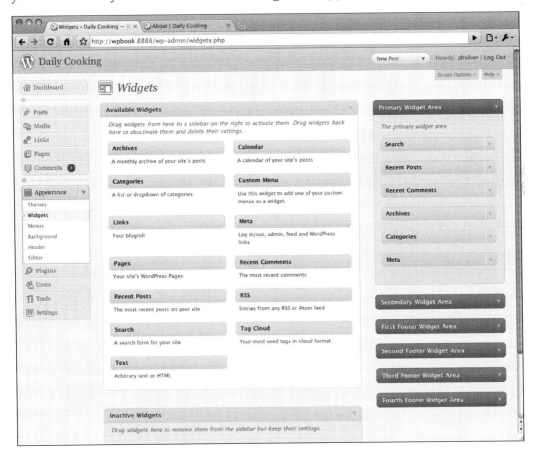

TwentyTen comes with a whopping SIX widget areas. One of them, which is your right sidebar, comes pre-loaded with six widgets in it:

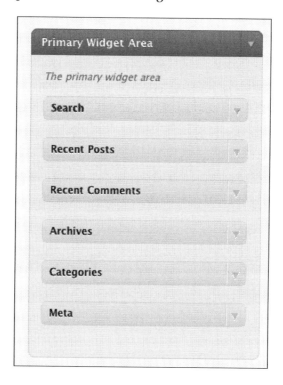

You can click on the little down arrow at the right of any widget to expand the details and see the options. You can drag a new widget in from the collection of **Available Widgets** on the left. You can drag existing widgets up and down to change their order. You can delete a widget by expanding it, and then clicking on **Delete**. Experiment with putting widgets into different widget areas and then refresh your blog to see how they look. Always be sure to click **Save** if you make changes to a widget. In the next section, we'll specifically look at the process of adding a **Links** widget to the sidebar.

Links

WordPress gives you a very powerful way of organizing external links or bookmarks on your site. This is a way to link other related blogs—websites you like, websites that you think your visitors will find useful, or just any category of link you want—to your blog. Speaking of categories, you can create and manage link categories that are separate from your blog categories.

When you installed WordPress, it created the link category **Blogroll**, along with a number of links in that category. You can see them on the main Links screen in the WP Admin:

Adding a new link

Let's add a new link to the **Blogroll** category. In your WP Admin, navigate to **Links | Add New**. This will take you to the **Add New Link** page, which has a number of boxes in which you can add information about your new link:

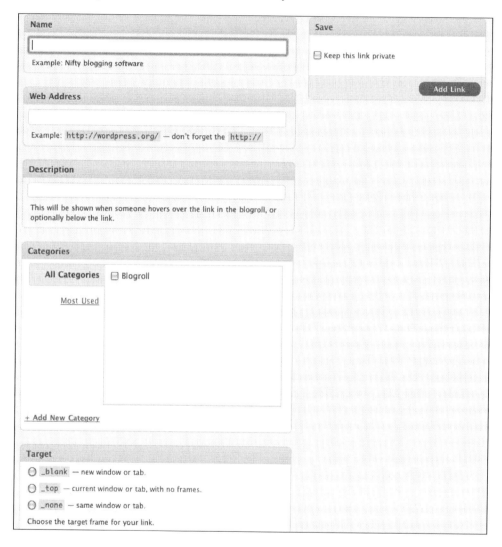

Of all the fields on this page, it's the top two that are the most important. You need to give your link a **Name**, which is the text people will see and can click on. You also need to give a **Web Address**, which is the URL of the website. You can optionally add a description, which will show up when visitors hover over the link and possibly in other places, depending on your theme.

The other two most-often used fields on this page are **Categories** and **Target**. The **Categories** box in the preceding screenshot should look familiar because it's very similar to the **Categories** selection box for Posts (However, Link Categories and Post Categories are completely separate from each other.). You can assign a category to the new link that you're adding or create a new category by clicking on the **+ Add New Category** link. Your links will be organized by the categories on your website.

The **Target** box lets you choose whether your **visitors** will be taken to a new window, or a new tab, when they click on the link. I generally recommend using **_blank** when sending people to an external website.

The other boxes on this page are used less commonly. You can use the **Link Relationship (XFN)** boxes to specify **XFN (XHTML Friends Network)** relationships between you and any individuals to which you link.

 Learning more: If you want to learn more about XFN take a look at this website: `http://gmpg.org/xfn/`.

The final **Advanced** box at the bottom of this page will allow you to specify:

- An image that belongs with this link (for example, the logo of the company whose site to which you are linking)
- The RSS feed for the website to which you're linking
- Any notes you have about the site, beyond what you entered into the **Description** box
- A rating for the site from **0** to **9**

To make use of any of these pieces of information, you need to have a theme that recognizes and makes use of them.

At the top right of the page is a **Save** box with a checkbox that you can check if you want to keep the link private; that is, if you don't want it to show up on your site to anyone but you. Click on the **Add Link** button in that box to save your new link.

Displaying links

The TwentyTen theme doesn't come with any feature that actually shows your links. The easiest way to display them is to add a Links widget to your sidebar. Other themes may have other built-in ways to display links.

To add a Links widget, navigate to the widgets page and drag the links widget over to the **Primary Widget Area** box:

After you click on the **Save** button, visit your website again and you'll see the list of links added to the sidebar:

Managing links and categories

You can manage your links just as you manage posts and pages by navigating to **Links**. From here, you can click on the name of a link to edit it, click on the URL to visit it, and see which categories you've chosen for it. Using the **View all Categories** pull-down menu, you can filter links by categories, change the order, and do bulk deletes.

Just as with post categories, you can manage and add new link categories on the **Link Categories** page. You can access this page by navigating to **Links | Link Categories**:

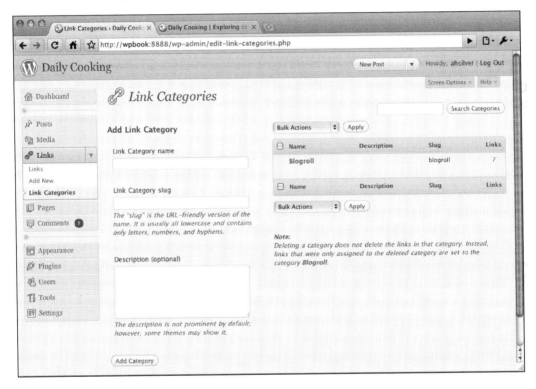

From this page, you can both add a new category using the form at the left, and also manage your existing categories using the table at the right.

Media library

The media library is where WordPress stores all of your uploaded files—images, PDFs, music, video, and so on. To see your media library, navigate to **Media** in the main menu:

This is the now-familiar management table. My media library has only two photos. I uploaded one to insert into the Butternut Squash soup post, and one to be the Featured Image for that post. As you can see from preceding screenshot, it shows me the following:

- A thumbnail of the image. If this were another type of media, I'd see an icon representing the type of media.

- The title that I gave the file when I uploaded it, along with the format extension.

- The author.

- Information about which post or page the file is attached to. This will be important when it comes to making an image gallery. The uploaded file will be attached to the post or page that you are editing while uploading a file.

- The number of comments waiting on the attached post or page.
- The date when the file was uploaded.

If you hover over the row with your mouse, links for **Edit, Delete Permanently**, and **View** will appear. You can click on the file's title or the **Edit** link to edit the **Title, Caption, Description, Alt text**, and even the image itself. More on that in a bit.

You can also add a new file to your media library. Navigate to **Media | Add New** to get a page similar to the upload media page that you got while uploading a file for a post. When you click on the **Select Files** button and select the file to be uploaded, it will upload it and then give you the same options you got when uploading an item through a page or post.

Enter a title, caption, and description if you want, and click on the **Save all changes** button.

Your new item will appear in the media library and will be unattached to any post or page. However, you'll still be able to use what you just uploaded in any post or page.

To do that, click on the **Upload/Insert** button as you did before on the **Add/Edit Post** or **Add/Edit Page** screen. However, instead of choosing a file **From Computer**, click on the **Media Library** tab on the top of the box:

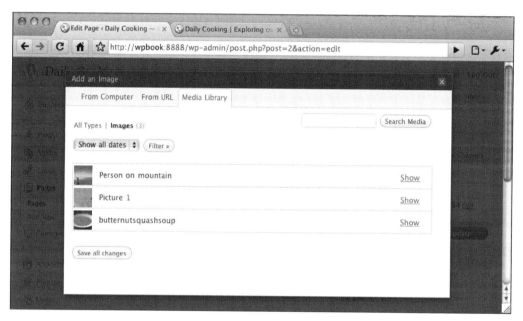

When you click on the **Show** link that is next to the image you want to use, you'll get the same set of options you got after uploading an image. Now you can click on the **Insert into Post** button. The media item will now show as **Attached to** that post or page.

Adding plugins

Plugins are little packages of code that you can add to WordPress to increase its functionality. Developers all over the world create plugins! Many of them are available for use at no cost; others ask for a donation or a small fee.

The steps for installing a plugin are simple:

1. Find your plugin.
2. Install and activate it.
3. Configure and/or implement it (if necessary).

Finding your plugin

The best place to find plugins is the WordPress **Plugin Directory** at `http://wordpress.org/extend/plugins/`. There are more plugins every day (as of this writing, there are 12,644) and millions of downloads (143,376,466 and counting). You can search plugins by topic and by tag, as well as see a list of the most popular, newest, and recently updated plugins. This is the best available plugin resource and you should always go here first when looking for a plugin.

You can also do Google searches. I recommend searching for the problem you're trying to solve and see what plugins other users recommend and why. Often, there are multiple plugins that perform similar functions, and you will find the feedback of other WordPress users valuable in choosing between them. However, as you do this, be sure to keep an eye out for malicious or poorly-coded plugins that could break your website or allow someone to hack into it. I am always wary of a new plugin with no reviews, comments, or feedback from users, in addition, of course, to those plugins that have bad feedback about them on the Internet.

For the purposes of this section of the book, I'll walk you through adding a plugin that I think everyone should have. It's called **WP-DB-Backup** and it adds the ability to easily create a complete database export of your blog.

Installing and activating the plugin

There are two ways to get the plugin into your WordPress installation.

- Install from within the WP Admin
- Install manually

The first option, installing from within the WP Admin, is generally quicker and easier, but it's not possible in all cases. You need to be using WordPress 2.7 or higher, and you have to be on a server that's configured correctly, in a way that lets WordPress add files. Plus, the plugin you want to install has to be available in the WordPress Plugin Repository.

In the following section, we'll go over auto-installation first, and then the manual method.

Auto-installation

If you meet the server and WordPress version requirements for auto-installation, then you can search for and install a new plugin from within the WP Admin. Just navigate to **Plugins | Add New**. If you already know the plugin you want, type its name into the search box.

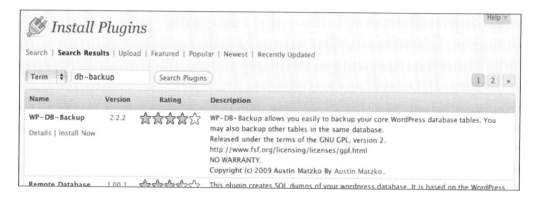

When you see the plugin, you can click **Details** to see the plugin's details:

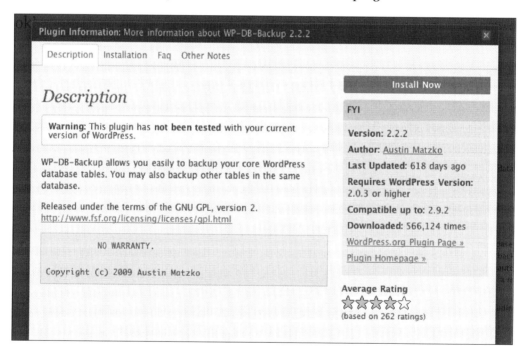

I recommend you always look at this information carefully. Be sure to watch for version compatibility. In this case, the details tell me that this plugin is not officially compatible with the latest version of WordPress, which means you should proceed with caution and be prepared for undocumented bugs. In this particular case, I have personally tested this plugin and know it works fine with this version of WordPress. At this point, you click **Install Now**, and you're done installing! The next screen you see will invite you to activate the plugin:

Installing Plugin: WP-DB-Backup 2.2.2

Downloading install package from http://downloads.wordpress.org/plugin/wp-db-backup.2.2.2.zip...

Unpacking the package...

Installing the plugin...

Successfully installed the plugin **WP-DB-Backup 2.2.2**.

Actions: Activate Plugin | Return to Plugin Installer

In the case of this plugin, I do recommend you go ahead and activate it. However, if you're running a live blog and are about to implement a plugin that will immediately change the appearance of your blog, you should be cautious.

Download, (unzip?), upload

If your situation doesn't match the three requirements above (plugin repository, 2.7+, server setup), then you'll need to install your plugin manually.

First, **download** the plugin from the plugin repository or other website. In this case you're downloading from the following page: `http://wordpress.org/extend/plugins/wp-db-backup/`.

Just click on the orange **Download** button, and save the resulting ZIP file on your computer where you can find it again. (Before downloading any plugin, check the plugin compatibility, just like in the section above on *Auto-installation*).

At this point, if your server is set up correctly, you'll be able to **upload** the ZIP file directly on the **Plugins | Add New | Upload** page:

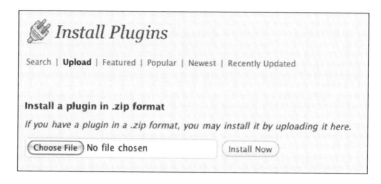

If this automatic uploader *doesn't* work for you, you can do this the old-fashioned way:

First **unzip**, that is, extract the ZIP file you downloaded so that it's a folder, probably named, in this case, `wp-db-backup`.

Using your FTP client, **upload** this folder inside the `wp-content/plugins/` folder of your WordPress installation. You'll also see the two plugins that WordPress came with in that folder—`akismet` and `hello.php`.

Now, go to your WP Admin and navigate to **Plugins**. You'll see the three plugins on this page. Just click on the **Activate** link in the **WordPress Database Backup** row:

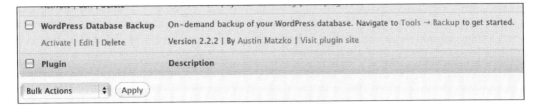

Now, you are ready for the final step, which is to actually make use of this plugin.

Configuring and/or implementing—if necessary

In the case of this plugin, all you have to do is use it. You'll have a new link in your menu to which you can navigate. It's **Tools | Backup**. When you go to this page, you'll be able to choose the tables to back up. If you've installed any plugins that add additional tables, you'll have the option to choose them as well; I always do. I also always check the two boxes to exclude spam comments and post revisions.

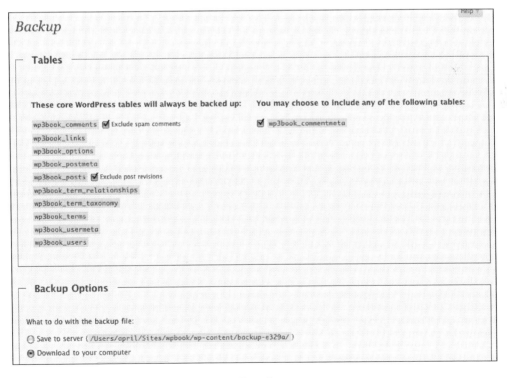

You can now decide if you want to save the backup to your server, download it, or have it e-mailed to you. I suggest downloading it every time.

There is also an option of scheduling regular backups. This is not 100% reliable, so you should probably set up a reminder to check if your backup has been e-mailed to you or not. The frequency you choose should depend on how often you edit your site—once a week is probably often enough for most people.

For other plugins, the configuration and/or implementation steps may be different.

- You may not have to do anything. Some plugins simply change the way WordPress does some things, and activating them is all you need to do.
- You may have to configure a plugin's details before it begins to work. Some plugins need you to make choices and set new settings.
- There may not be a configuration page, but you may have to add some code to one of your theme's template files.

If you're unsure of what to do after you've uploaded and activated your plugin, be sure to read the `readme` file that came with your plugin, or look at the **FAQ** on the plugin's website.

Many plugin authors accept donations. I strongly recommend giving donations to the authors of plugins that you find useful. It helps to encourage everyone in the community to continue writing great plugins that everyone can use.

In the next section, we'll add another useful plugin.

Adding an image gallery

You can add an image gallery to any page or post in your website using WordPress's built-in Image Gallery functionality. There are just three simple steps:

1. Choose a post or page for your image gallery.
2. Upload the images you want in that gallery.
3. Add the special code to the page or post, and save it.

Let's get started.

Choosing a post or page

For my food blog, I'm going to create a new page named **My Food Photos** for my image gallery. You can always do this on an existing page or post. Following is my new page:

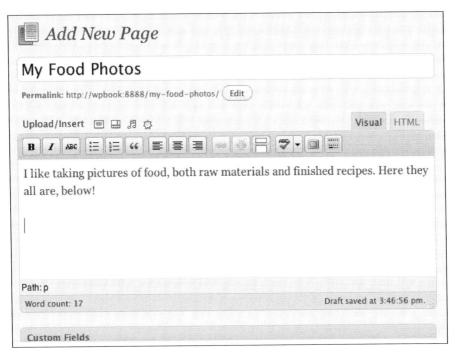

Note where I have left my cursor. I made sure to leave it in a spot on the page where I want my gallery to appear, that is, underneath my introductory text (After creating this page, I will also navigate to **Appearance | Menus** to add it as a subpage under **About**.).

Uploading images

Now click on the **Upload/Insert** image icon and upload some photos (you can choose multiple photos at once).

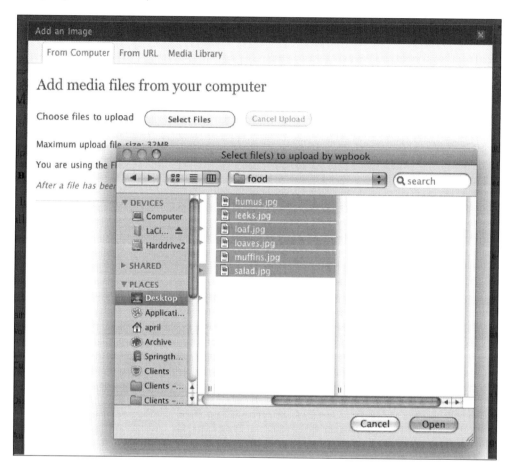

For each photo you upload, enter the title (and a caption if you'd like). When you're done, click on the **Save All Changes** button. You'll be taken to the **Gallery** tab, which will show all of the photos you've uploaded to be attached to this page:

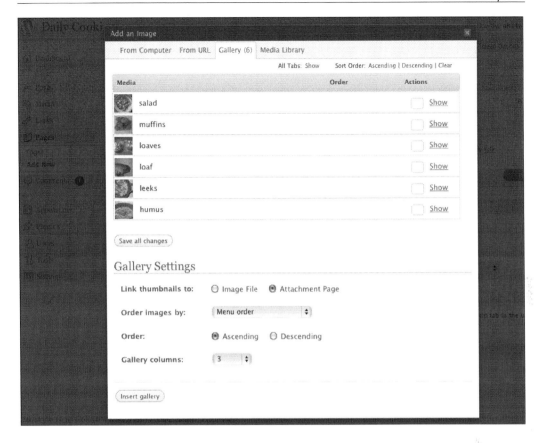

If you want to upload more photos at this point, just click on the **From Computer** tab at the top, and upload another photo.

When you've uploaded all the photos you want (you can add more later), you may want to change the order of the photos. Just enter the numbers 1 through 6 (or however many photos you have) in the **Order** column:

Make sure you click **Save All Changes**.

On most computers, you can, instead of entering numbers, simply drag-and-drop images. WordPress will then generate the order numbers for you automatically.

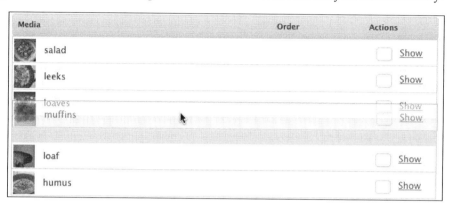

Then, you can review the **Gallery Settings**. There are a number of ways to use the gallery, but there is a single approach that I've found works for most people. You can experiment on your own with other settings and plugins, of course! I suggest you set **Link thumbnails to** to be **Image File** instead of **Attachment Page**. You can leave the other settings as they are for now.

Once all of your settings are done, click on the **Insert gallery** button. This overlay box will disappear, and you'll see your post again. The page will have the gallery icon placeholder in the spot where you left the cursor, as seen in the following screenshot:

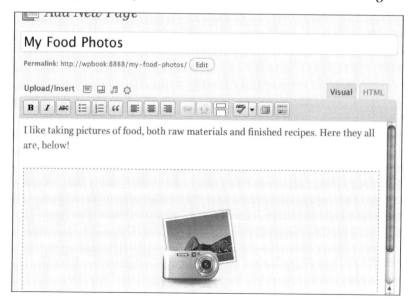

If you're in the HTML view, you'll see the gallery shortcode in that spot:

Note that because I'm uploading these photos while adding/editing this particular page, all of these photos will be "attached" to this page. That's how I know they'll be in the gallery on this page. Other photos that I've uploaded to other posts or pages will not be included in this gallery.

Learning more

The [gallery] shortcode is quite powerful! For example, you can actually give it a list of Media ID numbers—any Media item in your Media Library—to include, or you can tell it to just exclude certain items that are attached to this post or page. You can also control how the Thumbnail version of each image shows whether the medium or large. There is more! Take a look at the codex to get all of the parameters: http://codex.wordpress.org/Gallery_Shortcode.

Now, publish or save your page. When you view the page, there's a gallery of your images as follows:

If you click on one of the images, you'll be linked to the larger version of the image. Now, this is not ideal for navigating through a gallery of images. Let's add a plugin that will streamline your gallery.

Using a lightbox plugin

A lightbox effect is when the existing page content fades a little and a new item appears on top of the existing page. You've seen this effect already in the WP Admin when you clicked on Add/Insert image. We can easily add the same effect to your galleries by adding a plugin. There are a number of lightbox plugins available, but the one I like these days uses jQuery Colorbox. Find this plugin, either through the WP Admin or in the Plugins Repository (http://wordpress.org/extend/plugins/jquery-colorbox/), and install it.

Once you've activated the plugin, navigate to **Settings | jQuery Colorbox**:

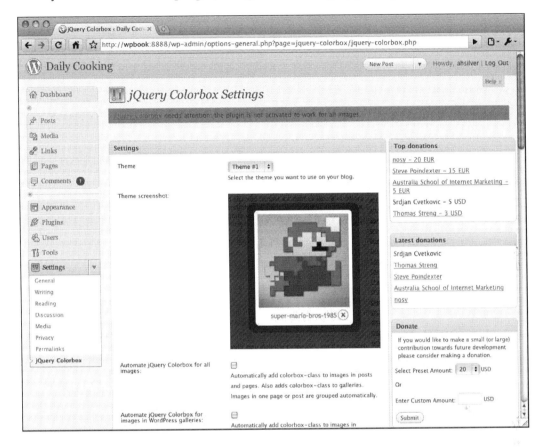

Use the **Theme** pull-down to choose the theme you want (the preview image will update to give you an idea of what it will look like); I've chosen **Theme #4**. Then you can choose to either **Automate jQuery Colorbox for all images** or **Automate jQuery Colorbox for images in WordPress galleries**. You can choose whether to automate for all images; I certainly suggest you automate for images in galleries. You can experiment with the other settings on this page (if you routinely upload very large images, you'll want to use the areas that let you set the maximum size of the colorbox and resize images automatically). You'll want to disable the warning (the very last check box on the page). Then, click on **Save Changes**.

Now, when I go to my image gallery page and click on the first image, the colorbox is activated, and I can click **Next** and **Back** to navigate through the images:

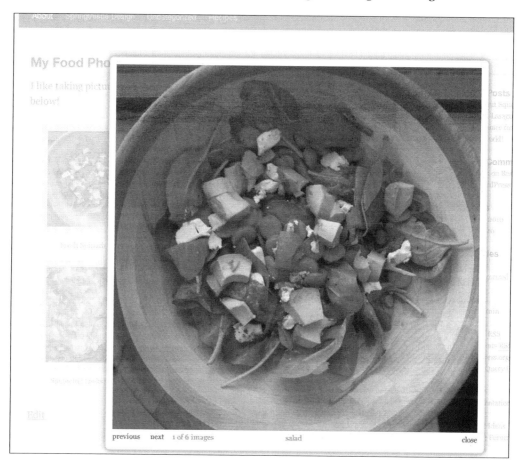

Making your website mobile-friendly

One last thing you might want to do before putting your new website live is to make it mobile-friendly. Mobile devices have very small screens—certainly much smaller than most computers. The design of your theme is probably not ideal for mobile devices. There are many plugins available that will detect if a visitor is using a mobile browser and serve up a different theme instead.

By far, the most popular plugin for this purpose is WPTouch, which you can find at `http://wordpress.org/extend/plugins/wptouch/`. It renders blogs especially quite nicely for the Iphone and Ipod touch.

You can do your own online research and experimentation to figure out which mobile plugin suits your website the best. You can start by looking at plugins with the **mobile** tag in the WordPress Plugins Repository:

`http://wordpress.org/extend/plugins/tags/mobile.`

Summary

This chapter explored all of the content WordPress can manage that's not directly about blogging. You learned about static pages, menus, bookmark links, the media library, image galleries, plugins, and more.

You are now fully equipped to use the WordPress Admin panel to control all of your website's content. Next, you'll want to control the display. In the next chapter, we will start discussing themes.

5
Choosing and Installing Themes

One of the greatest advantages of using a **CMS (Content Management System)** for your blog or website is that you are able to change the look and feel of your website without being knowledgeable about HTML and CSS. Almost every CMS allows users to customize the look of their site without having to worry about their content being changed. These managed looks are named **themes**. On other platforms (for example, Blogger, Joomla!, Drupal, and so on), themes are sometimes called **templates** or **layouts**.

Thousands of WordPress themes are available for download free of cost, and thousands more are available at a pretty low cost. Many of the free themes are developed by members of the WordPress community and listed on WordPress's main website at `http://wordpress.org/extend/themes/`.

Before you change the theme of your current site, you will want to know:

- Some basic things about the theme you're considering
- How to choose the theme that best suits your content and audience
- How to install a theme
- How to modify static content inside these themes

In this chapter, we will discuss all of these topics. This chapter is a ground-up guide to using themes. In the next chapter, we will discuss the advanced topic of developing your own themes.

If you are using `WordPress.com` to host your WordPress website, you cannot upload themes to your site; you have to choose from the hundred or so themes that `WordPress.com` makes available to you. So, you can skip forward to the *Previewing and activating* section of this chapter.

Finding themes

There are dozens of websites that offer WordPress themes for you to download and implement on your website. Many theme developers offer their themes for free, whereas some charge a small fee. Of course, if you cannot find a free theme that fits your needs, you can always hire a theme developer to create a customized theme for you, or you can be your own theme developer (see *Chapter 6*).

WordPress Theme Directory

The first place you should always go to when looking for a theme is the official WordPress **Theme Directory** at `http://wordpress.org/extend/themes/`. This is where everyone in the WordPress community uploads their free themes and tags them with keywords that describe the basic look, layout, and function of their theme. Look at the following screenshot:

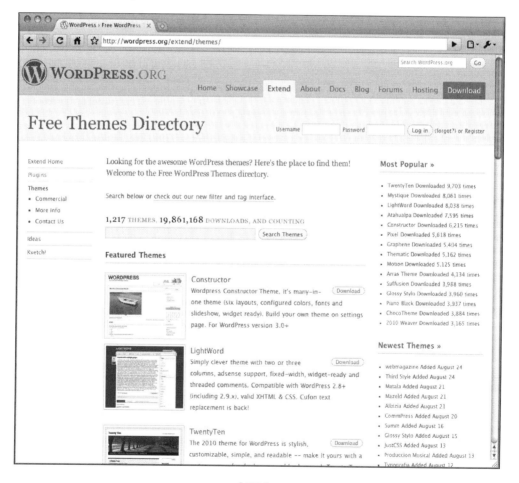

By looking at the list of popular themes on the right, you can see which themes are chosen most often. TwentyTen, as you already know, is the default theme that WordPress uses automatically when you first install it.

To get a better idea of what a theme will look like than what's offered by the thumbnail, just click on the title of the theme (in my case Graphene). You'll be taken to the theme's detail page:

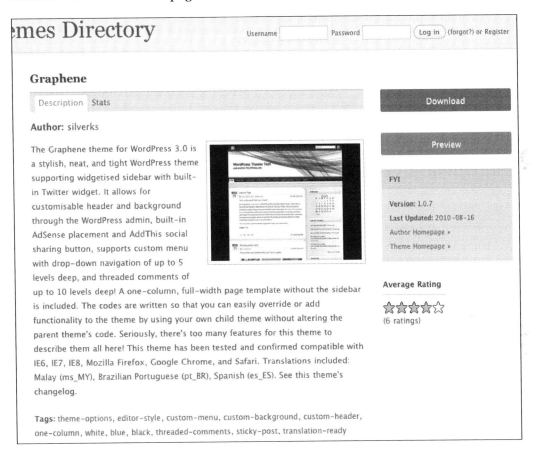

This page shows you the theme's description, all of the tags that apply to it, the average rating given to it by other users, and some comments on the theme. If you click on the **Preview** button, you'll get to see the theme actually in action. The theme in action will look as shown in the following screenshot:

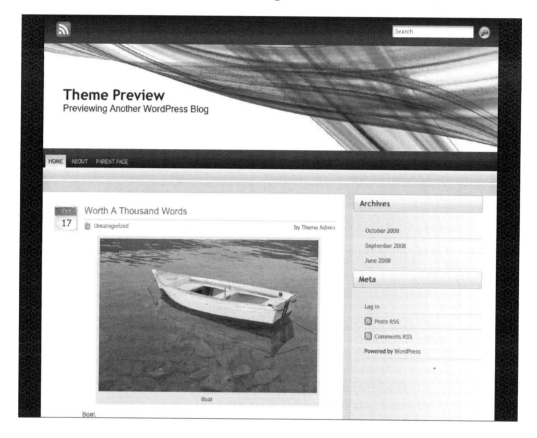

This preview is very useful. It not only shows you exactly what the theme will look like and what is included in the sidebar, but also includes examples of a variety of different HTML and element styles so that you can see how they'll look. These elements include:

- Images
- Headings (1, 2, 3, 4, 5, and 6)
- Paragraphs
- Lists
- Forms

- Tables
- Blockquote
- Code
- Links

If you browse through this site and find a theme you like, make note of it; we'll discuss how to add it to your WordPress site later on in this chapter.

Finding more themes

If you can't find a theme in the directory that you like, you have other options. There are other sites with free themes, and also sites that sell themes for a price. Most commercial themes are offered at two prices. The first price is simply the cost of buying the theme for your own use and can be anywhere from $30 to $80. The second price is the price you pay if you want to be the only user of the theme and that can be anywhere from $500 to $1,500.

Most good commercial theme sites let you see a preview of the theme in action before you buy it. Some also let you customize the theme before download. As with any other online shopping experience, do a little research before buying to make sure you'll be getting a quality theme with decent support. There are plenty of badly-coded themes out there, and even themes with malicious code. Before buying a theme, verify the source of the theme and see if you can find feedback or reviews from anyone else who has purchased it.

To find more sites that offer themes, just do a Google search for "WordPress themes" and you'll get over sixty million hits. Also, keep in mind that you can choose a basic theme now and customize it or create your own from scratch later as you build skills by reading this book.

Some theme basics

So that you'll be better informed when choosing and installing themes, let's take a quick look at some factors to consider when choosing a theme, and what actually makes a theme.

What makes a theme?

A WordPress **theme** is actually a collection of files in a folder. There are no special or unusual formats, just a few requirements for those files in the theme folder. The only requirements for a folder to be a valid WordPress theme are:

1. It should have a `style.css` file and an `index.php` file.
2. The `style.css` file must have the basic theme information in its first five lines.

There are a number of additional files that you'll find in most theme folders. They are:

- A `screenshot.png` file — this is the little thumbnail that shows what the theme looks like
- An `images` folder — this is where all images associated with the theme live
- A variety of files that are used for different purposes (for example, `header.php`, `footer.php`, `page.php`, `single.php`, `archive.php`, and so on)

You don't have to worry about these details now, but knowing them will help you identify what is going on in the themes you download for now. This will also be useful in the next chapter when we discuss making your own theme from scratch.

When you download a theme, you are actually just downloading a zipped folder.

Factors to consider when choosing a theme

As you look through all of the available themes, you'll see that there is quite a variety of both look and feel, and layout. When considering a theme, make sure to ask yourself the following questions:

- Do I like the design of the header?
- Are the sidebars (if any) flexible? Can I choose how many sidebars I want to display? Is it widget-ready?
- Is it complex or simple? Which do I prefer?
- How flexible is the content and layout? Can I choose the column count and widths?
- Does it offer a Theme Settings page where I can customize layout, category display, homepage, and other options?

At this point in WordPress's development, I recommend rejecting any theme that does not support widgets.

Installing and changing themes

Now that you've chosen the theme you want to use, you'll need to install it into your WordPress website.

You'll have two choices.

1. You'll have two choices, as you did when adding new plugins. If you are using WordPress 2.6.3 or above, and **if** the theme you want is in the WordPress theme directory, and **if** your server is set up properly, you can add the theme directly from within the WP Admin.

2. If any of those three conditions are not met, you'll have to download, extract, and then upload the theme.

Adding a theme within the WP Admin

As mentioned in the preceding section, you can add a theme directly from within your WP Admin if you've chosen a theme from the WordPress theme directory, if you're using a current-enough version of WordPress, and if your server settings allow. First, navigate to **Appearance**, and then click on the **Install Themes** tab:

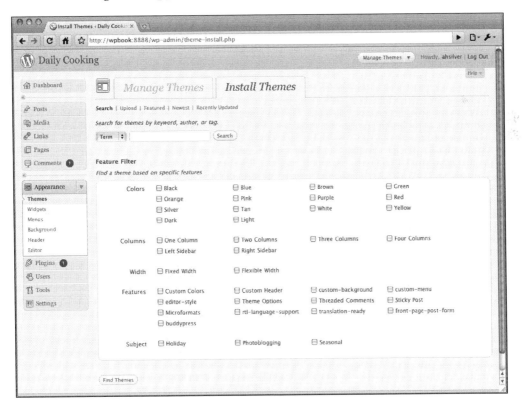

This will look similar to the **Add New Plugins** page because you have some sub-navigation links at the top (**Search, Upload, Featured, Newest, Recently Updated**) along with a search box. You also see checkboxes that will let you narrow down the type of theme for which you're looking (by color, by columns, by feature, and so on). The theme programmers tag their themes with this information, and this is how the theme directory knows which themes meet these criteria.

I've already found a theme I like, so I'll put its name in the search box:

If I click on **Preview**, I will see the same theme preview that I saw on the main theme directory page. Note that at this point, the theme preview will be the same as the preview on the theme directory page, rather than a preview of your own site's content. Until the theme is installed, you won't see a preview of your own site. If I click on **Install** and then confirm by clicking **Install Now**, this theme will be downloaded and added to my collection of themes:

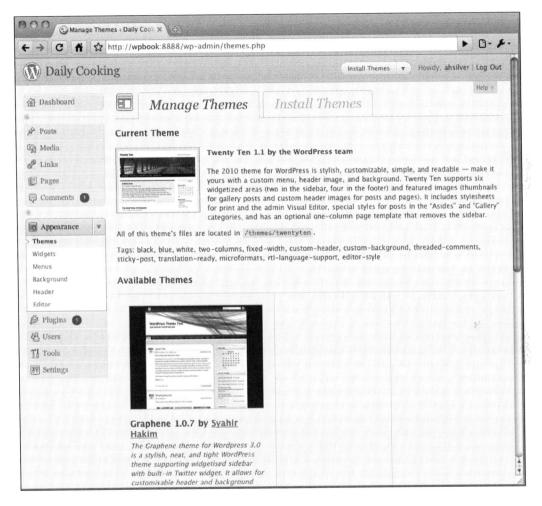

If I click on the thumbnail or the **Preview** link on this page (**Appearance**), I will see a preview of the theme with my own content in it:

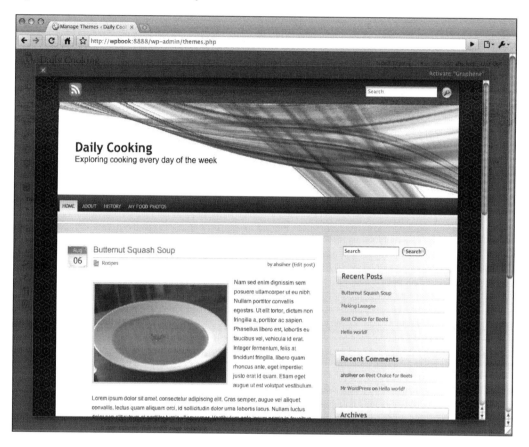

If I like it, I can activate the theme in one of two ways:

1. By clicking **Activate Graphene** in the upper-right corner of the preview window, or

2. By clicking **Activate** in the Graphene box on the main Appearance page

After activating, this theme will be used for my site instead of TwentyTen, the default WordPress theme.

Downloading, extracting, uploading

If you can't install a theme from within the WP Admin for one of the three reasons, you'll have to use the following steps instead.

Once you find a theme that you want to use, download it to your computer, to your desktop for example. When this is done, you'll see a ZIP file on your desktop (for example, `graphene.1.0.7.zip`).

At this point, you can upload the ZIP file through the WP Admin by navigating to **Appearance | Install Themes | Upload**.

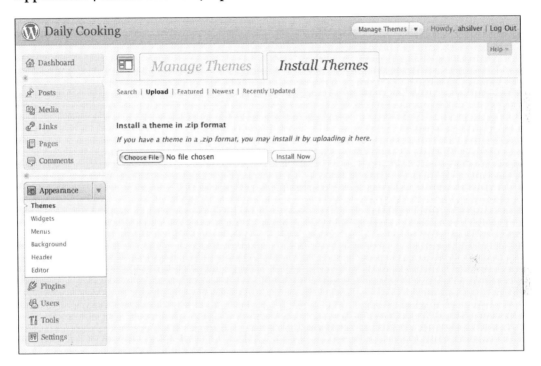

You can choose the ZIP file and upload it that way. If that doesn't work, continue with the steps below to extract and upload the theme files.

If you're using Mac, the ZIP file may have automatically been unzipped for you, in which case you'll see a folder on your desktop instead of the ZIP file or in addition to the ZIP file (for example, `graphene`). If not, then just do the extraction/unzipping manually so that you have the theme folder on your desktop.

Following are the file contents of the Graphene folder that I downloaded:

Name
404.php
▶ ▤ admin
changelog.txt
comments.php
editor-style.css
footer.php
functions.php
header.php
▶ ▤ images
index.php
▶ ▤ languages
license.txt
loop.php
page-onecolumn.php
readme.txt
screenshot.png
search-404.php
search.php
searchform.php
sidebar.php
single.php
style.css

It's got a `style.css` file and an `index.php` file, and so I know it's definitely a valid theme.

Now you need to upload the theme folder to your WordPress website. As you did in *Chapter 2*, you need to FTP to your server. Once there, navigate to your WordPress website's installation folder. Next, go to the `wp-content` folder and then to the `themes` folder. You'll see one theme folder in here already, named `twentyten` (and possibly others as well). These are the themes that come pre-installed with WordPress.

Upload the folder you just unzipped (for example, `graphene`) into the `themes` folder on your server. That's it!

Now when you go to **Appearance** in your WP Admin, the theme will appear. You can **Preview** and **Activate** just as if you'd added it from within the WP Admin (in the preceding section).

Summary

This chapter described how to manage the basic look of your WordPress website. You have learned where to find themes, why they are useful, and how to implement new themes on your WordPress website.

In the next chapter, you will learn, step-by-step, how to build your own theme from scratch.

6
Developing Your Own Theme

You know how to find themes on the Web and install them for use on your WordPress site. However, you may not be able to find the perfect theme, you may want to create a thoroughly personalized theme, or you may be a website designer with a client who wants a custom theme.

In this chapter, you'll learn how to turn your own design into a fully functional WordPress theme that you'll be able to use on your own site. You'll also learn how to convert your theme folder into a ZIP file that can be shared with other WordPress users on the Web.

All you will need before we get started is:

- Your own design
- The ability to slice and dice your design to turn it into HTML

We'll start out with tips on slicing and dicing, so that your HTML and CSS files are as WordPress-friendly as possible, and then cover the steps for turning that HTML build into a fully functional theme.

Note that I assume that you are already comfortable writing and working with HTML and CSS. You don't need to be familiar with PHP, because I'll be walking you through all of the PHP code.

This chapter covers only the very basics of theme creation. This topic actually deserves a whole book, and it has one! I highly recommend the book *WordPress 2.8 Theme Design* by Tessa Blakeley Silver (a 3.0 update to this book is due out soon). This book covers in detail everything you can possibly want to know about creating your own theme, including even such details as choosing a color scheme, considering typography, writing the best CSS, and laying out your HTML using Rapid Design Comping. If this chapter leaves you wanting more, go there!

Setting up your design

Just about any design in the world can be turned into a WordPress theme. However, there are some general guidelines you can follow—both in the design and the HTML/CSS build of your theme—which will easily convert the design into a theme.

Designing your theme to be WordPress-friendly

While you can design your blog any way that you want, a good way to start would be with one of the standard blog layouts.

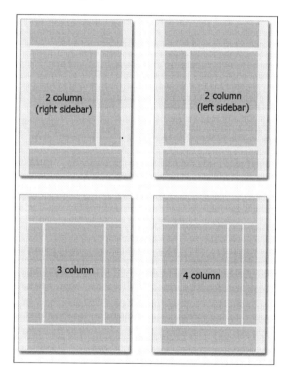

Note that while these different standard layouts have differing numbers of columns and column widths, they all have these essential parts:

- Header
- Main column
- Side column(s)
- Footer

WordPress expects your theme to follow this pattern, and so it provides functions that make it easier to create a theme that has this pattern. As you're designing your first blog theme, I suggest including these parts. Also, a design that stays within the same general design patterns of WordPress themes will most easily accommodate existing plugins and widgets.

The two-column layout is the simplest and the easiest to implement as a WordPress theme, so we'll be using this layout as an example in this chapter. Following is a screenshot of the design I created in Photoshop for my food blog:

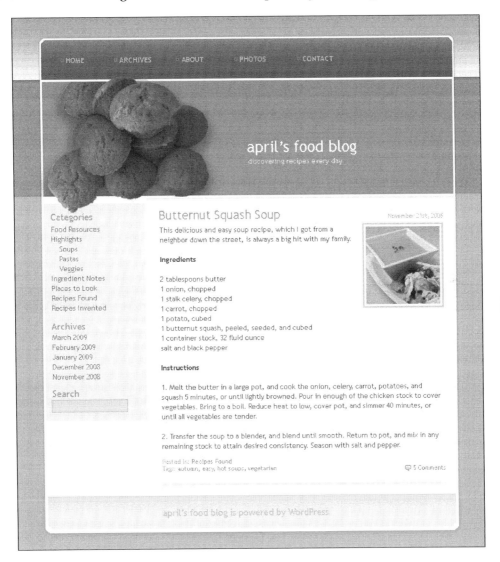

Note that this layout has a header, main column, side column, and footer:

Now that the design is complete, we're ready for the next step, namely, turning the design into code.

Converting your design to code

The next step towards turning your ideal design into a WordPress theme is to slice images out of your design and write HTML and CSS files that put it all together. For the purpose of this chapter, I assume that you already know basically how to do this, and let's also assume we're working with a tableless layout! We'll cover some pointers on how to do your slicing and dicing in a way that will fit best into WordPress.

> If you'd like to learn how to do Rapid Design Comping, which is *how to turn your design into HTML quickly and easily*, be sure to check out the book *WordPress 2.8 Theme Design*, by Tessa Blakeley Silver. She discusses this for a whole chapter.

The first thing I do is turn my design into HTML and put it in a folder. You can name this folder anything you like; I choose to call it HTML build. My HTML build folder, which has my HTML, CSS, and image files, looks like this:

We will now take a look at some of the choices I made when writing these HTML and CSS files so that you can take advantage of these tips and tricks.

Examining the HTML structure

Following is the very basic (not final) layout of my HTML file for my food blog design:

```
<!DOCTYPE html>
<html dir="ltr" lang="en-US">
<head>
    <meta charset="UTF-8" />
    <title>Blog title</title>
    <style type="text/css">@import url("style.css");</style>
</head>
<body>

<div id="container">
    <div id="header">
        <div id="mainnav">
            <ul>
                <li>Navigation list item</li>
            </ul>
        </div><!-- /mainnav -->
        <h1><a href="#">My Blog Title</a></h1>
        <div id="description">this is My subtitle</div>
    </div><!-- /header -->

    <div id="content">
        <div id="copy">
            <div class="post">
                <h2><a href="#">Post Title</a></h2>
                <div class="post-date">Post Date</div>
                <p>Post Content</p>
```

```
                    <div class="categories">Categories</div>
                    <div class="tags">Tags</div>
                    <div class="comments">Comments</div>
                </div>
            </div>
            <div id="sidebar">
                <h3>Categories</h3>
                <ul>
                    <li>category list item</li>
                </ul>
                <h3>Archives</h3>
                <ul>
                    <li>archive list item</li>
                </ul>
            </div><!-- /sidebar →
            <div style="clear: both"> </div>
        </div><!-- /content -->

        <div id="footer">
            Footer text
        </div><!-- /footer -->
    </div><!-- /container -->

</body>
</html>
```

You can see that I've separated out these four major parts:

- The header is in the div with id="header"
- The side column is in the div with id="sidebar"
- The main column is in the div with id="copy"
- The footer is in the div with id="footer"

I'd like to call your attention to a few other things I've done here:

- The mainnav is in an unordered list (ul)

  I did this because WordPress has a function that spits out the navigation of your site in the order you choose. When WordPress spits out the list, every linked item is in a list item tag (li).

- **Archives** and **Categories** are similar

  There are going to be a number of items that you may want to add to your sidebar, including widgets. Many of these items will be lists with titles, so I've prepared for that in my HTML.

- Within the `div id="copy"` is a `div` with `class="post"`

  Even though this basic layout has just one post in it, I know that I'll want to show more than one post at a time. I've created this `div` expecting that it'll be repeated for each post. Also, WordPress expects this `div` to be named `post`. (We'll get into that later.)

Now that I've got my basic layout, I'm going to add a few more HTML elements to flesh it out a bit, including more information in the `<head>` as well as the search box, and some additional CSS. Then, I'll fill up the sidebar, header, content, and footer with a bunch of dummy text so that it looks almost exactly like my theme's design in Photoshop. I'm not including the complete HTML here, but you can find it in the code bundle for this chapter (in the folder named `HTML_build`) if you'd like to do the same. However, note that I've left most of the text a little different. This is my trick to remind myself, later, to replace the static text with dynamic WordPress-generated text.

Examining the CSS

Let's now take a look at the CSS. First, we'll review the CSS that displays everything you see in the design. Note that I've got styles for my five key parts, namely, header, sidebar, copy, post, and footer. They are as follows:

```css
body {
    margin: 0px;
    background: #ddd url('images/bg-body.gif') repeat-x;
    font-family:  "Trebuchet MS", Helvetica, Arial, sans-serif;
    font-size: 14px;
}

a, a:visited {
    color: #397cc6;
    text-decoration: none;
}

a:hover {
    text-decoration: underline;
}

/*** STRUCTURAL PLACEMENT - - - - - - - - - - -- - - - - - - */

#container {
    margin: 0 auto;
    width: 837px;
}

#header {
    margin: 35px 0 0 0;
    height: 343px;
    background: url('images/header.jpg') no-repeat;
}

#mainnav {
    padding: 40px 0 0 30px;
}

#content {
    background: #fff url('images/bg-content.gif');
    padding: 0 10px 0 10px;
}
```

```
#copy {
   width: 590px;
   float: right;
}

#sidebar {
   width: 200px;
   float: left;
   background-color: #F7F7F7;
}

#footer {
   background: url('images/footer.gif') no-repeat;
   height: 79px;
}

/*** STYLING PIECES - - - - - - - - - - - - - - - - - - - - */

/* header title */
#header h1 {
   color: #fff;
   font-size: 24px;
   font-weight: normal;
   margin: 140px 0 5px 500px;
   text-transform: lowercase;
}

#header h1 a {
   color: #fff;
   text-decoration: none;
}

#header h1 a:hover {
   background-color: #9A8A71;
}

#header #description {
   color: #fff;
   margin: 0 0 5px 500px;
   text-transform: lowercase;
}

/* main (top) navigation */
#mainnav ul {
```

```
      margin: 0;
      padding: 0;
   }


   #mainnav li {
      margin: 0;
      padding: 0 30px 0 0;
      display: inline;
      color: #82aedf;
   }

   #mainnav ul li:before {
      content: "\00A4 \0020 \0020";
   }

   #mainnav a, #mainnav a:visited {
      color: #bad2ee;
      text-transform: uppercase;
      text-decoration: none;
   }

   #mainnav a:hover {
      text-decoration: underline;
   }


   /* sidebar */

   #sidebar {
      padding: 0 0 20px 0;
   }

   #sidebar h3 {
      color: #b7b6b6;
      font-weight: normal;
      font-size: 18px;
      margin: 30px 0 5px 10px;
   }

   #sidebar h3.first {
      margin-top: 0;
   }
```

```
#sidebar ul {
   margin: 0 0 0 10px;
   padding: 0;
}

#sidebar li {
   margin: 0;
   padding: 0;
   list-style-type: none;
}

#sidebar input {
   background-color: #ededed;
   border: 1px solid #ccc;
   padding: 4px;
   margin-left: 10px;
}

/* posts */
.post {
   border-bottom: 3px solid #f7f7f7;
   padding: 0 0 15px 0;
}

.post h2 {
   color: #c1ae90;
   font-weight: normal;
   margin: 0;
}

.post h2 a {
   color: #c1ae90;
}

.post .categories, .post .tags, .post .post-date {
   color: #bababa;
   font-size: 12px;
}
.post .tags { width: 480px; }

.post .post-date {
   float: right;
   margin-top: -18px;
}
```

```css
.post .comments {
   font-size: 12px;
   float: right;
   margin-top: -20px;
}

.post .comments a, .post .comments a:visited {
   background: url('images/icon-comments.gif') no-repeat 0 3px;
   padding: 1px 0 1px 18px;
}

.post img {
   padding: 5px;
   border: 4px solid #e2e2e2;
   margin: 10px;
}

/* footer */

#footer {
   color: #dedede;
   font-size: 20px;
   text-align: center;
   padding-top: 20px;
   text-transform: lowercase;
}

#footer a, #footer a:visited {
   color: #dedede;
}


#footer a:hover {
   color: #bbb;
}
```

However, beyond this, there are some other styles we should add. When WordPress spits out items that include page lists, category lists, archive lists, images, galleries, and so on, it gives many of these items a particular class name. If you know these class names, you can prepare your stylesheet to take advantage of them.

When you add an image to a post or page, WordPress gives you the option to have it to the right, left, or at the center of the text. Depending on what you choose, WordPress will give the image the class `alignleft`, `alignright`, or `aligncenter`. Let's add `alignleft` and `alignright` to the stylesheet:

```
/* WordPress styles */
.alignright {
    float: right;
}

.alignleft {
    float: left;
}

.aligncenter {
    display: block;
    margin: 0 auto;
}
```

When you add an image with a caption, WordPress gives it the class `wp-caption`. There are three essential entries you'll want to make in your stylesheet to style the caption box, which are:

```
.wp-caption {
    padding-top: 5px;
    border: 4px solid #e2e2e2;
    text-align: center;
    background-color: #fff;
    margin: 10px;
}

.wp-caption img {
    margin: 0;
    padding: 0;
    border: 0 none;
}

.wp-caption p.wp-caption-text {
    font-size: 11px;
    line-height: 17px;
    padding: 0 4px 5px;
    margin: 0;
}
```

I've designed my caption box to match my images without caption that I styled in `.post img`.

Another useful class is `current_page_item`. WordPress adds this to the list item in the pages menu, on the page that you are currently working. This gives you the ability to visually mark a page that the user is currently viewing. I'll mark it with an underline using the following code:

```
#mainnav .current_page_item a, #mainnav .current_page_item a:visited {
    text-decoration: underline;
}
```

We'll be coming back to the `#mainnav`'s CSS later when we enable the theme for Menus.

WordPress uses many other classes that you can take advantage of when building your stylesheet. I've listed a few of them in *Chapter 11*.

Now that you've got your HTML and CSS lined up, you're ready for the next step: turning the HTML build into a WordPress theme.

Converting your build into a theme

You'll be turning your HTML build into a theme, which is composed of a number of template files and other scripts. We are going to first dig into the inner workings of a theme so as to get familiar with how it's put together. Then we'll actually turn the HTML build into a theme folder that WordPress can use. Finally, we'll replace the dummy text in your build with WordPress functions that spit out content. As I mentioned in an earlier chapter, doing development for your WordPress website on a local environment can make the whole process much smoother. Consider getting a server up and running on your home computer using WAMP, MAMP, or some other way to install Apache and MySQL.

Creating the theme folder

The first step to turning your HTML build into a theme is to create your theme folder, and give it everything it needs to be recognized as a theme by WordPress. Let's look at an overview of the steps and then take them one by one:

1. Name your folder, and create backup copies of your build files.
2. Prepare the essential files.
3. Add a screenshot of your theme named `screenshot.png`.

4. Upload your folder.

5. Activate your theme.

Let's take these steps one by one now:

1. Name your folder, and make backup copies.

   You'll want to give your build folder a sensible name. I'm naming my theme **Muffin Top** because of the muffins in my header image. I'll name the folder `muffintop`.

   Now I suggest creating backup copies of your HTML and CSS files. As you'll eventually be breaking up your build into template files, you can easily lose track of where your code came from. By keeping a copy of your original build, you'll be able to go back to it for reference.

2. Prepare the essential files.

   WordPress has only the following two requirements to recognize your folder as a theme:

   ◦ A file called `index.php`

   ◦ A file called `style.css` with an introductory comment

   Just re-name `index.html` to `index.php`, and that takes care of the first requirement.

   To satisfy the second requirement, your stylesheet needs to have an introductory comment that describes the basic information for the whole theme: title, author, and so on. Also, it has to be at the very top of the stylesheet. I've added this comment to my `style.css` file.

   ```
   /*
   Theme Name: Muffin Top
   Theme URI: http://springthistle.com/wordpress/projects
   Description: Design created especially for April's Food Blog
   for
       WordPress Complete.
   Version: 1.0
   Author: April Hodge Silver
   Author URI: http://springthistle.com/
   Tags: brown, blue, fixed width, two columns, widgets, food
   */
   ```

   When you add this comment section to your stylesheet, just replace all of the details with those that are relevant to your theme.

3. Add a screenshot.

   Remember when we first learned how to activate a new theme that there were thumbnail versions of the themes in your **Appearance** tab? You'll want a thumbnail of your own design. It has to be a PNG file and with the name `screenshot.png`. Just do the following:

   ° Flatten a copy of your design in Photoshop.

   ° Change the image width to 300px and the height to 225

   ° **Save for web** as a PNG-8.

4. Name your file `screenshot.png`, and save it in your build folder.

   Now that I've got my theme ready to upload, my theme folder looks like this:

5. Upload your folder.

   Using your FTP software, upload your template folder to `wp-content/themes/` in your WordPress build. It will share the `themes` folder with `twentyten` and any other theme you've added as you installed WordPress. In the following screenshot, you can see my **muffintop** theme (highlighted in the following screenshot) living in the **themes** folder:

6. Activate your theme.

    You've got the absolute basic necessities in there now, so you can activate your theme (though it won't look like much yet). Log in to your WP Admin and navigate to **Appearance**. There you'll see your theme waiting for you.

When you click on the thumbnail or **Activate** link of your theme, an overlay window will appear on top of the page with a preview of what your site will look like. Don't be alarmed if it's not perfect. The stylesheet is not yet being pulled in correctly.

Click on the link in the upper-right corner to activate your theme. This is another good reason to have a development server. You wouldn't want to have this incomplete theme active on a live site while you finish the final pieces!

Speaking of final pieces, your theme is now ready to have all of the WordPress content added.

Adding WordPress content

Right now, your `index.php` file is your only theme file. We'll be breaking it up into template files a bit later. First, we need to replace the dummy text with WordPress functions that will spit out your actual content into your theme.

The <head> tag

First we'll set up the `<head></head>` section of your HTML file. Let's start with the stylesheet. WordPress provides a function that knows where your stylesheet lives. Replace the code that calls in the stylesheet (`style.css`) in your `index.php` file with this:

```
<link rel="stylesheet" href="<?php bloginfo('stylesheet_url'); ?>"
type="text/css" media="screen" />
```

Using this function instead of a hardcoded call to the stylesheet will come in handy if you ever have a need to rename your theme folder. Now, when you look at your site, you see your theme, along with the dummy text, in all its glory.

Next, you'll want WordPress to be able to place your blog's name in the title bar of your browser. So replace your dummy title with the following code in the `title` tag:

```
<title><?php bloginfo('name'); ?></title>
```

This will spit out the title of the current page, then an arrow, and then the title of your blog. Later, you may want to download the All-in-one-SEO plugin, which will change the `<title>` page by page, depending on what's appropriate.

You need to add another important chunk of code to put header tags into your theme for the RSS feed, the Atom feed, the **pingback** URL, and other miscellaneous WordPress stuff. Add the following three lines in your `<head>` section:

```
<link rel="alternate"
      type="application/rss+xml"
      title="<?php bloginfo('name'); ?> RSS Feed"
      href="<?php bloginfo('rss2_url'); ?>" />
<link rel="alternate"
      type="application/atom+xml"
      title="<?php bloginfo('name'); ?> Atom Feed"
      href="<?php bloginfo('atom_url'); ?>" />
<link rel="pingback"
      href="<?php bloginfo('pingback_url'); ?>" />
```

Add the following line right before the closing `</head>` tag:

```
<?php wp_head(); ?>
```

Now add the `body_class()` function to the body tag, so it looks like this:

```
<body <?php body_class() ?>>
```

Your header now looks something like this:

```
<head>
   <title><?php bloginfo('name'); ?></title>
   <meta name="robots"
         content="index, follow"></meta>
   <meta name="distribution"
         content="global"></meta>
   <meta name="description"
         content="discovering new recipes and food daily"></meta>
   <meta name="keywords"
         content="april hodge silver, food, recipes"></meta>
   <link rel="stylesheet" href="<?php bloginfo('stylesheet_url'); ?>"
type="text/css" media="screen" />
   <link rel="alternate"
         type="application/rss+xml"
         title="<?php bloginfo('name'); ?> RSS Feed"
         href="<?php bloginfo('rss2_url'); ?>" />
   <link rel="alternate"
         type="application/atom+xml"
         title="<?php bloginfo('name'); ?> Atom Feed"
         href="<?php bloginfo('atom_url'); ?>" />
   <link rel="pingback"
         href="<?php bloginfo('pingback_url'); ?>" />
   <?php wp_head(); ?>
</head>
<body <?php body_class() ?>>
```

The header and footer

It's time to start adding the content that you can see. Let's first replace the dummy text in the main navigation bar and header with WordPress content tags.

WordPress will generate a linked list of pages for you, as I mentioned earlier. Just replace your dummy text with this code, replacing the whole <ul></ul> tag:

```php
<?php
    if (function_exists('wp_nav_menu')) wp_nav_menu('depth=2');
    else {
        echo '<ul>';
        wp_list_pages('title_li=&sort_column=menu_order&depth=2');
        echo '</ul>';
    }
?>
```

What's this code saying? First, it checks to see if the wp_nav_menu() function exists. It was added in WordPress 3.0, so some older installations might not have it. If that function doesn't exist, the code calls an older function that lists pages. The arguments tell the functions to not print a greater depth than 2, because the CSS isn't prepared to handle it.

Next, you can replace your dummy blog title and dummy blog description with the following two tags:

```php
<?php bloginfo('name'); ?>
<?php bloginfo('description'); ?>
```

These tags pull information from where you set the blog name and description in the WP Admin, and you can simply change them from the **Settings | General** page.

Finally, if you want to link the blog title in the header to the homepage of the blog, use the following for the URL:

```php
<?php bloginfo('url'); ?>
```

Now, the part of your HTML that describes the header looks like this:

```html
<div id="header">
    <div id="mainnav">
        <?php
            if (function_exists('wp_nav_menu')) wp_nav_menu('depth=2');
            else {
                echo '<ul>';
                wp_list_pages('title_li=&sort_column=menu_order&depth=2');
                echo '</ul>';
            }
        ?>
    </div><!-- /mainnav -->
```

```
    <h1><a href="<?php bloginfo('url'); ?>"><?php bloginfo('name');
?></a></h1>
    <div id="description"><?php bloginfo('description'); ?></div>
</div><!-- /header -->
```

Are you wondering why you should bother with some of this when you could have just typed your blog title, URL, and description to the theme? One reason is that if you ever want to change your blog's title, you can just do it in one quick step in the WP Admin and it will change all over your site. The other reason is that if you want to share your theme with others, you'll need to give them the ability to easily change the name through their own WP Admin panel. Keep in mind, anything, anything at all, that will change from site to site based on the site's purpose and content, should not be hard-coded into the theme but should be to be dynamically generated.

Now when I refresh the site, my dummy text in the header has been replaced with actual content from my blog:

Just to tie things up, I'm going to add the same code to my footer for displaying the home URL and blog title, and also the important function `wp_footer()`, which many plugins need to hook into. My footer section now looks like the following:

```
<div id="footer">
    <a href="<?php echo get_option('home'); ?>/">
        <?php bloginfo('name'); ?></a> is powered by wordpress
</div><!-- /footer -->

</div><!-- /container -->

<?php wp_footer() ?>
</body>
</html>
```

The sidebar

Now we can move along to adding WordPress-generated content in the sidebar, which still has just the dummy text:

Starting at the top, replace your dummy text for the list of categories with the following WordPress categories tag. Again, be sure to place it within the `<ul></ul>` tag.

```
<?php wp_list_categories('title_li='); ?>
```

Just like with pages, you need to turn off the default title by using `title_li=`.

Now, replace your dummy text for the list of archives with this tag:

```
<?php wp_get_archives(); ?>
```

The final item in the sidebar is the search box. This can be entirely replaced by a WordPress function.

```
<?php get_search_form(); ?>
```

Now, the part of your HTML that describes the sidebar looks something like the following:

```
<div id="sidebar">
    <h3 class="first">Categories</h3>
    <ul>
        <?php wp_list_categories('title_li='); ?>
    </ul>
```

```
<h3>Archives</h3>
<ul>
    <?php wp_get_archives(); ?>
</ul>

<h3>Search</h3>
<?php get_search_form(); ?>
</div><!-- /sidebar -->
```

(Later in the chapter, we'll be making this a widget-ready area, but for now, we'll keep it like this.)

Save this file and reload your theme, and you'll see that your dummy text has been replaced with WordPress output for the **Categories** and **Archives** lists, and the **Search** form.

In my case, the search form doesn't look quite the way I want. So I'm going to add these WordPress styles to my stylesheet to hide the label and the submit button:

```
.screen-reader-text, #searchsubmit {
    display: none;
}
```

Main column—the loop

The most important part of the WordPress code comes next. It's called the *loop*, and it's an essential part of your theme. The *loop*'s job is to display your posts in chronological order, choosing only those posts which are appropriate. You need to put all of your other post tags inside the *loop*. The basic *loop* text, which has to surround your post information, is displayed using the following code:

```php
<?php if (have_posts()) : ?>

    <?php while (have_posts()) : the_post(); ?>
        <div id="post-<?php the_ID(); ?>" <?php post_class() ?>>
            <!-- individual post information -->
        </div>
    <?php endwhile; ?>

    <div class="navigation">
        <div class="alignleft">
            <?php next_posts_link('&laquo; Older Entries') ?></div>
        <div class="alignright">
            <?php previous_posts_link('Newer Entries &raquo;') ?></div>
    </div>
<?php else : ?>
    <h2 class="center">Not Found</h2>
    <p class="center">Sorry, but you are looking for something that
        isn't here.</p>
    <?php get_search_form(); ?>
<?php endif; ?>
```

There are three basic parts of the *loop*:

- Individual post information
- Next and previous posts links
- What to do if there are no appropriate posts

Note that you can style your next and previous post links using the `navigation` class. We already added `alignright` and `alignleft`, so we're all set with them. Also, we will reuse the handy `get_search_form()` function that we used in the sidebar.

We are going to paste the loop we just saw into our `index.php` file in the place where the main column lives. In my case, that's the `div` with `id="copy"`. First, however, let's replace the comment `<!-- individual post information -->` with the dummy text from our HTML build. Now, the part of your HTML that describes your main column looks something like the following:

```html
<div id="copy">

    <?php if (have_posts()) : ?>

        <?php while (have_posts()) : the_post(); ?>
            <div id="post-<?php the_ID(); ?>" <?php post_class()
?>>

                <h2><a href="#">Butternut Squash Soup</a></h2>
                <div class="post-date">November 21st, 2008</div>

                <p>My first paragraph.</p>
                <p>My second paragraph.</p>

                <div class="categories">Posted in:
                    <a href="#">Recipes Found</a></div>
                <div class="tags">Tags:
                    <a href="#">autumn</a>,
                    <a href="#">easy</a>,
                    <a href="#">soups</a>
                </div>
                <div class="comments">
                <a href="#">5 Comments</a></div>
            </div>
        <?php endwhile; ?>

        <div class="navigation">
            <div class="alignleft">
                <?php next_posts_link('&laquo; Older Entries') ?>
            </div>
            <div class="alignright">
                <?php previous_posts_link('Newer Entries &raquo;') ?>
            </div>
        </div>
    <?php else : ?>
        <h2 class="center">Not Found</h2>
        <p class="center">Sorry, but you are looking for
            something that isn't here.</p>
        <?php get_search_form(); ?>
    <?php endif; ?>

</div><!-- /copy -->
```

Now that we've got the basic *loop* in the theme, we can replace our dummy text with more WordPress tags.

The post title and the URL that links to the post can be replaced with these two WordPress tags:

```
<?php the_permalink() ?>
<?php the_title(); ?>
```

The date of the post is expressed by this tag:

```
<?php the_time('F jS, Y') ?>
```

The funny-looking code, F jS, Y, is PHP date formatting code.

Learning more:
You can look up for more options on how to display the date on a PHP website at: http://us3.php.net/manual/en/function.date.php.

Now replace your dummy placeholder text for the actual content of the post with this code:

```
<?php the_content(); ?>
```

Your categories and tags lists get expressed by the following two tags:

```
<?php the_category(', ') ?>
<?php the_tags(); ?>
```

By default, the the_category() function spits out your categories in a linked list. Since I want them to display categories separated by comments, I have to add the ', ' argument that tells the function to put something else. In this case, it is a comma and a space between category names.

Finally, you can set up your comments link with this tag:

```
<?php comments_popup_link('Leave a Comment &#187;',
                          '1 Comment &#187;',
                          '% Comments &#187;'); ?>
```

Here, you can see that there are three arguments passed, separated by commas:

- The first option tells WordPress the text that it has to display when there are no comments.
- The second option tells WordPress the text that it has to display when there is just one comment.

- The third option tells WordPress text that it has to display for more than one comment. The percent symbol (%) gets replaced with the actual number of existing comments.

The section of your HTML that contains your main *loop* now looks something like this:

```
<div id="copy">

    <?php if (have_posts()) : ?>

    <?php while (have_posts()) : the_post(); ?>
        <div id="post-<?php the_ID(); ?>" <?php post_class() ?>>
            <h2>
                <a href="<?php the_permalink() ?>">
                    <?php the_title(); ?></a>
            </h2>
            <div class="post-date">
                <?php the_time('F jS, Y') ?></div>

            <?php the_content(); ?>

            <div class="categories">Posted in:
                <?php the_category(', ') ?>
            </div>
            <div class="tags">Tags:
                <?php the_tags(); ?>
            </div>
            <div class="comments">
             <?php comments_popup_link('Leave a Comment
                                            &#187;',
                                    '1 Comment &#187;',
                                    '% Comments &#187;'); ?>
            </div>
        </div>
    <?php endwhile; ?>

    <div class="navigation">
        <div class="alignleft">
            <?php next_posts_link('&laquo; Older Entries') ?>
        </div>
        <div class="alignright">
         <?php previous_posts_link('Newer Entries &raquo;') ?>
        </div>
    </div>
```

```php
<?php else : ?>
   <h2 class="center">Not Found</h2>
   <p class="center">Sorry, but you are looking for
      something that isn't here.</p>
   <?php get_search_form(); ?>
<?php endif; ?>


</div><!-- /copy -->
```

Phew! Now save your `index.php` and reload your website. Your theme is in action!

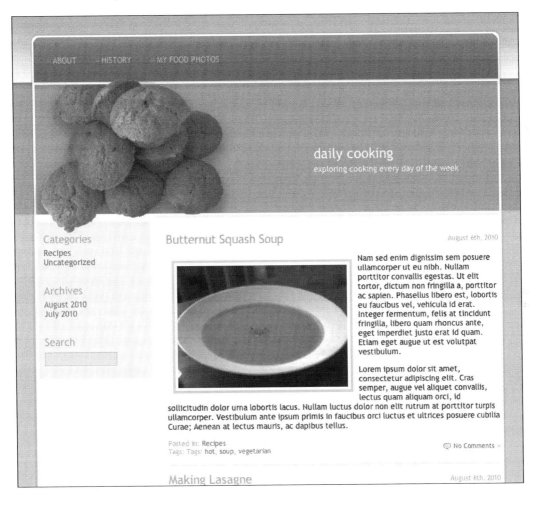

> **Learning more**:
>
> If you'd like to learn more about the useful built-in WordPress template tags and functions you can implement when building up your theme, you can find it in *"WordPress 2.8 Theme Design"*, *by Tessa Blakeley Silver.*

Creating templates within your theme

You've now got a functional basic template for your theme. It works great on the main blog page and successfully loads content for anything you can click on in your site.

However, we want slightly different templates for other types of content on our site. For example, a single post page needs to have a comments form where visitors can post comments; the Page page doesn't need to show the date, category, or tags; and the category page should show the category name.

Before we can create other templates, we need to break up the main index.php file into parts so that these different templates can share the common elements. I've mentioned many times the importance of the header, sidebar, and footer. We're going to break them up now. First, let's take a quick look at how it works.

Understanding the WordPress theme

The WordPress theme is actually composed of a number of template files. This allows the different parts of the site (such as the frontend, blog archive, page, single post, search results, and so on) to have different purposes. Breaking the index.php file into template files allows us to not only share some common parts of the design, but also have different code in the different parts.

As I mentioned earlier, we'll soon be breaking up the four main pieces of the design (header, sidebar, main column, and footer) so that WordPress can make good use of them. That's because while the header and footer are probably shared by all pages, the content in the main column will be different. Also, you may want the sidebar on some pages, but not on others.

We'll first create these template files, and then move on to other, more optional template files.

Breaking it up

We're going to break up the `index.php` file by removing some of the code into three new files:

```
header.php
footer.php
sidebar.php
```

header.php

First, cut out the entire top of your `index.php` file. This means cutting the `doctype` declaration, the `<head>`, any miscellaneous opening tags, and the header `div`. In my case, I'm cutting out all the way from this, the first few lines:

```
<!DOCTYPE html PUBLIC "-//W3C//DTD XHTML 1.0 Transitional//EN"
"http://www.w3.org/TR/xhtml1/DTD/xhtml1-transitional.dtd">
<html xmlns="http://www.w3.org/1999/xhtml">
<head>
```

through and including these lines:

```
</div><!-- /header -->

<div id="content">
```

Then, paste this text into a new file named `header.php` that you created within your `theme` folder.

Now at the very top of the `index.php` file (that is, where you just cut the header text from) write in this line of WordPress PHP code:

```
<?php get_header(); ?>
```

This is a WordPress function that includes the `header.php` file you just created. If you save everything and reload your website now, nothing should change. If something changes, then you've made a mistake.

footer.php

Next, we will create the footer file. To create this, first cut out all of the text at the very bottom of the `index.php` file, from the clearing div just inside the `#content` div, and all the way through the `</html>` tag. In my case, this is the entire text I cut:

```
    <div style="clear: both"> </div>
</div><!-- /content -->

<div id="footer">
<a href="<?php echo get_option('home'); ?>/">
```

```
        <?php bloginfo('name'); ?></a> is powered by wordpress
    </div><!-- /footer -->

</div><!-- /container -->
<?php wp_footer() ?>
</body>
</html>
```

Paste the text you just cut into a new `footer.php` file that you create within your `theme` folder.

Now, at the very bottom of the `index.php` file (from where you just cut the footer text) write in the following line of WordPress PHP code:

```
<?php get_footer(); ?>
```

This is a special WordPress function that includes the `footer.php` file you just created. Again, you should save everything and reload your website to make sure nothing changes.

sidebar.php

There is just one more essential template file to create. For this one, cut out the entire `div` containing your sidebar. In my case, it's the following text:

```
<div id="sidebar">
    <h3 class="first">Categories</h3>
    <ul>
        <?php wp_list_categories('title_li='); ?>
    </ul>

    <h3>Archives</h3>
    <ul>
        <?php wp_get_archives(); ?>
    </ul>

    <h3>Search</h3>
    <?php get_search_form(); ?>
</div><!-- /sidebar -->
```

Paste this text into a new file in your `theme` folder named `sidebar.php`.

Now in `index.php`, add this function in the place you just cut your sidebar from:

```
<?php get_sidebar(); ?>
```

This will include the sidebar. In the case of my design, I will want the sidebar on every page. So it's not very crucial for it to be a separate file. I could have included it in the footer.php file. However, in some templates, including the default template that came with your WordPress installation, the designer prefers to not include the sidebar in some views such as the **Page** and single posts.

Your four template files

You've now got four template files in your theme folder, namely, header.php, footer.php, sidebar.php, and the now-much-shorter index.php. By the way, my index.php file now has only the three WordPress functions and the *loop*. Following is the entire file:

```php
<?php get_header(); ?>

<div id="copy">

    <?php if (have_posts()) : ?>

        <?php while (have_posts()) : the_post(); ?>
            <div id="post-<?php the_ID(); ?>" <?php post_class() ?>>
                <h2><a href="<?php the_permalink() ?>">
                    <?php the_title(); ?></a></h2>
                <div class="post-date"><?php the_time('F jS, Y') ?></div>

                <?php the_content(); ?>
                <div class="categories">Posted in:
                    <?php the_category(', ') ?></div>
                <div class="tags">Tags: <?php the_tags(); ?></div>
                <div class="comments">
                    <?php comments_popup_link('No Comments &#187;',
                                              '1 Comment &#187;',
                                              '% Comments &#187;'); ?>
                </div>
            </div>
        <?php endwhile; ?>

        <div class="navigation">
            <div class="alignleft">
                <?php next_posts_link('&laquo; Older Entries') ?></div>
            <div class="alignright">
                <?php previous_posts_link('Newer Entries &raquo;') ?>
            </div>
        </div>
    <?php else : ?>
```

```
        <h2 class="center">Not Found</h2>
        <p class="center">Sorry, but you are looking for something
               that isn't here.</p>
        <?php get_search_form(); ?>
    <?php endif; ?>

</div><!-- /copy -->

<?php get_sidebar(); ?>

<?php get_footer(); ?>
```

After creating individual template files, my `theme` folder looks like this:

This whole cutting-and-pasting process to create these four files was just to set the scene for the real goal of making alternative template files.

Archive template

WordPress is now using the `index.php` template file for every view on your site. Let's make a new file—one that will be used when viewing a monthly archive, category archive, or tag archive.

To create your archive template, make a copy of `index.php` and name this copy `archive.php`. When someone is viewing a category or a monthly archive of my site, I want them to see an excerpt of the post content instead of the full post content. So, I edit `archive.php` and replace `the_content()` with `the_excerpt()`.

Now navigate to a monthly archive on the site by clicking on one of the month names in the sidebar. Following is how it will look now:

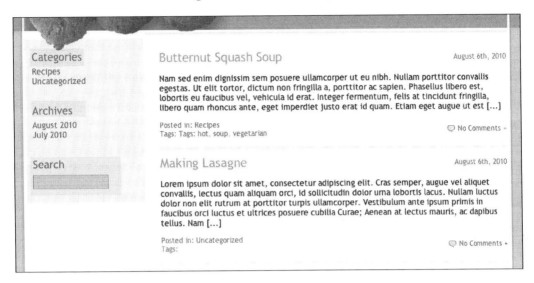

Instead of showing the full body of the post, WordPress has printed the first 55 words of the content followed by **[...]**. However, if you go back to the main page of the blog, you can see that it still displays the full content. This is the power of template files.

Learning more:

You can alter the appearance of the excerpt in your theme if you don't like the 55 words and [...] display. Take a look in the codex for details: http://codex.wordpress.org/Function_Reference/the_excerpt.

Let's make one more change to the archive template. I'd like it to display a message that lets the users know what type of archive page they are on. To do that, just add this code inside `copy div`:

```
<h2 class="pagetitle">
    <?php if (is_category()) { ?>
    Archive for the '<?php single_cat_title(); ?>' Category
    <?php } elseif( is_tag() ) { ?>
    Posts Tagged '<?php single_tag_title(); ?>'
    <?php } elseif (is_month()) { ?>
    Archive for <?php the_time('F, Y'); ?>
    <?php } ?>
</h2>
```

I also added a new style to my stylesheet to color this class dark grey.

Now, when I click on a month, category, or tag, I see a new heading at the top of the page that lets me know where I am:

Single template

The next template we need to create is for the single post view. To view a single post, you can usually just click on the post title. Right now, the single post page looks like the site's front page (because it's using `index.php`); except with just one post. At the very least, this page should have a comment form added!

To get started, again make a copy of `index.php`, and name the copy `single.php`. This is the template that WordPress will look for first when it's serving a single post. If it doesn't find `single.php`, it'll use `index.php`.

To add a comment form to `single.php`, simply add the following code just before `<?php endwhile; ?>`:

```php
<?php comments_template(); ?>
```

Now, when you view an individual post, you'll see that the list of comments and the comment form have both appeared.

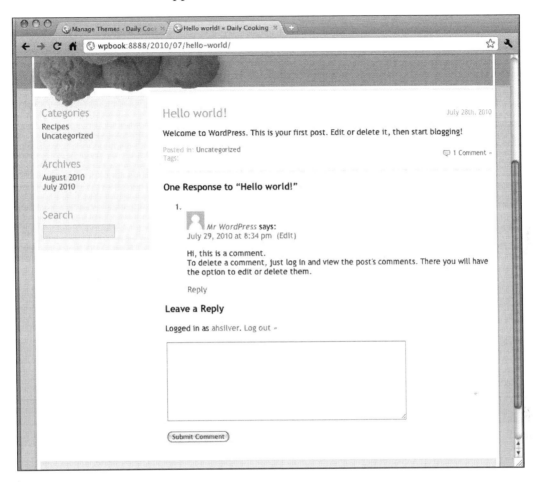

At this point, you may want to add some CSS to handle styling the comments list. You could start by copying the comments-related CSS from the twentyten theme.

There are two other changes I recommend for `single.php`:

- Remove the code for next posts and previous posts.
- Add code to display links for next post and previous post.

To remove the code for the previous and next posts, which is only relevant on pages that show multiple posts at a time, just delete the entire `div` with `class="navigation"`:

```
<div class="navigation">
   <div class="alignleft">
      <?php next_posts_link('&laquo; Older Entries') ?></div>
   <div class="alignright">
      <?php previous_posts_link('Newer Entries &raquo;') ?></div>
</div>
```

To add links to the next and previous single post, insert this code near the top of the page just above the `div` with the `post_class()` function:

```
<div class="navigation">
   <div class="alignleft">
      <?php previous_post_link('&laquo; %link') ?></div>
   <div class="alignright">
      <?php next_post_link('%link &raquo;') ?></div>
</div>
```

I also added some additional CSS to handle the navigation div. Now your next and previous posts are linked to the current post page by their titles like this:

Page template

The last template we're going to create is for the static page view. On my food blog site that would be the **About** page, for example:

I want to get rid of the date, categories, tags, and comments because they don't apply to my pages, only to my posts. Make a copy of index.php and name the copy page.php. When you edit the file, remove the code for the date, categories, and tags:

```
<div class="post-date"><?php the_time('F jS, Y') ?></div>
<div class="categories">Posted in: <?php the_category(', ') ?></div>
<div class="tags">Tags: <?php the_tags(); ?></div>
```

I do not want to let visitors comment on pages, I'll remove the comments link as well:

```
<div class="comments"><?php comments_popup_link('No Comments &#187;',
'1 Comment &#187;', '% Comments &#187;'); ?></div>
```

For extra credit, you can remove the anchor tag from the page title, and also remove the entire `div` with `class="navigation"` because it's not relevant to static pages. Now my **About** page looks much cleaner.

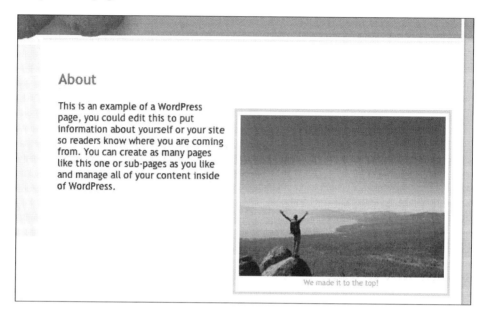

Generated classes for body and post

As you're modifying your theme to make accommodations for different types of pages, you should also know about the CSS classes that WordPress will put into your theme. One of them is classes in the `body` tag and the others are classes in the post `div`. If you look carefully at the code we've been using, you'll see these two functions:

- `body_class()`
- `post_class()`

The `body_class()` function adds a whole bunch of classes to the body tag, depending on the page you're viewing. For example, the main page of my site has these classes in the body:

```
<body class="home blog logged-in">
```

My Butternut Squash Soup single post page's body tag looks like this:

```
<body class="single single-post postid-15 logged-in">
```

My About page page looks like this:

```
<body class="page page-id-2 page-template page-template-default
logged-in">
```

If I wanted to style anything differently on different pages, I could do it largely with CSS, without having to create another template.

The post_class() function does something similar with the post div, giving the div different classes depending on the characteristics of the post itself. For example, my Butternut Squash Soup post's div has these classes:

```
<div id="post-15" class="post-15 post type-post hentry category-
recipes tag-hot tag-soup tag-vegetarian">
```

and my About page's post div has these:

```
<div id="post-2" class="post-2 page type-page hentry">
```

By using these classes in my stylesheet, I could style every post differently depending on its category, tag, post-type, and so on. Keep that in mind as you design your next theme!

Other WordPress templates

In addition to archive.php, single.php, and page.php, there are a number of other standard template files that WordPress looks for before using index.php for particular views. We're not going to create those files here, but you should feel free to experiment on your WordPress installation. These files are:

- archive.php trumps index.php when a *category*, *tag*, *date*, or *author* page is viewed
- single.php trumps index.php when an *individual post* is viewed
- page.php trumps index.php when looking at a *static* page
- search.php trumps index.php when the results from a *search* are viewed
- 404.php trumps index.php when the URI address finds *no existing content*.
- front-page.php trumps index.php when the *home* page is viewed
- A custom template page, selected via the WP Admin, trumps page.php when that *particular page* is viewed
- category.php trumps archive.php, which trumps index.php when a *category* is viewed
- A custom category-ID.php page trumps category.php when a *particular category* is viewed

- `tag.php` trumps `archive.php`, which trumps `index.php` when a *tag page* is viewed

- A custom `tag-tagname.php` page trumps `tag.php` when a *particular tag* is viewed

- `author.php` trumps `archive.php` when an *author* page is viewed

- `date.php` trumps `archive.php` when a *date* page is viewed

In addition to what's listed above, there are also template files that would be applicable in a situation that includes a custom taxonomy or a custom post type.

Learning more:

You can find a detailed flow chart of the template hierarchy here: `http://codex.wordpress.org/Template_Hierarchy`. You can get a more detailed discussion of creating these built-in template pages in *"WordPress 2.8 Theme Design"*, by Tessa Blakeley Silver.

In this chapter, we've experimented with the uses of quite a number of WordPress template tags. In *Chapter 11*, I have listed more of the most useful template tags.

Next, we'll explore making custom templates for pages.

Creating and using a custom template

WordPress allows you to create custom templates. These can be used only for pages (not for posts). A custom template allows you to display the content differently, or easily use built-in WordPress functions within a template.

Up to WordPress version 2.9.2, the bundled theme was named default, and it had an archives template. Let's create an archives template for this new theme. We want our archives template to display a complete list of categories, monthly archives, and tags in use on the site.

To do this, we need to create a template. These are the steps we'll take:

1. Create the template file by copying an existing file in the custom theme.

2. Add WordPress functions to the template file.

3. Tell the **Blog Archives** page to use the custom template file instead of `page.php`.

Let's get started.

1. Create the template file.

   Make a copy of `page.php` within your theme, and give it a new name. I like to prepend all of my custom template files with `tmpl_` so that they are sorted separately from all the WordPress template files that I will create. I'll name this file `tmpl_archives.php`.

   In order for WordPress to be able to identify this file as a template file, we need to add a specially styled comment to the top of the page (just as we did with `style.css`). The comment needs to be formatted like this:

   ```php
   <?php
   /* Template Name: Blog Archives */
   ?>
   ```

   In the WP Admin panel, the template will be identified by this template name, so make sure the name signals to you for what the template is used.

2. Add WordPress functions.

   Edit your new template file and remove the *loop* entirely. That is, remove it from `<?php if (have_posts()) : ?>` to `<?php endif; ?>`, and everything in between. Instead of the *loop*, we'll add some WordPress functions that will display what we want. Because we are creating a custom template, we can add any of the WordPress functions we discovered earlier in the chapter, as well as any other WordPress function (see *Chapter 11*).

   First, let's add a complete list of categories and monthly archives. In the spot where the *loop* was present, insert this code:

   ```php
   <h3>Categories</h3>
   <ul>
       <?php wp_list_categories('title_li='); ?>
   </ul>

   <h3>Archives</h3>
   <ul>
       <?php wp_get_archives(); ?>
   </ul>
   ```

   This should look familiar—I copied and pasted it directly from `sidebar.php`.

3. Apply the template to a page.

   Leave your HTML editor, and log in to your WP Admin. You need to edit or create the page in which you want to use this template. In this case, I will create a page and name it **Blog Archives**.

On the **Edit Page** page, look for the **Template** menu within the **Attributes** box (at the right, by default).

Change it from **Default Template** to **Blog Archives**, and click on **Update Page**. (Note that you can also change a page's template using **Quick Edit** on the **Pages | Edit** page). Now, when you return to the frontend of your website and click on the **Blog Archives** page, you'll see that the categories and monthly archives are as follows:

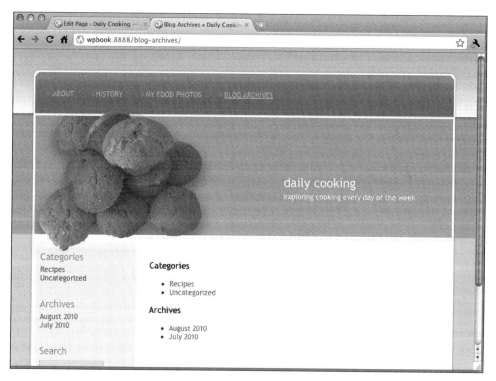

To make this a bit more exciting, let's add one more WordPress function to `tmpl_archives.php`. Underneath the monthly list, add this code:

```
<h3>Tags</h3>
<?php wp_tag_cloud(''); ?>
```

This function prints all of the tags in use on the site, one after the other (inline, not in a list format), and increases the font size of the tags that have been used more often. Save the template file and re-load the **Blog Archives** page to see the tag cloud (not so impressive right now because I have very few posts and tags in use), as shown in the following screenshot:

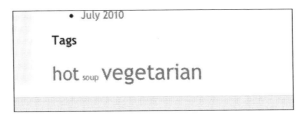

There is no limit to the number of custom templates you can make in your WordPress theme.

Now that we are done making templates for the muffintop theme, take a look at how the theme directory has grown:

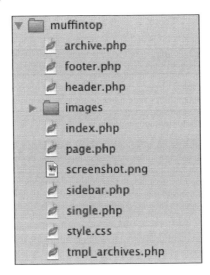

Making your theme widget-friendly

If you want to be able to use the widgets in your theme, you will need to make your theme widget-friendly (also know as **widgetizing** your theme). Widgetizing is actually pretty easy, and involves just the following three steps:

1. Ensure that your sidebar is one big, unordered list.

2. Add a `functions.php` file with a special function in it.

3. Add conditional code to your sidebar.

Nearly all of the PHP code you need to add in steps 2 and 3 can be pasted from already existing files, so the non-programmers out there shouldn't be too intimidated! Let's get started.

Making sure your sidebar is one big <ul> tag

This is actually not a requirement, but it's becoming the standard for WordPress sidebars among the theme-writing community. As we will be editing the sidebar anyway, let's modify it first to be one big `<ul>` tag. Another standard is that the headings should be `<h2>`s, so I'll make that change as well.

For your sidebar to be one long UL, every item in the UL will contain a Header and another UL.

```
<div id="sidebar">
   <ul>
      <li>
         <h2 class="first">Categories</h2>
         <ul>
            <?php wp_list_categories('title_li='); ?>
         </ul>
      </li>

      <li>
         <h2>Archives</h2>
         <ul>
            <?php wp_get_archives(); ?>
         </ul>
      </li>

      <li>
         <h2>Search</h2>
         <?php get_search_form(); ?>
      </li>
   </ul>
</div><!-- /sidebar -->
```

All I did to change my `sidebar.php` was add a `<ul>` at the beginning of the `sidebar` `div` and a `</ul>` at the end, and I put each item (categories, archives, and search) into a `<li></li>` tag.

After making these changes, I also tweaked my stylesheet so that the display isn't affected negatively.

Adding functions.php

Your `theme` folder now needs a new file named `functions.php` with the following as its contents:

```php
<?php
if ( function_exists('register_sidebar') )
    register_sidebar();
?>
```

If your `sidebar.php` is not in a single big `<ul>`, or your headers are not `<h2>`s, then you're going to need slightly more complicated code in your `functions.php` file. You can look up those details in the WordPress Codex. (Refer to the next *Learning more* section.)

Adding conditional code to sidebar

The third and final step is to add conditional code to your `sidebar.php`. This code says, "If the person using this theme wants to use widgets, don't show this stuff. If he or she doesn't want to use widgets, do show this stuff." That way, a person not using widgets will see whatever default items you put into the `sidebar.php`.

At the top of the `sidebar.php`, just under the opening `<ul>` tag, add this line of code:

```php
<?php if ( !function_exists('dynamic_sidebar')
        || !dynamic_sidebar() ): ?>
```

At the bottom of the sidebar, just above the closing `</ul>`, add this line of code:

```php
<?php endif; ?>
```

Adding some widgets

Your theme is ready for widgets! You can now go to WP Admin, navigate to **Appearance | Widgets,** and add widgets (when you do, the three default items will disappear). For example, as you see in the following screenshot I added three widgets:

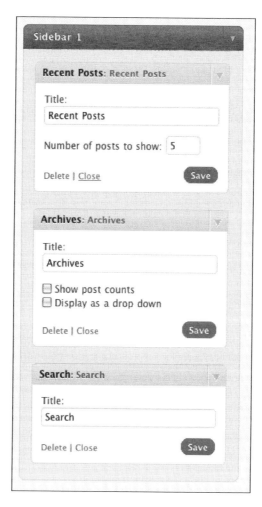

Be sure to click on **Save**, and then return to your website and reload the page. The default items you had placed in the sidebar have been replaced with widgets, as shown in the following screenshot:

Further widgetizing options

What we just covered is the simplest way to widgetize a theme. There are actually a lot of options that you could utilize when adding the code to your `sidebar.php` and `functions.php` pages. For example, there are options that allow you to:

- Widgetize more than one sidebar, giving each a name
- Widgetize a part of your sidebar, but leave in some default items
- Widgetize a sidebar that is not one big long `<ul>`
- Widgetize a sidebar whose item titles are not `<h2>`s
- Customize the search form widget

Learning more

To learn about the variety of options available and how to take advantage of them, take a look at the Codex: `http://codex.wordpress.org/Widgetizing_Themes`.

Enabling a menu in your theme

As of WordPress 3, users can now control more easily what appears in menus. Instead of having to show "all pages" in the menu, you can choose to show a selection of pages and/or categories, and/or other options (as we saw in *Chapter 4*).

Because we used the `wp_nav_menu()` function in the header of the site (in the file `header.php`), if the user creates a menu in **Appearance | Menus**, the first menu they create will show up in that spot.

For example, here is the Muffin Top theme with the menu I created in *Chapter 4*:

It looks a little like a disaster, but that just means I need to clean up my CSS to allow for subpages. Another change in the CSS is that the list item's `<li>`s are no longer given the page-item class, but instead get the menu-item class. Once I clean up my CSS and add a rollover menu, my nav is ready to go:

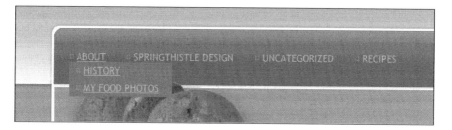

(You can find the CSS changes I made in the code packet for this chapter.)

If you want to have more than one navigation menu in your theme, you can register multiple navigation menu locations and let the user create multiple menus and choose which menu goes in which location. To learn more about that, check out this page of the codex: `http://codex.wordpress.org/Navigation_Menus`.

Learning more: The `wp_nav_menu()` function is quite powerful, and can take a number of parameters that will let you control the classes and IDs, the name of the menu, and more. Take a look here in the codex for details: `http://codex.wordpress.org/Function_Reference/wp_nav_menu`.

Creating a child theme

If you can find an existing theme or theme framework that you like, and you just want to use your CSS and HTML skills, you can create a child theme. A child theme uses the parent theme as a starting point and, without changing the theme framework itself, alters just the bits you want to alter. There are some themes, named **theme frameworks**, that were created specifically with the idea that you would come along and make child themes for them.

Let's take a quick look at how to make a child theme.

Creating the new theme directory

Since it comes bundled, let's make a child theme of twentyten and call it twentyeleven. Create a new folder in `wp-content/themes/`, and name it `twentyeleven`.

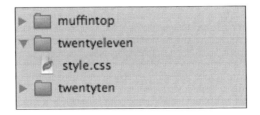

Creating the stylesheet

The only file you need to start with in this directory is the stylesheet. The stylesheet needs the usual header, plus a new line:

```
/*
Theme Name: Twenty Eleven
Description: A Child Theme of Twenty Ten
Version: 1.0
Author: April Hodge Silver
Author URI: http://springthistle.com/
Template: twentyten
*/
```

The key line in that code is `Template: twentyten`. This tells WordPress that your new theme is a child theme of `twentyten`, the directory name of the `twentyten` theme. To make your child theme start out with the CSS from the parent theme, add this code below the comment:

```
@import url(../twentyten/style.css);
```

Using your child theme

That's it! Your new theme now shows up on the **Appearance** page:

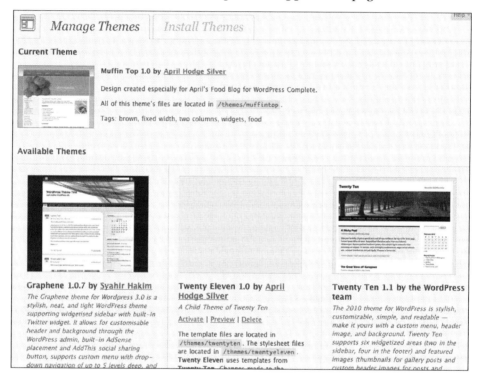

You have a child theme. It will use all of the Twenty Ten styles, template files, functions and everything else. If you activate it, it will present your site as if you were using Twenty Ten.

If you want to change anything, do so in your `twentyeleven` folder. You will override the Twenty Ten original template file if you create a template file (for example, `single.php`, `index.php`, `archive.php`, and so on). The `functions.php` file works a little differently, however. If you create a `functions.php` file, it will be in addition to the Twenty Ten original `functions.php` file; it will not override. If you want to override a specific function in the Twenty Ten `functions.php` file, just create a function with the same name; your new one will take precedence.

In the future, you can update Twenty Ten when it has updates available without worrying about overwriting the changes you made through the Twenty Eleven child theme.

 Learning more: The WordPress codex has a page devoted to learning about child themes: `http://codex.wordpress.org/Child_Themes`. There's also a page with a list of popular theme frameworks: `http://codex.wordpress.org/Theme_Frameworks`. Of course, you can always do a search on the web for both free and paid theme frameworks.

Sharing your theme

If you want to turn your template into a package that other people can use, you just have to take the following steps:

1. Make sure you have the rights to redistribute images, icons, photos, and so on, that you included in your theme.

2. Remove all unnecessary files from your theme's folder. Be sure you don't have backup versions or old copies of any of your files. If you do delete any file, be sure to retest your theme to ensure you didn't accidentally delete something important.

3. Make sure the comment at the top of the `style.css` file is complete and accurate.

4. Create a `Readme.txt` file. This is a good place to let future users know with what version of WordPress your theme is compatible and if it has any special features or requirements.

5. Zip the folder and post your theme ZIP file on your own website for people to download, or post it directly in the WordPress **Theme Directory** at `http://wordpress.org/extend/themes`.

These steps are outlined in a rather general way. If you'd like more details on the process of preparing and sharing your theme in the WordPress community, I highly recommend taking a look at the book *"WordPress 2.8 Theme Design", by Tessa Blakeley Silver*. In this book, the author spends an entire chapter discussing the details involved with sharing your theme and makes recommendations regarding licensing, alternative packaging techniques, getting feedback, versioning, and tracking theme usage.

Summary

You have now crossed to the other side of the theming world. You have learned how to make your own theme. With just the most basic HTML and CSS abilities, you can create a design and turn it into a fully functional WordPress theme.

In this chapter we saw how to:

- Turn your HTML build into a basic theme
- Create WordPress templates to influence the display of a variety of views on your site
- Create custom templates to be applied to pages within your site
- Make your new theme widget-ready
- Create a child theme
- Share your theme with everyone else in the WordPress community

7
Feeds and Podcasting

Let's start out with a definition. For those of you who aren't sure, this is what a "feed" is (when it comes to websites):

> A **web feed** is a data format used for providing users with frequently updated content. (Wikipedia)

Let's take a closer look at this concept. The key idea here is "frequently updated content". A website that features a blog or updated news or any type of content that changes regularly will want to offer users a **feed**. This is because most users will not want (or remember) to visit every such website every day, and users will lose track of which websites have new content today, which don't, what they've already seen, and so on.

Instead, they'll use a **feed aggregator** (or **feed reader**). The users tells the feed reader about all of the regularly updated websites in which they are interested, and the feed reader grabs the updated content and displays it all in one place. I, for example, use a reader named **Google Reader**, and I have given it the feeds for the Planet Money blog, a craigslist search for "wheelbarrow", lifehacker's mac-os-x tag, my sister's family blog, and more. I just have to visit my Google Reader page once a day to see which items have been updated, and I'm done. No need to visit multiple websites. This also adds up to a saving in terms of page load time, as feeds contain fewer advertisements and have only the textual content in which you'll be interested, you don't have to wait for website design elements or ads to render.

What this all boils down to is this: If YOU are going to create a website with frequently updated content, you'll want to offer your users a feed so that they can add it to their reader. Also, you'll want to be sure you are familiar with feeds and feed readers so that you can both understand what your users are seeing and also offer your users everything they are likely to want.

In this chapter, you will learn about feeds, how to provide feeds for your own website's content, and some useful plugins to make all this happen.

Feed basics

Feeds are pure content (or just summaries of content) presented in a structured way via XML, and are usually organized with the most recent information on top. You can always stay up-to-date using feed **aggregators** (software that can read feeds). Using them, you can also have the content you want delivered or collected for you in the way and place you want. This applies not only to written content from blogs or new websites, but also audio and video content (that is, podcasts).

Typically, web feeds are either in **RSS (Really Simple Syndication)** or Atom format. RSS has changed over the past decade, and thus is often referred by a version number. The most up-to-date version of RSS is RSS 2.0.1. The older versions that are still somewhat in use are 0.91 and 1.0. For our purposes in this book, we'll use RSS 2; but you should know that some software is only capable of reading the older versions. If you ever find that you have readers on your blog who write to you complaining that their feed reader can't read your RSS feed, then you could consider publishing links for the older formats (we'll review how to do that later in the chapter), or using a web tool (such as FeedBurner). Tools such as these can serve up feeds in different formats, so your visitors can receive your content in whichever way they choose.

Feed readers

Your subscribers will read your content using a feed reader. **Feed readers** are either web-based or client-side software, which grab the XML content from all the feeds you want and format it legibly. WordPress was programmed with this need in mind and it automatically helps you format your posts so that they come in nicely through the feed readers.

You may want to take a look at your blog in a few feed readers to see how your content looks. There are a few different basic types of feed readers—online, desktop, mobile, and so on.

Bloglines and Google Reader are the most popular online feed-reading tools. You can easily add new feeds, organize them into folders and sections, see which feeds have been updated, and also see which items within each feed you have already read. Following is a screenshot of Google Reader:

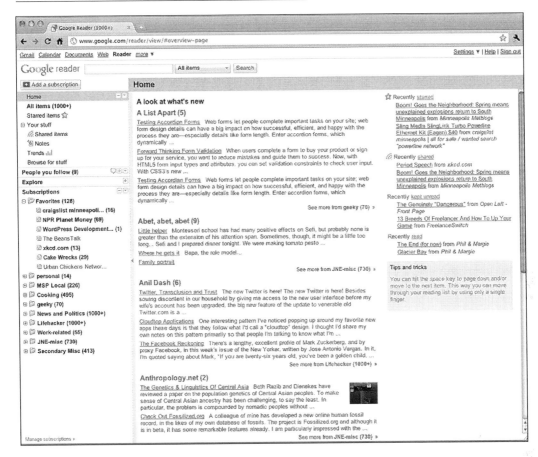

Feedreader and **Thunderbird** are two easy-to-use and free desktop feed readers. You can download and install them on your computer to control your feed reading at home.

There are also feed readers for iPhones and smart phones.

The Firefox browser comes with a built-in feed reader that displays a formatted feed instead of the source XML (Safari does this, too). While Firefox doesn't provide the organizational or tracking features in real feed readers, it can be useful for quickly checking what your own feed looks like.

Learning more

You can find an extensive list of these and other feed readers on Wikipedia: http://en.wikipedia.org/wiki/List_of_feed_aggregators.

Your built-in WordPress feeds

Luckily for you, feed generation is automated in WordPress. The WordPress installation has a feed generator included. The feed generator generates feeds from posts, comments, and even categories. It also generates all versions of RSS and Atom feeds.

You can find the feed generator for your WordPress blog (that we created in the previous chapter) if you point your browser to any of the following URLs (replace wpbook:8888 with the URL of your WordPress installation), and if you have pretty permalinks turned on for your site:

- RSS 2 — `http://wpbook:8888/feed/`
- RDF/RSS 1.0 feed — `http://wpbook:8888/feed/rdf/`
- RSS 0.92 feed — `http://wpbook:8888/feed/rss/`
- Atom — `http://wpbook:8888/feed/atom/`
- Comments — `http://wpbook:8888/comments/feed/`

If you do not have permalinks turned on for your site, you will need to use the following URLs instead:

- RSS 2 — `http://wpbook:8888/?feed=rss2`
- RDF/RSS 1.0 feed — `http://wpbook:8888/?feed=rdf`
- RSS 0.92 feed — `http://wpbook:8888/?feed=rss`
- Atom — `http://wpbook:8888/?feed=atom`
- Comments — `http://wpbook:8888/?feed=comments`

This is what I see in Firefox 3 when I browse to the RSS 2 URL:

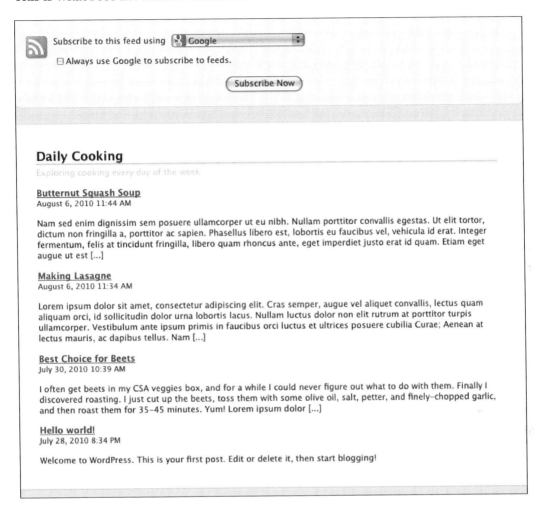

Adding feed links

WordPress automatically generates even the feed links that you see in the preceding screenshot, so you don't have to type them in or remember what they are for. If you're using an existing theme, there's a good chance it's already got the feed links in it, in which case you can skip the following section. If it doesn't, or if you want to learn more about adding feed links to your own templates, continue on here!

You can use handy built-in WordPress functions to add feeds to your theme. Let's add a variety of feeds to the theme we created in *Chapter 6*. We'll add a feed for the whole website, the individual categories, and the comments on posts.

Feeds for the whole website

First, let's add feeds for all the posts and all the comments on the website. If you're not already using the theme we created in *Chapter 6*, you may want to download it now from `http://www.packtpub.com/files/code/4101_Code.zip` and install it on your blog, because that is where we'll be adding the feeds.

Using your FTP software or the built-in WordPress theme editor, edit the `footer.php` file in your `muffintop` folder. Just after the "is powered by wordpress" text, add this:

```
<a href="<?php bloginfo('rss2_url'); ?>" class="rss">Posts</a>
<a href="<?php bloginfo('comments_rss2_url'); ?>"
class="rss">Comments</a>
```

I've also added an RSS icon in GIF format to the theme's `images` folder, and the following CSS to the stylesheet:

```
.rss, p.rss a {
    background: url('images/rss.gif') no-repeat;
    padding: 0 0 0 17px;
    color: #E69730;
}


p.rss { background: none; padding: 0; }

#footer .rss {
    background-position:  0 7px;
    padding: 0 8px 0 17px;
    filter:alpha(opacity=50);
    opacity: .5;
    -moz-opacity:.5;
    color: #999;
}

#footer .rss:hover {
    color: #999;
    filter:alpha(opacity=100);
    opacity: 1;
    -moz-opacity:1;
}
```

Now when you reload your site, you'll see links for those two feeds in the footer. See the following screenshot:

WordPress will generate the feed URLs for you based on your site settings so that you don't have to hardcode them into your template. If you want to add links for other kinds of feeds, replace `rss2_url` in the earlier mentioned link with the following:

- For RSS 1.0 — `rdf_url`
- For RSS 0.92 — `rss_url`
- For Atom — `atom_url`

There's another important way to offer full site feeds on your site. When you look at blog websites, you often see the feed icon in the browser's address bar:

You can click on that icon and see a list of feeds offered by the site:

The code for this is inserted in the `<head>` tag of the HTML where you need to have special `<link>` tags that communicate about the site's feeds to the browser. We actually included them in the previous chapter when we wrote the `<head>` for the **muffintop** theme. They look like this:

```
<link rel="alternate"
    type="application/rss+xml"
    title="<?php bloginfo('name'); ?> RSS Feed"
```

```
           href="<?php bloginfo('rss2_url'); ?>" />
<link rel="alternate"
      type="application/atom+xml"
      title="<?php bloginfo('name'); ?> Atom Feed"
      href="<?php bloginfo('atom_url'); ?>" />
```

Again, if you have a reason to make other types of feeds available, just add new lines with the options I offered above, and replace `rss2_url`, `atom_url`, and so on.

Feeds for categories

Some site visitors may want to only subscribe to posts in a particular category. Let's add an RSS feed that is category-specific.

Using your FTP software or the built-in WordPress theme editor, edit the `archive.php` file in your `theme` folder. (Remember that this is the proprietary template file that WordPress uses for the category page). Add the following code just before `<?php if (have_posts()) : ?>`:

- If you're using permalinks, your category feed code will be this:

```
<?php if (is_category()) { ?>
        <p><a href="<?php echo get_category_link($cat);?>/feed"
class="rss"><?php single_cat_title(); ?> feed</a></p>
<?php } ?>
```

- If you're not using permalinks, your category feed code will be this:

```
<?php if (is_category()) { ?>
        <p><a href="<?php echo get_category_
link($cat);?>&feed=rss" class="rss"><?php single_cat_title(); ?>
feed</a></p>
<?php } ?>
```

I am using permalinks, and so I added the code in the first item to the `archive.php`. Now, here is one of my category pages with the feed link I just added:

Feeds for post comments

On the individual posts page, we can add a feed to allow users to subscribe to the comments on a particular post. Sometimes a single post on a blog can draw a lot of attention, with dozens or hundreds of people adding comments. People who comment, and even those who don't comment, may be interested in following the thread, or subscribing to it.

Using your FTP software or the built-in WordPress theme editor, edit the `single.php` file in your `theme` folder. If you're using the theme we built during *Chapter 6*, find the code that we added in it, which includes the comments template `<?php comments_template(); ?>` and add this code just before it:

```
<p class="rss">
    <?php post_comments_feed_link('Subscribe to these comments'); ?>
</p>
```

(If you are not using the theme we built in *Chapter 6*, you can add the preceding text anywhere in `single.php` so long as it is inside the `if` and `while` loops of the *loop*.) Now, when you look at a single post page, you'll see the subscription link just above the comments form:

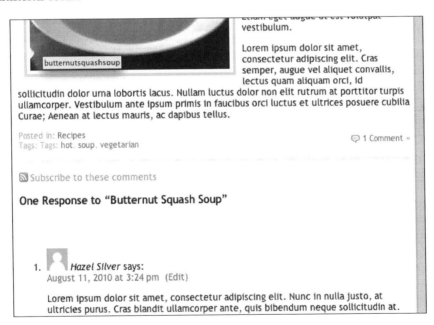

Learning more: More built-in feed are available within WordPress. Learn about them here: `http://codex.wordpress.org/WordPress_Feeds`.

Tracking subscribers with FeedBurner

Unlike visitors to your website's pages, your feed users cannot be tracked through normal site-tracking software such as Google Analytics or Site Meter. The most popular way to track feed users is through the free services provided by **FeedBurner**.

To use FeedBurner, you will need to divert all of your feed links through FeedBurner instead of sending people directly to your WordPress RSS feeds. FeedBurner will then keep a track of the number of subscribers for you and provide you with a separate dashboard, statistics, and other features.

Burn your feed on FeedBurner

I'll need to create a FeedBurner account before you can start using it. Just go to `http://feedburner.google.com/`, log in with your Google account, and follow the sign up instructions. You'll have the option to choose your FeedBurner URL.

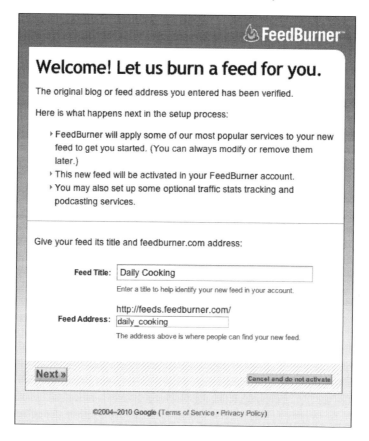

Then click on **Next**, and you're done.

FeedBurner plugin

You're going to need the **FeedBurner plugin**. This plugin will tell WordPress that when someone clicks on one of your feed URLs, which are generated by WordPress, redirect them through FeedBurner. You can download the plugin here: `http://wordpress.org/extend/plugins/feedburner-plugin/`.

Upload and activate the plugin as you learned in *Chapter 4*. Then go to the configuration screen by navigating to **Settings | FeedBurner**. Enter your FeedBurner URL into the appropriate text box.

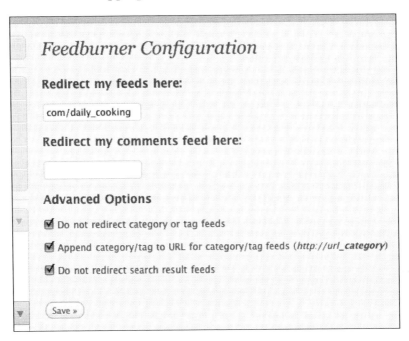

As you can see, you can add a comments feed if you want to track that as well.

Starting immediately, the feed URLs that WordPress generates (though they look the same) will actually redirect the user to FeedBurner so that it can collect stats.

You won't be able to see your user data right away. FeedBurner will take a few days to collect statistics on your subscribers. Once it has enough data, you'll be able to log in and see how many subscribers you have, which feed readers they are using, and a lot of other data.

Podcasting

A **podcast** is a special feed that includes a reference to an audio or video file instead of just text. People use a podcasting client (like iTunes or Juice) to collect and listen to the episodes.

[**Fun fact**: The word "podcast" is a combination of iPod and broadcasting.]

Have you ever considered creating your own podcast? It's like having your own radio or TV show. Your subscribers, instead of reading your posts at their computers, can listen through their headphones to your content at any time.

Adding a podcast to your WordPress blog is outrageously easy. While generating your blog's RSS feeds, WordPress automatically adds an `<enclosure>` tag (available in RSS 2.0) if a music file is linked within that post, and this tag is read by podcast clients. Therefore, all you have to do is make a post; WordPress will do the rest for you.

Creating a podcast

For basic podcasting, there are just two steps you have to take:

1. Record.
2. Post.

Let's look at these steps in detail.

Record yourself

You can record your voice, a conversation, music, or any other sound you'd like to podcast using any commercial or free software and save it as an MP3 file. You may also find that you need to do some editing afterwards.

Some good free software to consider using are as follows:

- I recommend using Audacity, which is a free, cross-platform sound recorder, and editor. You can download Audacity from `http://audacity.sourceforge.net/`. You may have to do a bit of extra fiddling to get the MP3 part working, so pay attention to the additional instructions at that point. You may also want to use a leveling tool such as the Levelator, which can be found at `http://www.conversationsnetwork.org/levelator`.

- Another option is a free application that runs on Windows named WavePad. You can download WavePad from `http://www.nch.com.au/wavepad/`.

- If you are working on a Mac and want some free software, take a look at Garage Band. It comes with the OS, so it will already be installed on your computer.

- If you are working on Mac and want to use a commercial software, Sound Studio is an excellent choice. You can find it at `http://www.apple.com/downloads/macosx/audio/soundstudio.html`.

Make a post

Now that you've created an MP3 file and it's sitting on your computer, you're ready to make a WordPress post that will be the home for the first episode of your podcast.

1. In the WP Admin, click on **New Post** on the top menu. Enter some initial text into your post if you want to provide an explanation of this episode. I suggest you also, at this point, add a new category to your blog called **Podcast**.

2. Next, click on the music icon in the media uploader:

3. When the form fields appear, click on **Browser uploader** or **Select Files** to find your MP3 file. WordPress will upload it, and then show you this screen with options:

You can enter a caption and description in this area. However, none of it will be used in your default podcast. You can use plugins, which we'll discuss in a few pages, to take advantage of the information you type in here.

4. If the **Link URL** field is empty, click on **File URL**, and WordPress will put the URL of the MP3 file you just uploaded in that space.

5. Click on **Insert into Post**.

6. Make any other changes or additions you want to make to your post, publish the post, and you're done.

That's it. Your website's RSS 2.0 feed and its Atom Feed can now be used by podcast clients to pick up your podcast.

You can use your own podcast client (iTunes, in my case) to subscribe right away. In iTunes, I go to **Advanced | Subscribe to podcast** and paste in the RSS URL of the new Podcast category I just created (`http://wpbook:8888/category/podcast/feed`). My podcast shows up like this:

√	Podcast	Time	Plays	Rele... ▼	Description
●	▼ Daily Cooking » Podcast			9/22/10	Exploring cooking every day of the week
● √	Podcast: Sizzling Lasagne	0:18		9/22/10	In this, the first episode of the Daily Cooking podcast, we

Here's how things map out:

WordPress item	Podcast item	Example
Blog or Category title	Podcast title	Daily Cooking	Podcast
Blog description	Podcast description	Exploring cooking every day...
Post title	Podcast episode title title	Podcast: Sizzling Lasagne
Post content	Podcast description	In this, the first episode of...

Dedicated podcasting

Setting up a dedicated podcast is easy—we already did it above! You just need to use a separate category for all of your podcast posts. Whenever you post a podcast episode, be sure to assign it to this category only. Furthermore, in addition to providing a link to the podcast feed on the archive page, you'll want to make this link available in the sidebar of your site.

First, go to the archive page for your podcast category and copy the URL. In my case it's `http://wpbook:8888/category/podcast/feed`. Also, to make things easier for iTunes users, you can add an iTunes-specific link. It is the same as your other link, but replace `http://` with `itpc://`.

Now create a new text widget for your sidebar, and add this HTML to it:

```
<ul>
<li><a href="http://wpbook:8888/category/podcast/feed">The Podcast</a></li>
<li><a href="itpc://wpbook:8888/category/podcast/feed">iTunes Podcast feed</a></li>
</ul>
```

Like this:

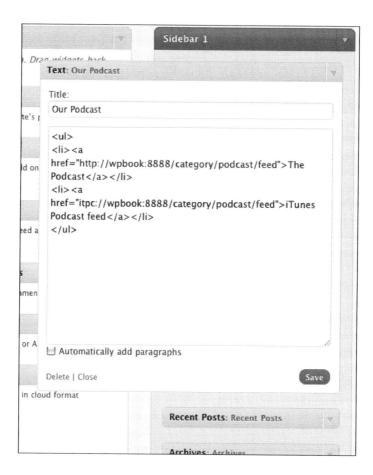

Now, that part of my sidebar looks like this:

Learning more: The WordPress codex has a section on getting started with podcasting. Take a look here: `http://codex.wordpress.org/ Podcasting`.

Podcasting plugins

We just learned that it's quite easy to add a podcast to your WordPress website. However, if you want additional features, you may want to use a podcasting plugin. Some additional features might be:

- Automatic feed generation
- Preview of what your podcast will look like in iTunes
- Download statistics
- Automatic inclusion of a player within your post on your website
- Support for separate category podcasts

There are quite a number of podcast-related plugins available in the WordPress Plugin Repository. The two most popular are:

- PodPress: `http://wordpress.org/extend/plugins/podpress/`
- Podcasting Plugin by TSG: `http://wordpress.org/extend/plugins/ podcasting/`

Also there are hundreds more, which you can find by looking at all plugins tagged **podcasting**: `http://wordpress.org/extend/plugins/tags/podcasting`. You'll have to read the plugin descriptions and user reviews to decide which of these might be the best match for you.

If you want to have your podcast listed in the iTunes podcast directory, take a look at **iPodCatter**. It helps users create a valid feed for the iTunes podcast directory and specify the `itunes:duration` and `itunes:explicit` tags on a per-episode basis. You can download this plugin from `http://garrickvanburen.com/wordpress-plugins/wpipodcatter`.

Using a service to host audio files for free

If you anticipate having a large number of subscribers, or if you plan on producing such a large volume that you'll run out of space on your own server, you can use an external hosting service that will host your audio files either for a fee or even free of cost. Some options to consider are:

- `archive.org`
- `libsyn.org`
- `podbean.com`

If you choose to do this, first upload your file to the service you chose, and make a copy of the URL it gives you for the file.

Now you need to insert it into your WordPress post. However, some services, such as `archive.org`, give you a URL that actually redirects to the music content behind the scenes. This interferes with WordPress's file-detection process. Tom Raftery proposes a good solution on this blog at `http://www.tomrafteryit.net/wordpress-podcasts-not-showing-up-fixed/`.

To implement the fix, do the following when creating a post:

- Scroll down to the section named **Custom fields**.
- Select **enclosure** from the **Name** drop-down menu (if there isn't one already, click on **Enter new**, and just type **enclosure** into the **Name** box), paste the URL of your music file in the **Value** box, and finally, click on **Add Custom Field**.

That's all you have to do because WordPress takes care of the rest.

Summary

Feeds are an easy and popular way to syndicate content—be it written blog content or audio or video podcast content. In this chapter, we learned what an RSS feed is and how to make feeds available for our WordPress blog. We also explored how to syndicate a whole blog or just posts within a certain category, and how to create your own podcast with or without the help of plugins.

Although different versions of RSS are available, RSS 2.0 is the most up-to-date and feature-rich format.

8
Developing Plugins and Widgets

Earlier in this book, you learned how to install plugins. **Plugins** are essentially a way to add to or extend WordPress's built-in functionality. There are thousands of useful plugins available from the online WordPress community, and they perform all different kinds of functions. In the earlier chapters, we installed plugins that catch spam, allow FeedBurner to track RSS followers, add a lightbox to your photo galleries, backup the WordPress database, and more. You can also get plugins that manage your podcasts, create a Google XML site map, integrate with social bookmarking sites, track your stats, translate into other languages, and much more.

Sometimes, however, you'll find yourself in a situation where the plugin you need just doesn't exist. Luckily, it's quite easy to write a plugin for WordPress that you can use on your own site and share with the larger community if you want. All you need is some basic PHP knowledge, and you can write any plugin you want.

This chapter is divided into three major parts. In the first part, we'll create two plugins using an easy-to-follow step-by-step process. In the second part, we'll create a widget using the built-in WordPress Widget class. In the third part, we'll look at shortcodes.

Plugins

In this section, we'll create a plugin via a simple step-by-step process. We'll first see what the essential requirements are, then try out the plugin, and then briefly discuss the PHP code.

Plugin code requirements

Just as there were requirements for a theme, there are requirements for a plugin. At the very least, your plugin must have:

- A PHP file with a unique name
- A specially structured comment at the top of the file

That's it. Then, of course, you must have some functions or processing code, but WordPress will recognize any file that meets these two requirements as a plugin.

Basic plugin—adding link icons

As a demonstration, we will create a simple plugin that adds icons to document links within WordPress. For example, in an earlier chapter we added a link to an MP3 file. It looks like the following now:

Once this plugin is complete, the link will look like the following instead:

To accomplish this, we have to do the following:

1. Provide images of the icons that will be used.
2. Have a PHP function that identifies the links to documents and adds a special CSS class to them.

3. Have a PHP function that creates the CSS classes for displaying the icons.

4. Tell WordPress that whenever it prints the content of a post (that is, using the `the_content()` function), it has to run the first PHP function.

5. Tell WordPress to include the new styles in the `<head>` tag.

Keep this list in mind as we move forward. Once all these five requirements are met, the plugin will be done.

Let's get started!

Naming and organizing the plugin files

Every plugin should have a unique name so that it does not come into conflict with any other plugin in the WordPress universe. When choosing a name for your plugin and the PHP file, be sure to choose something unique. You may even want to do a Google search for the name you choose in order to be sure that someone else isn't already using it.

In this case, as my plugin will be composed of multiple files (a PHP file and some image files) I'm going to create a folder to house my plugin. I'll name the plugin **Add Document Type Styles**, and the folder name, `ahs_doctypes_styles`, will be prefixed with my initials as extra security to keep it unique. The PHP file, `doctypes_styles.php`, will live in this folder. I've also collected a number of document type icons.

The folder I created for my plugin now looks like this:

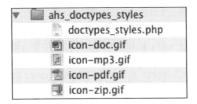

Now that I've got the images in my folder, I've taken care of the *first requirement* in the list of requirements my plugin has to meet.

Note: If your plugin has any unusual installation or configuration options, you may also want to include a `readme.txt` file in this folder that explains this. This `readme` file will be useful both as a reminder to you and as an instructional document to others who may use your plugin in the future. If you plan to submit your plugin to the WordPress plugin directory, you will be required to create a `readme` file.

As mentioned earlier, your plugin has to start with a special comment that tells WordPress how to describe the plugin to users on the plugins page. Now that I've got my folder and a blank PHP file created, I'll insert the special comment. It has to be structured like this:

```
/*
Plugin Name: Add Document Type Styles
Plugin URI: http://springthistle.com/wordpress/plugin_doctypes
Description: Detects URLs in your post and page content and applies
style to those that link to documents so as to identify the document
type. Includes support for: pdf, doc, mp3 and zip.
Version: 1.0
Author: April Hodge Silver
Author URI: http://springthistle.com
*/
```

Another good piece of information to have in your plugin is about licensing. Most plugins use the GPL (GNU General Public License). This license essentially means that anyone can use, copy, and enhance your code, and that they are not allowed to prevent anyone else from redistributing it. I've also added a note about the GPL to my plugin's PHP file.

That's all about the introductory code. Now we can add the meat.

Writing the plugin's core functions

The core of any plugin is the unique PHP code that you bring to the table. This is the part of the plugin that makes it what it is. Since this plugin is so simple, it only has a few lines of code in the middle.

The *second requirement* the plugin has to meet is "Have a PHP function that identifies links to documents and adds a special class to them". The following function does just that. Note that in keeping with my efforts to ensure that my code is unique, I've prefixed both of my functions with `ahs_doctypes_`:

```
function ahs_doctypes_regex($text) {
    $text = ereg_replace(
        'href=([\'|"][[:alnum:]|[:punct:]]*)
           \.(pdf|doc|mp3|zip)([\'|"])',
        'href=\\1.\\2\\3 class="link \\2"',
           $text);
    return $text;
}
```

When the function is given some `$text`, it will perform a search for any HTML anchor tag linking to a PDF, DOC, MP3, or ZIP file, and replace it with a class to that anchor. Then the function returns the altered `$text`.

The third requirement the plugin has to meet is "Have a PHP function that creates classes for displaying the icons". The following function does just that:

```
function ahs_doctypes_styles() {
    echo "<!-- for the plugin Document Type Styles -->\n";
    echo "<style>\n.link { background-repeat: no-repeat; padding: 2px
0 2px 20px; }\n";
    echo ".pdf { background-image: url('".WP_PLUGIN_URL."/ahs_
doctypes_styles/icon-pdf.gif'); }\n";
    echo ".doc { background-image: url('".WP_PLUGIN_URL."/ahs_
doctypes_styles/icon-doc.gif'); }\n";
    echo ".mp3 { background-image: url('".WP_PLUGIN_URL."/ahs_
doctypes_styles/icon-mp3.gif'); }\n";
    echo ".zip { background-image: url('".WP_PLUGIN_URL."/ahs_
doctypes_styles/icon-zip.gif'); }\n";
    echo "</style>\n\n";
}
```

That's it.

Adding hooks to the plugin

We get our code to actually run when it is supposed to by making use of WordPress **hooks**. The way in which plugin hooks work is—at various times while WordPress is running, it checks to see if any plugins have registered functions to run at that time. If there are, the functions are executed. These functions modify the default behavior of WordPress. The WordPress Codex says it best:

> *[...] There are two kinds of hooks:*
>
> 1. **Actions**: *Actions are the hooks that the WordPress core launches at specific points during execution, or when specific events occur. Your plugin can specify that one or more of its PHP functions are executed at these points, using the Action API.*
>
> 2. **Filters**: *Filters are the hooks that WordPress launches to modify text of various types before adding it to the database or sending it to the browser screen. Your plugin can specify that one or more of its PHP functions is executed to modify specific types of text at these times, using the Filter API.*

This means you can tell WordPress to run your plugin's functions at the same time when it runs any of its built-in functions. In our case, we want our plugin's first function, `ahs_doctypes_regex()`, to be run as a filter along with WordPress's `the_content()`. (This is the *fourth requirement* a plugin has to meet.)

Now add the following code to the bottom of the plugin:

```
add_filter('the_content', 'ahs_doctypes_regex');
```

This uses the `add_filter` hook that tells WordPress to register a function named `ahs_doctypes_regex()` when it is running the function called `the_content()`. By the way, if you have more than one function that you want added as a filter to the content, you can add a third argument to the `add_filter()` function. This third argument would be a number from 1-9, and WordPress would run your functions in the order from smallest to largest.

All that's left in our list of requirements that a plugin has to meet is the *fifth requirement*, "Tell WordPress to include the new styles in the `<head>` tag". Now, we need to add a hook using `add_action()` to WordPress's `wp_head()` function, which is included in the `<head></head>` tag of every decent WordPress theme.

```
add_action('wp_head', 'ahs_doctypes_styles');
```

Here is the complete plugin PHP file (minus the license, which I removed for space considerations):

```php
<?php
/*
Plugin Name: Add Document Type Styles
Plugin URI: http://springthistle.com/wordpress/plugin_doctypes
Description: Detects URLs in your post and page content and applies
style to those that link to documents so as to identify the document
type. Includes support for: pdf, doc, mp3 and zip.
Version: 1.0
Author: April Hodge Silver
Author URI: http://springthistle.com
*/

function ahs_doctypes_regex($text) {
    $types = ereg_replace(',[:space:]*','|',$types);
    $text = ereg_replace('href=([\'|"][[:alnum:]|[:punct:]]*)\
.(pdf|doc|mp3|zip)([\'|"])','href=\\1.\\2\\3 class="link \\2"',$text);
    return $text;
}

function ahs_doctypes_styles() {
    echo "<!-- for the plugin Document Type Styles -->\n";
    echo "<style>\n.link { background-repeat: no-repeat; padding: 2px
0 2px 20px; }\n";
    echo ".pdf { background-image: url('".WP_PLUGIN_URL."/ahs_
doctypes_styles/icon-pdf.gif'); }\n";
    echo ".doc { background-image: url('".WP_PLUGIN_URL."/ahs_
doctypes_styles/icon-doc.gif'); }\n";
```

```
    echo ".mp3 { background-image: url('".WP_PLUGIN_URL."/ahs_
doctypes_styles/icon-mp3.gif'); }\n";
    echo ".zip { background-image: url('".WP_PLUGIN_URL."/ahs_
doctypes_styles/icon-zip.gif'); }\n";
    echo "</style>\n\n";
}

add_filter('the_content', 'ahs_doctypes_regex');
add_action('wp_head', 'ahs_doctypes_styles');
?>
```

 Please make sure that there are no blank spaces before <?php and after ?>. If there are any spaces, the PHP will break, complaining that headers have already been sent.

Make sure you save and close this PHP file. You can now do one of two things:

- Using your FTP client, upload ahs_doctypes_styles/ to your wp-content/plugins/ folder
- Zip up your folder into ahs_doctypes_styles.zip and use the plugin uploader in the WP Admin to add this plugin to your WordPress installation

Once the plugin is installed, it will show up on the plugins page:

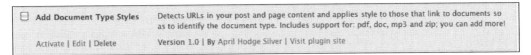

Now you can activate it. That's all you have to do! Let's take a look at the plugin.

Trying out the plugin

If you look at the podcast post we created in an earlier chapter, you'll notice that an MP3 icon has been added to it.

You can also try adding a new post with links to PDF, ZIP, or DOC files. This can be done by uploading the files and clicking on **Insert into Post**.

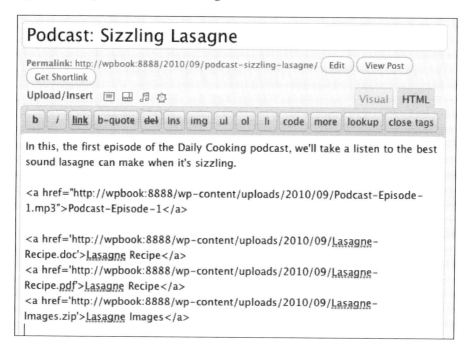

When you view this post, you'll see that icons have been automatically added to it by the plugin:

Now that you've learned about a basic plugin that uses hooks to piggyback on the existing WordPress functionality, let's enhance this plugin by giving the user some controls.

Adding an admin page

As you have already seen, some plugins add a page to the WP Admin where you or the user can edit plugin options. We've seen this with Akismet, DB Backup, FeedBurner, and jQuery Colorbox. Now let's modify our plugin to give the user some control over which document types are supported.

First, deactivate the plugin we just wrote. We'll make changes to it and then reactivate it.

Following is what the new management page will look like when we are done:

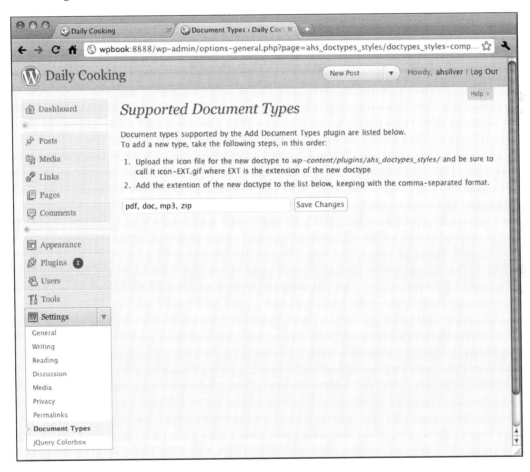

Following are the steps we'll carry out to modify the plugin in order to make this new page possible:

- Add functions that create an admin page and save the user's input in a new option.

- Modify the `ahs_doctypes_regex()` and the `ahs_doctypes_styles()` function so that they retrieve and use the user's input.

- Add hooks for the admin page functions.

Let's get started!

Adding management page functions

The management page that we will create is going to add an option to the WP Admin. This uses the existing space in the WordPress options table in the database, so no database modifications are required. The name of the new option has to be unique. I'm going to call the new option `ahs_supportedtypes`, and I'll be sure to use `supportedtypes_` in all of my function names to ensure that they are unique.

There are six functions we need to add to the plugin so that an admin page can be added to the WP Admin. Let's take a look at the first two.

```
function set_supportedtypes_options() {
    add_option("ahs_supportedtypes","pdf,doc,mp3,zip");
}

function unset_supportedtypes_options () {
    delete_option("ahs_supportedtypes");
}
```

The *first function* adds the new option `ahs_supportedtypes` when the plugin is activated, and also sets the default value. *The second function* removes the new option when the plugin is deactivated.

Let's look at the new *third function*:

```
function modify_menu_for_supportedtypes() {
    add_submenu_page(
        'Document Types', // Page <title>
        'Document Types', // Menu title
        7,                // What level of user
        __FILE__,              //File to open
        'supportedtypes_options'  //Function to call
        );
}
```

This function adds a new item to the **Settings** menu in the WP Admin using
`add_submenu_page`. This takes five arguments, namely, page title, menu link text,
the user at the maximum level who can access the link, what file to open (none, in
this case), and the function to call, `supportedtypes_options()`, which is the *fourth
new function* we are adding.

```
function supportedtypes_options () {
    echo '<div class="wrap"><h2>Supported Document Types</h2>';
    if ($_REQUEST['submit']) {
        update_supportedtypes_options();
    }
    print_supportedtypes_form();
    echo '</div>';
}
```

This function actually displays our new page. It prints a title, checks to see
if someone has clicked on the submit button, and if it is clicked, the
`supportedtypes_options()` function updates options, and then prints the form.

The new *fifth function* we have to add is responsible for updating options if the
submit button has been clicked.

```
$updated = false;
if ($_REQUEST['ahs_supportedtypes']) {  update_option('ahs_
supportedtypes', $_REQUEST['ahs_supportedtypes']); $updated = true; }

if ($updated) {
        echo '<div id="message" class="updated fade">';
        echo '<p>Supported Types successfully updated!</p>';
        echo '</div>';
    } else {
        echo '<div id="message" class="error fade">';
        echo '<p>Unable to update Supported Types!</p>';
        echo '</div>';
    }
}
```

The last function we need to add, the new *sixth function*, prints the form that users
will see.

```
function print_supportedtypes_form () {
    $val_ahs_supportedtypes = stripslashes(get_option('ahs_
supportedtypes'));
    echo <<<EOF
<p>Document types supported by the Add Document Types plugin are
listed below.<br />To add a new type, take the following steps, in
this order:
```

```
<ol>
    <li>Upload the icon file for the new doctype to <i>wp-content/
    plugins/ahs_doctypes_styles/</i> and be sure to call it icon-EXT.gif
    where EXT is the extension of the new doctype</li>
    <li>Add the extention of the new doctype to the list below,
    keeping with the comma-separated format.</li>
</ol>
</p>

<form method="post">
    <input type="text" name="ahs_supportedtypes" size="50"
value="$val_ahs_supportedtypes" />
    <input type="submit" name="submit" value="Save Changes" />
</form>
EOF;
}
```

Those six functions together will take care of adding a link in the menu, adding the management page for that link, and updating the new option.

Modifying the regex() function

Now that the users are able to edit the list of supported document types by appending the document types they want, we should have a way of telling the regex() function to use the user's list instead of a built-in list. To do that, we need to use get_option('ahs_supportedtypes') in our regex() function. The get_option() function will retrieve the value that the user has saved in the new option we just created. Modify your regex() function so that it looks like this:

```
function ahs_doctypes_regex($text) {
    $types = get_option('ahs_supportedtypes');
    $types = ereg_replace(',[ ]*','|',$types);
    $text = ereg_replace('href=([\'|"][[:alnum:]|[:punct:]]*)\
.('.$types.')([\'|"])','href=\\1.\\2\\3 class="link \\2"',$text);
    return $text;
}
```

We also have to tell the function that prints the styles into the <head> tag to use the user's list. Modify the ahs_doctypes_styles() function so that it looks like this:

```
function ahs_doctypes_styles() {
    $types = split(",[ ]*",get_option('ahs_supportedtypes'));
    echo "<!-- for the plugin Document Type Styles -->\n";
    echo "<style>\n.link { background-repeat: no-repeat; padding: 2px
0 2px 20px; }\n";
    foreach ($types as $type) {
```

```
        echo ".$type { background-image: url('".WP_PLUGIN_URL."/ahs_
doctypes_styles/icon-$type.gif'); }\n";
    }
    echo "</style>\n\n";
}
```

Adding hooks

We have added our management page functions, but now we have to tell WordPress to use them. To do that, we just need to add the following three new hooks:

```
add_action('admin_menu','modify_menu_for_supportedtypes');
register_activation_hook(__FILE__,"set_supportedtypes_options");
register_deactivation_hook(__FILE__,"unset_supportedtypes_options");
```

The first hook tells WordPress to add our link to the menu when it creates the menu with `admin_menu()`. The next two hooks tell WordPress to call the activation and deactivation functions when the plugin is activated or deactivated.

Trying out the plugin

We have added all of the new functions. Now, I'll change the version number in my initial comment from `1.0` to `1.1`, change the description, and save the file. Next, I will go to the plugin page and see the updated plugin information:

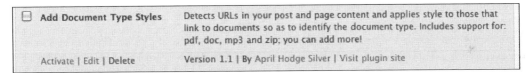

Now, I can reactivate the plugin. Now when you look at the **Settings** menu, you will see that the new link has been added.

Click on it to see the management page.

Supported Document Types

Document types supported by the Add Document Types plugin are listed below.
To add a new type, take the following steps, in this order:

1. Upload the icon file for the new doctype to *wp-content/plugins/ahs_doctypes_styles/* and be sure to call it icon-EXT.gif where EXT is the extension of the new doctype

2. Add the extention of the new doctype to the list below, keeping with the comma-separated format.

pdf, doc, mp3, zip   Save Changes

If you follow the two steps here on the management page (upload the file icon and add the extension to the option), then that new document type will be supported.

There are already a number of ways in which this plugin could be improved. Some of them are:

- Instead of making the user upload his or her new icon using FTP, the plugin could allow the user to upload the new icon directly via the new management page
- The plugin could display the icons for the supported document types on the management page, so the users can see what they look like
- The plugin could check to make sure that for every document type in the option field there is an existing icon, else it displays an error to the user

Perhaps you'd like to try to make these changes yourself!

Plugin with DB access—capturing searched words

We're going to leave the doctypes plugin behind now, and create a new plugin, featuring active use of the database. Let's create a simple plugin that stores all the words that visitors search for using the blog's search function.

The database table structure for this plugin will be as follows:

table wp_searchedwords:

Field	Type	Null	Key	Default	Extra
id	int(11)	YES	PRI	NULL	auto_increment
word	Varchar(255)			NULL	

Now, let's write the plugin code.

Getting the plugin to talk to the database

The first part of this plugin has to be run only when the plugin is activated. This will be the initialization function, and it has to check to see if the database table exists; and if not, create it.

```
function searchedwords_init($content) {
    if (isset($_GET['activate']) && $_GET['activate'] == 'true') {
        global $wpdb;
        $result = mysql_list_tables(DB_NAME);
        $current_tables = array();
        while ($row = mysql_fetch_row($result)) {
            $current_tables[] = $row[0];
        }
        if (!in_array("wp_searchedwords", $current_tables)) {
            $result = mysql_query(
            "CREATE TABLE `wp_searchedwords` (
                id INT NOT NULL AUTO_INCREMENT PRIMARY KEY,
                word VARCHAR(255)
            )");
        }
    }
    if (!empty($_GET['s'])) {
        $current_searched_words = explode(" ",urldecode($_
GET['s']));
        foreach ($current_searched_words as $word) {
            mysql_query("insert into wp_searchedwords values(null
,'{$word}')");
        }
    }
}
```

The preceding function also stores the searched word in the database table if a search has just been performed.

Adding management page functions

We now need a familiar-looking function that adds a management page to the admin menu. In this case, we're using `add_management_page()` instead of `add_submenu_page()` because this plugin is more of a tool than something that needs settings.

```
function modify_menu_for_searchedwords() {
    if (function_exists('add_submenu_page')) {
        add_management_page(
            "Searched Words",
```

```
                        "Searched Words",
                        1,
                        __FILE__,
                        'searchedwords_page'
            );
      }
}
```

We also need a function that retrieves the information from the database and displays it on the new management page.

```
function searchedwords_page() {
     $result = mysql_query('SELECT COUNT(word) AS occurence, word FROM
wp_searchedwords GROUP BY word ORDER BY occurance DESC');
     echo '<style>.searchwords { padding: 0px; border: 3px solid #ddd}
.searchwords td { border-top: 2px solid #e0e0e0; padding: 3px; margin:
0;  }  .searchwords th { background-color: #e0e0e0; padding: 5px 3px
1px 3px; margin: 0; }</style>';
     echo '<div class="wrap"><h2>Searched Words</h2>';
     echo '<table class="searchwords">';
     if (mysql_num_rows($result)>0) {
            echo '<tr><th>Search words</th><th># searches</th></tr>';
            while ($row = mysql_fetch_row($result)) {
                   echo "<tr><td>{$row[1]}</b></td><td>{$row[0]}</td></
tr>";
            }
     } else {
            echo '<tr><td colspan="2"><h3>No searches have been
preformed yet</h3></td></tr>';
     }
     echo '</table></div>';
}
```

That's it, only two. The previous plugin had more functions because data was being captured from the user and being saved. Here, that's not necessary.

Adding hooks

Lastly, we just need to add two hooks:

```
add_filter('init', 'searchedwords_init');
add_action("admin_menu","modify_menu_for_searchedwords");
```

The first hook tells WordPress to run the initialization function when the plugin is activated, or when a search is performed. The second hook modifies the admin menu to add a link to the new management page.

Trying out the plugin

As with the last plugin, you can now either upload your plugin using FTP to `wp-content/plugins`, or you can turn it into a ZIP file and add it using the uploader in the WP Admin.

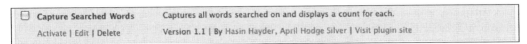

Once you've installed it, activate it. Look at the menu under **Tools** and you'll see a link to the new management page:

When you click on **Searched Words**, you'll see a new page that the plugin created:

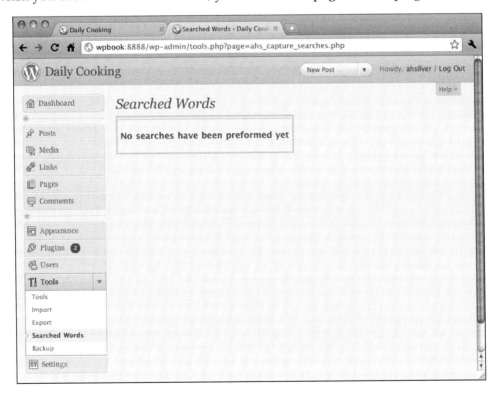

The new page shows that no searches have been performed since the plugin was activated. Do a few searches on your site and return to this page:

Learning more

There are hundreds of hooks available in WordPress—way too many to cover in this book. You can learn more about the hooks discussed in this book, as well as learn about all of the other hooks available, by going online. Start out at these online reference sites:

- The **Plugin API** contains very thorough information about writing plugins and using hooks:

    http://codex.wordpress.org/Plugin_API

- For a complete list of *action* hooks:

    http://codex.wordpress.org/Plugin_API/Action_Reference

- For a complete list of *filter* hooks:

  `http://codex.wordpress.org/Plugin_API/Filter_Reference`

- You may also want to take a step back and look at the general **Plugin Resources** page in the WordPress **Codex**:

  `http://codex.wordpress.org/Plugin_Resources`

- If you want to submit your plugin to the WordPress Plugin Repository, you'll have to take steps similar to those you took when preparing a theme, and you'll also have to get hooked up to the WordPress SVN repository. Learn more about how to submit a plugin to the WordPress Plugin Repository at:

  `http://codex.wordpress.org/Plugin_Submission_and_Promotion`

Widgets

Writing a widget bears some similarities to writing a plugin, but in some ways it's easier because there is a widget class that you can leverage for some of the functionality.

Recent posts from a Category Widget

In this section, we will see how to write a widget that displays recent posts from a particular category in the sidebar. The user will be able to choose how many recent posts to show and whether or not to show an RSS feed link. It will look like the following screenshot:

Let's get started!

Naming the widget

Widgets, like plugins, need to have a unique name. Again, I suggest you search the Web for the name you want to use in order to be sure of its uniqueness. Because of the widget class, you don't need to worry so much about uniqueness in your function and variable names, since the widget class unique-ifies them for you.

I've given this widget the filename `ahs_postfromcat_widget.php`.

As for the introduction, this comment code is the same as what you use for the plugin. For this widget, the introductory comment is this:

```
/*
Plugin Name: April's List Posts Cat Widget
Plugin URI: http://springthistle.com/wordpress/plugin_postfromcat
Description: Allows you to add a widget with some number of most
recent posts from a particular category
Author: April Hodge Silver
Version: 1.0
Author URI: http://springthistle.com
*/
```

Widget structure

When building a widget using the widget class, your widget needs to have the following structure:

```
class UNIQUE_WIDGET_NAME extends WP_Widget {

    function UNIQUE_WIDGET_NAME() {
            $widget_ops = array();
            $control_ops = array();
            $this->WP_Widget();
    }

    function form ($instance) {
            // prints the form on the widgets page
    }

    function update ($new_instance, $old_instance) {
            // used when the user saves their widget options
    }

    function widget ($args,$instance) {
            // used when the sidebar calls in the widget
    }
```

```
}

// initiate the widget

// register the widget
```

Of course, we need an actual unique widget name. I'm going to use `Posts_From_Category`. Now, let's flesh out this code one section at a time.

Widget initiation function

Let's start with the widget initiation function. Blank, it looks like this:

```
function Posts_From_Category() {
        $widget_ops = array();
        $control_ops = array();
        $this->WP_Widget();
    }
```

In this function, which has the same name as the class itself and is therefore the constructor, we initialize various things that the `WP_Widget` class is expecting. The first two variables, to which you can give any name you want, are just a handy way to set the two array variables expected by the third line of code.

Let's take a look at these three lines of code:

- The `$widget_ops` variable is where you can set the class name, which is given to the widget div itself, and the description, which is shown in the WP Admin on the widgets page.

- The `$control_ops` variable is where you can set options for the control box in the WP Admin on the widget page, like the width and height of the widget and the ID prefix used for the names and IDs of the items inside.

- When you call the parent class' constructor, `WP_Widget()`, you'll tell it the widget's unique ID, the widget's display title, and pass along the two arrays you created.

For this widget, my code now looks like this:

```
function Posts_From_Category() {
    $widget_ops = array(
            'classname' => 'postsfromcat',
            'description' => 'Allows you to display a list of recent
posts within a particular category.');

    $control_ops = array(
            'width' => 250,
```

```
            'height' => 250,
            'id_base' => 'postsfromcat-widget');

    $this->WP_Widget('postsfromcat-widget', 'Posts from a Category',
$widget_ops, $control_ops );
}
```

Widget form function

This function has to be named `form()`. You may not rename it if you want the widget class to know what it's purpose is. You also need to have an argument in there, which I'm calling `$instance`, that the class also expects. This is where current widget settings are stored.

This function needs to have all of the functionalities to create the form that users will see when adding the widget to a sidebar. Let's look at some abbreviated code and then explore what it's doing:

```php
<?php
function form ($instance) {

    $defaults = array('catid' => '1', 'numberposts' => '5');
    $instance = wp_parse_args( (array) $instance, $defaults ); ?>

    <p>
        <label for="<?php echo $this->get_field_id('title');
?>">Title:</label>
        <input type="text" name="<?php echo $this->get_field_
name('title') ?>" id="<?php echo $this->get_field_id('title') ?> "
value="<?php echo $instance['title'] ?>" size="20">       </p>

    <p>
        <label for="<?php echo $this->get_field_id('catid');
?>">Category ID:</label>
        <?php wp_dropdown_categories('hide_empty=0&hierarchical=1&id
='.$this->get_field_id('catid').'&name='.$this->get_field_name('catid'
).'&selected='.$instance['catid']); ?>
    </p>

    <p>
        <label for='<?php echo $this->get_field_id('numberposts');
?>">Number of posts:</label>
        <select id="<?php echo $this->get_field_id('numberposts');
?>" name="<?php echo $this->get_field_name('numberposts'); ?>">
        <?php for ($i=1;$i<=20;$i++) {
```

```
                echo '<option value="'.$i.'"';
                if ($i==$instance['numberposts']) echo '
    selected="selected"';
                echo '>'.$i.'</option>';
            } ?>
            </select>
        </p>

        <p>
            <input type="checkbox" id="<?php echo $this->get_field_
    id('rss'); ?>" name="<?php echo $this->get_field_name('rss'); ?>"
    <?php if ($instance['rss']) echo 'checked="checked"' ?> />
            <label for="<?php echo $this->get_field_id('rss'); ?>">Show
    RSS feed link?</label>
        </p>

        <?php
    }
    ?>
```

First, I set some defaults, which in this case is just for the number of posts, which I think it would be nice to set to 5. You can set other defaults in this array as well.

Then you use a WordPress function named `wp_parse_args()`, which creates an `$instance` array that your form will use. What's in it depends on what defaults you've set and what settings the user has already saved.

Then you create form fields. Note that for each form field, I make use of the built-in functions that will create unique names and IDs and input existing values.

- `$this->get-field_id` creates a unique ID based on the widget instance (remember, you can create more than one instance of this widget).
- `$this->get_field_name()` creates a unique name based on the widget instance.
- The `$instance` array is where you will find the current values for the widget, whether they are defaults or user-saved data.

All the other code in there is just regular PHP and HTML. Note that if you give the user the ability to set a title, name that field "title", WordPress will show it on the widget form when it's minimized. The widget form this will create will look like this:

Widget save function

When a user clicks the save button on the widget form, WordPress uses AJAX to run your save function. You need to be sure to save whatever the user types in, which is all we're doing in this case, but you can put other functionalities here if it's appropriate for your widget (for example, database interactions, conversions, calculations, and so on). The final code for this function is as follows:

```
function update ($new_instance, $old_instance) {
    $instance = $old_instance;

    $instance['catid'] = $new_instance['catid'];
    $instance['numberposts'] = $new_instance['numberposts'];
    $instance['title'] = $new_instance['title'];
    $instance['rss'] = $new_instance['rss'];

    return $instance;
}
```

Be sure this function is named `update()` and is prepared to accept two instances, one with old data and one with the just-submitted data. You can write your code to check the `$new_instance` for problems, and thus return the `$old_instance` if the new one isn't valid. The `$instance` you return will be what's shown in the update widget form.

Widget print function

The third main function in your widget class is the one that is called by the sidebar when it's time to actually show the widget to people visiting the website. It needs to retrieve any relevant saved user data and print out information for the website visitor. In this case, our final print function looks like this:

```
function widget ($args,$instance) {
    extract($args);

    $title = $instance['title'];
    $catid = $instance['catid'];
    $numberposts = $instance['numberposts'];
    $rss = $instance['rss'];

    global $wpdb;
    $posts = get_posts('numberposts='.$numberposts.'&category='.$catid
);
    $out = '<ul>';
    foreach($posts as $post) {
        $out .= '<li><a href="'.get_permalink($post->ID).'">'.$post-
>post_title.'</a></li>';
    }
    if ($rss) $out .= '<li><a href="'.get_category_
link($catid).'feed/" class="rss">Category RSS</a></li>';
    $out .= '</ul>';

    echo $before_widget;
    echo $before_title.$title.$after_title;
    echo $out;
    echo $after_widget;
}
```

The first thing I do is extract the data in the instance, which has the information the website administrator had saved when filling out the widget form. Then, the widget contacts the database to get the posts in the category and prints them out in a nice bulleted list.

The last four lines are important. There are four variables that the theme developer set when activating the sidebar as a widget-ready area. We set them ourselves, back in *Chapter 6*. They are:

- $before_widget
- $before_title
- $after_title
- $after_widget

Be sure to use those so that theme developers are happy with your widget.

Initiate and hook up the widget

That's it for widget functionality! Now you just need to add a little code that will hook the widget up to the rest of WordPress.

```
function ahspfc_load_widgets() {
    register_widget('Posts_From_Category');
}


add_action('widgets_init', 'ahspfc_load_widgets');
```

This tells WordPress that when it initiates widgets, it should be sure to register our new widget.

Final widget code

Here is the complete widget code:

```php
<?php
/*
Plugin Name: April's List Posts Cat Widget
Plugin URI: http://springthistle.com/wordpress/plugin_postfromcat
Description: Allows you to add a widget with some number of most
recent posts from a particular category
Author: April Hodge Silver
Version: 1.0
Author URI: http://springthistle.com
*/


class Posts_From_Category extends WP_Widget {

    function Posts_From_Category() {
        /* Widget settings. */
        $widget_ops = array(
                'classname' => 'postsfromcat',
                'description' => 'Allows you to display a list of
recent posts within a particular category.');

        /* Widget control settings. */
        $control_ops = array(
                'width' => 250,
                'height' => 250,
                'id_base' => 'postsfromcat-widget');

        /* Create the widget. */
```

```php
        $this->WP_Widget('postsfromcat-widget', 'Posts from a
Category', $widget_ops, $control_ops );
    }


    function form ($instance) {

        /* Set up some default widget settings. */
        $defaults = array('numberposts' => '5');
        $instance = wp_parse_args( (array) $instance, $defaults );
?>


        <p>
            <label for="<?php echo $this->get_field_id('title');
?>">Title:</label>
            <input type="text" name="<?php echo $this->get_field_
name('title') ?>" id="<?php echo $this->get_field_id('title') ?> "
value="<?php echo $instance['title'] ?>" size="20">
        </p>


        <p>
            <label for="<?php echo $this->get_field_id('catid');
?>">Category ID:</label>
            <?php wp_dropdown_categories('hide_empty=0&hierarchic
al=1&id='.$this->get_field_id('catid').'&name='.$this->get_field_name(
'catid').'&selected='.$instance['catid']); ?>
        </p>


        <p>
            <label for="<?php echo $this->get_field_
id('numberposts'); ?>">Number of posts:</label>
            <select id="<?php echo $this->get_field_
id('numberposts'); ?>" name="<?php echo $this->get_field_
name('numberposts'); ?>">
                <?php for ($i=1;$i<=20;$i++) {
                    echo '<option value="'.$i.'"';
                    if ($i==$instance['numberposts']) echo '
selected="selected"';
                    echo '>'.$i.'</option>';
                } ?>
                </select>
        </p>

        <p>
```

```
                    <input type="checkbox" id="<?php echo $this->get_
field_id('rss'); ?>" name="<?php echo $this->get_field_name('rss');
?>" <?php if ($instance['rss']) echo 'checked="checked"' ?> />
                    <label for="<?php echo $this->get_field_id('rss');
?>">Show RSS feed link?</label>
            </p>

            <?php
    }


    function update ($new_instance, $old_instance) {
            $instance = $old_instance;

            $instance['catid'] = $new_instance['catid'];
            $instance['numberposts'] = $new_instance['numberposts'];
            $instance['title'] = $new_instance['title'];
            $instance['rss'] = $new_instance['rss'];

            return $instance;
    }

    function widget ($args,$instance) {
            extract($args);

            $title = $instance['title'];
            $catid = $instance['catid'];
            $numberposts = $instance['numberposts'];
            $rss = $instance['rss'];

            // retrieve posts information from database
            global $wpdb;
            $posts = get_posts('numberposts='.$numberposts.'&category='.
$catid);
            $out = '<ul>';
            foreach($posts as $post) {
                    $out .= '<li><a href="'.get_permalink($post-
>ID).'">'.$post->post_title.'</a></li>';
            }
            if ($rss) $out .= '<li><a href="'.get_category_
link($catid).'feed/" class="rss">Category RSS</a></li>';
            $out .= '</ul>';

            //print the widget for the sidebar
            echo $before_widget;
            echo $before_title.$title.$after_title;
```

```
            echo $out;
            echo $after_widget;
        }

    }

    function ahspfc_load_widgets() {
        register_widget('Posts_From_Category');
    }

    add_action('widgets_init', 'ahspfc_load_widgets');

    ?>
```

Trying out the widget

Your widget is ready to go! Save all of your changes, and upload your widget to wp-content/plugins. Go to the **Installed Plugins** page, and you'll see your widget waiting to be activated:

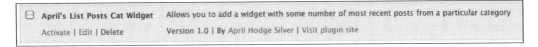

Activate it, and then navigate to **Appearance | Widgets**. You'll see the widget waiting to be added to a sidebar:

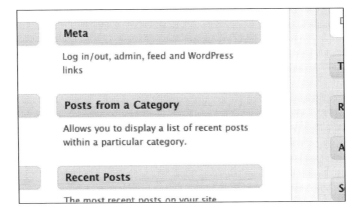

Drag the widget to a sidebar, and then click on the little down arrow to edit it. You'll see the options slide down, as shown in the following image:

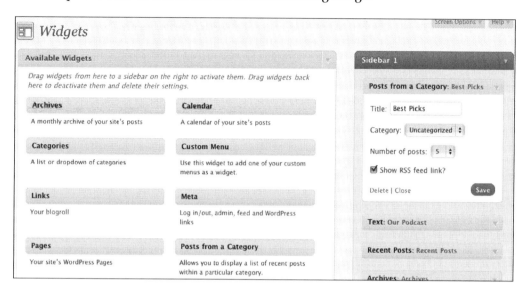

You can enter a **Title** or leave it blank for the default, choose the **Category** to use, choose the **Number of posts,** and choose whether or not to **Show RSS feed link.** Then click on **Save** as you would with any widget. When you return to the frontend of the site and reload, posts from the category you chose are displayed in the sidebar as follows:

Learning more

You can browse the following online reference sites to learn more about widgets:

- The WordPress **Widgets API** is located at:
  `http://codex.wordpress.org/Widgets_API`

- WordPress lists a number of widgets on the following page:
  `http://codex.wordpress.org/WordPress_Widgets`

- If you want to find more widgets to install on your website, visit the widgets section of the Plugin Repository at: `http://wordpress.org/extend/plugins/tags/widget`

Bundling a widget with a plugin

If you're writing a plugin and you'd like to make a widget available with it, you don't have to create a separate widget plugin. Just include all of the widget code, like what we created in the preceding section, in with your plugin's PHP file. When the user activates the plugin, the widget you created will automatically show up on the widgets page in the WP Admin. No need for a separate file!

Shortcodes

Shortcodes are a handy way to let a nontechnical person, that is, the editor of the website, include dynamic functionality within pages and posts, without having to actually use any PHP.

How do shortcodes work?

The way a shortcode works is that you tell WordPress to look at text within square brackets ([]) and evaluate it by running a PHP function. That PHP function can live in your `functions.php` file of your theme, or in a plugin file, or in a widget file. Let's create a simple shortcode and include it in with our theme by adding it to `functions.php`.

Creating a simple shortcode

Let's say you want to add a page with your bio on it and the text of your most recent post. Your bio won't change every day, but your most recent post will. We can create a shortcode for that.

First, let's write a function (with a unique name!) that grabs the data for the most recent post on the blog and put it in the theme's `functions.php` file. It looks like this:

```
function recent_post_func() {
    $posts = get_posts('numberposts=1');
    $out = '';
    foreach ($posts as $post) {
        setup_postdata($post);
        $out .= '<div class="ahs_recentpost"';
        $out .= '<h4><a href="'.get_permalink($post->ID).'">'.get_
the_title($post->ID).'</a></h4>';
        $out .= apply_filters('the_content', get_the_content());
```

```
        $out .= '</div>';
    }
    return $out;
}
```

Note that this function does not echo or print anything. It just returns a string. If you let your function print, it won't look right on the website.

Now, we tell WordPress that this function is a shortcode, and we tell it what the shortcode is using a hook. Be sure to choose something unique! I've chosen ahs_recentpost as the name for this shortcode, so the hook looks like this:

```
add_shortcode('ahs_recentpost', 'recent_post_func');
```

If you look at the function itself, you'll see I've put a unique class on that div so that the blog user can add some custom CSS if they want to style the div. For example:

```
.ahs_recentpost {
    border: 1px solid #ccc;
    background: #f0f0f0;
    padding: 15px;
    margin: 0 10px 15px 0;
}

.ahs_recentpost h4 {
    margin: 0;
}
```

Finally, create the bio page and include the shortcode in it.

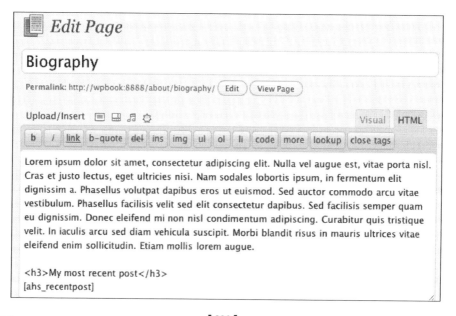

When you view the page, you'll see the most recent post has been included:

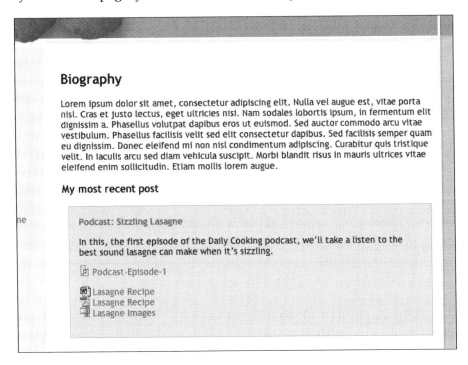

Adding options to the shortcode

Perhaps the user will want to choose to show their own most recent post, rather than the most recent post on the blog, if they share the blog with other writers. To enable them to do that, we need to add options to the shortcode.

Modify the first few lines of your shortcode function so that it looks like this:

```
function recent_post_func($atts) {
    extract(shortcode_atts(array(
            'authorid' => null,
            'numberposts' => 1,
    ), $atts));

    $args = 'numberposts='.$numberposts;
    if ($authorid) $args .= '&author='.$authorid;

    $posts = get_posts($args);

// no change below this point
```

As you can see, we've added an `$atts` argument to the function (WordPress will hand this off automatically), and used `extract()` to turn the options the user submits into variables available in the function. The values in the array passed to `extract()` sets the defaults, in case the user chooses no options. The last three lines just act on the information the user has submitted.

Now, the user can, instead of just using `[ahs_recentpost]` in their page, tell it how many recent posts to show, and which author ID, if any, to use:

```
[ahs_recentpost numberposts="2" authorid="1"]
```

Now my bio page looks like this:

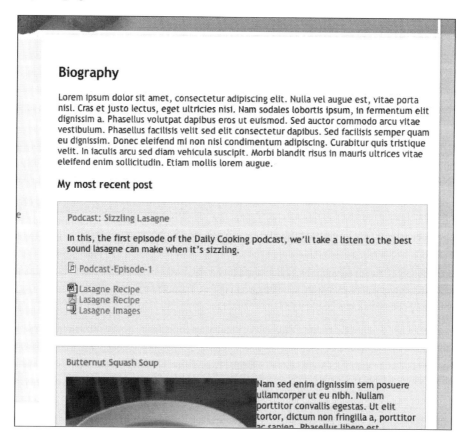

Obviously, there is no limit to the number of options that you can make available to the shortcode users. Also, if you want to make a shortcode available with a plugin or widget, you can just include the function and hook in your plugin or widget PHP file.

Enabling shortcodes in widgets

By default, shortcodes are ignored in widget. So, if you were to add a Text widget with your shortcode in it, as shown in the following screenshot:

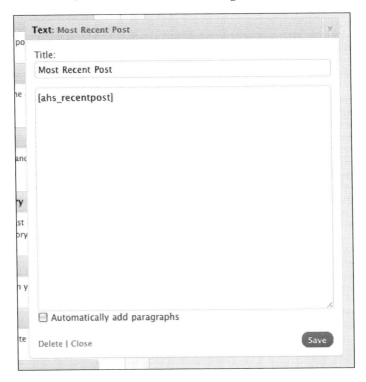

Then all that would show is the shortcode itself:

Add a single line to your `functions.php` file (or plugin or widget file):

```
add_filter('widget_text', 'do_shortcode');
```

And now all shortcodes on the site will be evaluated in widgets:

Summary

In this chapter, you learned everything you needed to know about creating basic plugins and widgets. Now you know how to structure the PHP file, where to put your functions, and how to use hooks. You also learned about adding management pages and enabling plugins and widgets to have database access. On top of all that, you learned how to create shortcodes, a powerful tool that lets you make dynamic functionality available to all WordPress users. With your already-existing knowledge of PHP and HTML, you now have tools to get started with writing every plugin and widget your heart may desire.

9
Community Blogging

So far in this book, we've focused on looking at a personal website, one that belongs to and is used by just one person. However, many blogs are used in a different way—there may be a single blog or website with a variety of writers, editors, and administrators. This makes the site more like a community project or even an online magazine.

In this chapter, we'll discuss allowing a blog to have multiple authors with differing levels of control over blog administration and content. We'll explore user management for multiple users on one blog, as well as other aspects of blogging as a member of a community. We'll also take some time to look at using a non-blog website with multiple users.

As of WordPress 3.0, multi-blog capability is now built into Wordpress directly (previously, it was necessary to set up a separate piece of software, named WordPress MU (multi-user)). We'll touch on this topic briefly in this chapter as well.

Concerns for a multiuser blog

A multiuser blog is useful when a group of people with similar interests want to collaborate and share space to publish their writing, or if an organization or company wants to have an online magazine. If that group wants to publish news on a particular topic, or on many topics in a broad sense, then they'll each need to be able to log in and post their content, update their profile, and so on. For example, I can decide that I want every member of my family to be able to contribute to my Daily Cooking blog. Each of my sisters and brothers and cousins and aunts and uncles can add their recipes and discoveries regarding food, which has the potential to make my food blog a richer and more exciting place for visitors.

However, content moderation is also of essential importance to a multiuser blog. The best way to keep a blog clean and on topic is by using a moderation flow that restricts the display of content until it travels through an approval process.

Users roles and abilities

WordPress includes the ability to have an unlimited number of users. Each of the users can be assigned one of the five roles. Let's look at these roles one at a time, starting with the most powerful.

Administrator

When you installed WordPress, it created a user for you with administrative powers. This role is called **administrator**, and every WordPress site must have at least one admin (you will not be allowed to delete them all). As you have already seen in the earlier chapters, administrators can do everything.

 The **administrator's** primary purpose is to manage everything about the website.

In general, you're not going to want to have a lot of administrators on a single blog or website. It is best to keep just one administrator for a blog with 10 to 20 authors and editors or perhaps up to three administrators for a blog with dozens of users.

Some examples of actions that only a user with an administrator role can take are:

- Switch blog theme
- Add, edit, activate, or deactivate plugins
- Add, edit, or delete users
- Manage general blog options and settings

Editor

After the administrator, the editor has the most powerful role. This role is for users who need to manage everything about the content of a website, but don't need to be able to change the basic structure, design or functionality of the blog itself (that's for administrators).

 The **editor's** primary purpose is to manage all of the content of the blog.

To get an idea of how the screen looks when a user logs in as an editor, let's take a look at the editor's menu (on the right) in comparison with the administrator's menu (on the left):

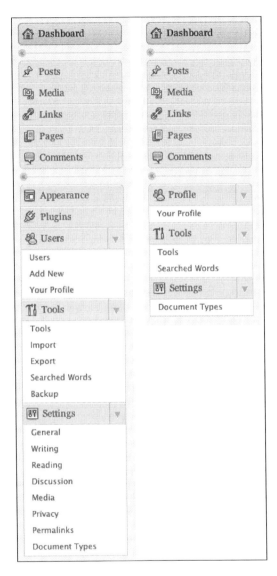

As you can see, the top section is unchanged. However, nearly the entire bottom menu, with **Appearance**, **Plugins**, **Users** (which is replaced by **Profile**), and **Settings**, has disappeared. We can see that the editor is left only with the ability to edit his or her own profile, and to access the **Tools** section, which includes any plugin pages that allow editor-level access (for example, **Searched Words**, **Document Types**).

The examples of actions that a user with an editor role can take are:

- Moderate comments
- Manage categories and links
- Edit other users' content

Author

Authors have much less access than editors. Authors can add and edit their own posts, and manage posts made by their subordinates. However, they can neither edit posts made by other authors, nor manage comments on posts that don't belong to them.

 The **author**'s primary purpose is to manage his or her own content.

To get an idea of the experience of a user with an author role, let's take a look at the author's menu (on the right) in comparison with the editor's menu (on the left):

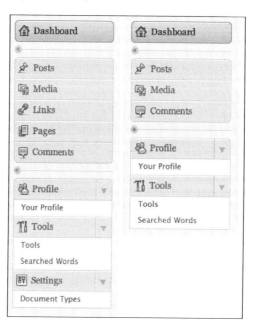

As you can see, the **Links** and **Pages** sections have disappeared, and so has the management page, which was available to editors (**Document Types**). The **Tags** and **Categories** sublinks have also disappeared. Additionally, if the author looks at the complete list of posts, he or she will only have the ability to **View**, and not **Edit**, **Quick Edit**, or **Delete**, posts that he or she did not author:

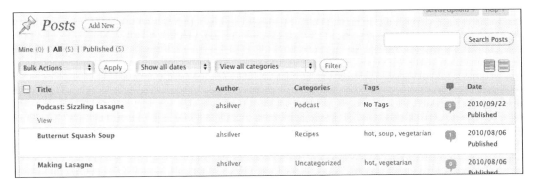

Contributor

Contributors are only able to write posts and submit them for review. These posts will be in **Pending Review** status until an author, editor, or administrator publishes them. Contributors cannot upload images or other files, cannot view the media library, add categories, and edit comments, or any of the other tasks available to more advanced users.

 The **contributor**'s primary purpose is to submit content for consideration.

Subscriber

Subscribers have no ability to do anything at all. They can log in and edit their profile, that's it. Depending on the permissions set in **Settings | Discussion**, blog visitors may have to sign up as subscribers in order to be able to post comments. Also, there are some plugins that handle sending informational updates to subscribers, such as newsletters or e-mail notifications of new posts.

Managing users

To manage users, log in (as an administrator, of course) and navigate to **Users**. You'll see a list of your existing users:

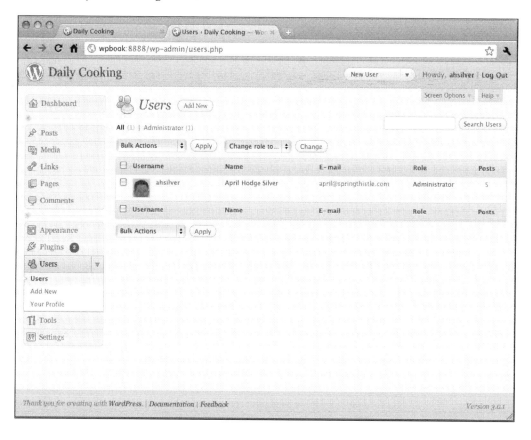

When we installed WordPress, it created only your first user (which is how you've been logging in all this time). Let's create a new user, and assign that user the next most powerful role of editor. To do this, navigate to **Users | Add New**. You'll see the **Add New User** form:

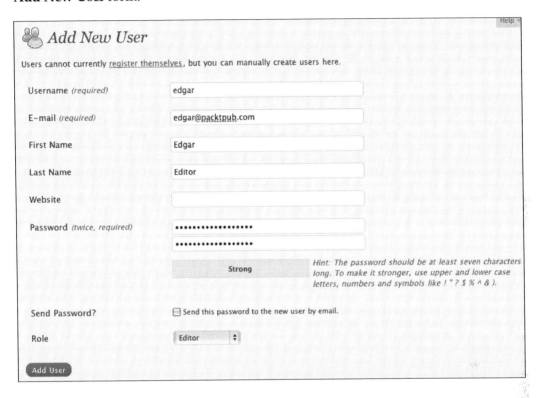

As you can see, only the **Username**, **E-mail** address, and **Password** are required. You can also change the **Role** from the default (**Subscriber**) to one of the other roles. In this case, I've selected **Editor**. Then, I click on the **Add User** button.

I can repeat this process to add an author, a contributor and a subscriber. When I'm done, the **Users** page (where the users can be managed) will look like this:

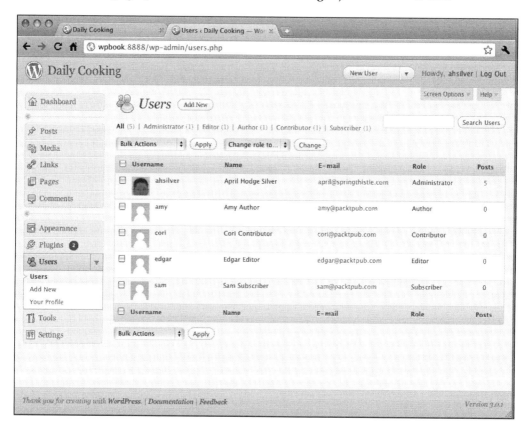

As with any other management list in WP Admin, you can roll over a row to see the management links. In this case, you can **Edit** or **Delete** users. You can use the checkboxes and the **Bulk Actions** menu, or use the filter links to view only users with particular roles. You can change the role of one or more users on this page by checking the box (or boxes) and using the **Change role to...** drop-down menu.

Enabling users to self-register

Adding users yourself is not the only way to add users to your WordPress website. You can also give your users the ability to register themselves. First, navigate to **Settings | General** and make sure you've checked **Anyone can register** next to **Membership**:

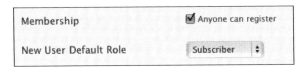

I strongly recommend leaving **New User Default Role** as **Subscriber**, though **Contributor** could also be fine if the purpose of your blog requires it. However, allowing new users to automatically be assigned a role with more power than that is just asking for trouble.

Next, add a link somewhere on your blog that links users to the login and registration pages. The easiest way to do this is to use the widget named **Meta**, which comes with your WordPress installation. It will add a widget to your sidebar with a few useful links, including **Log in** and **Register**.

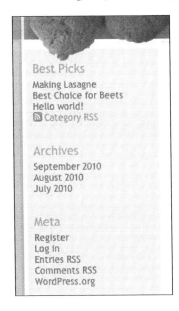

Of course, if this is not exactly the collection of links you want, you can create your own widget! Users clicking on **Register** will be taken to the following basic registration page that asks for only **Username** and **E-mail**:

After submitting this form, the user will be e-mailed a password, and the main site administrator will be sent an e-mail notification of the new registration. The user can now log in and edit his/her profile, or do more if an administrator changes their role.

Learning more

You can learn more about the built-in WordPress roles and capabilities here:
`http://codex.wordpress.org/Roles_and_Capabilities`.

User management plugins

At the time of this writing, there were over 100 plugins tagged **users** in the WordPress **Plugin Directory**: `http://wordpress.org/extend/plugins/tags/users`. They add functionality that allows you to do the following things (among many others):

- Send an e-mail to registered blog users

- Assign multiple authors to a single post

- Generate and display user profiles of registered users

- Restrict which categories different roles of users can use on their posts

- Track which pages your logged-in users are viewing

There are three plugins that people often find useful when a number of people edit a website, especially if they have a range of authority over final website content.

- **Peter's Post Notes**: `http://www.theblog.ca/wordpress-post-notes` allows each user to add a note whenever they edit a post.

- **Peter's Collaboration Emails**: `http://www.theblog.ca/wordpress-collaboration-emails` allows you to set up sending of e-mails (along with the note that has been included, via the first plugin above) whenever a contributor authors a new post, when the post is published, and if the post's status is changed again.

- **Genki Pre-Publish Reminder**: `http://ericulous.com/2007/03/19/wp-plugin-genki-pre-publish-reminder/` allows you to create a list of reminder steps to complete before publishing a post. This reminder appears on the Add Post page.

Even more powerful are the plugins that let you control what certain users are allowed to do within the WP Admin if the exact structure of the five roles WordPress offers you by default aren't quite right. The two most commonly used are:

- **Role Manager**: `http://www.im-web-gefunden.de/wordpress-plugins/role-manager/`. This very powerful plugin allows you to control exactly which of the capabilities each of your existing five roles has. For example, if you want your Authors to be able to edit other people's posts this plugin would allow you to add that capability to that role. It also lets you create entirely new roles. For example, you could create a new role named PowerAuthor that is also allowed to edit widgets.

- **Adminimize**: `http://wordpress.org/extend/plugins/adminimize/`. Without digging too deeply into the backend of roles and capabilities, this plugin lets you streamline the administration interface. You can hide certain menu items and also some boxes on the Add/Edit screens.

Creating a multi-site website

As I mentioned on the first page of this chapter, there used to be a separate version of WordPress named **WordPress MU** (pronounced myoo) that allowed you to create a master blog with many subblogs—essentially giving each user their own (limited) blog.

Well, as of WordPress 3.0, this capability is built directly into every download of WordPress, and just has to be enabled. If you go to the old WordPress MU URL, you'll see this:

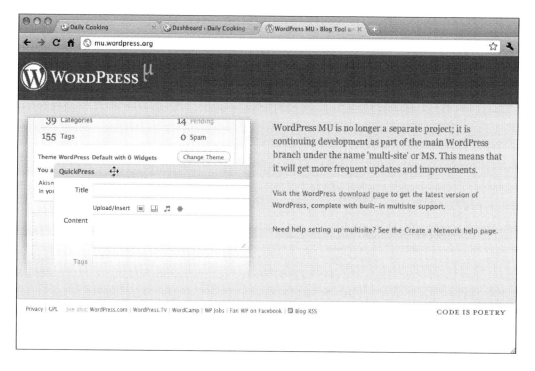

You may be wondering what makes a WordPress site, which can have multiple users, different from a WordPress MU site. WordPress MU is now thought of as MS, or **Multi-Site**, rather than multiuser. It allows you to have a main website and for every user to have their own subsite, which gets its own subdomain or subdirectory. As the administrator of the site, you can choose how much flexibility to give users:

- How much control they have over their own sidebars and widgets
- How many themes they can choose from (if any)
- How many plugins they can choose from (if any)

Websites that use WordPress MS include:

- `wordpress.com`
- `blogs.nytimes.com`
- `metblogs.com`
- `trueslant.com`
- `blog.mozilla.com` and more

A full discussion on setting up and administering the WordPress MS capabilities is outside of the scope of this book. However, you can find a thorough and helpful tutorial in the WordPress codex here: `http://codex.wordpress.org/Create_A_Network`.

Summary

In this chapter, we learned how to manage a group of users working with a single blog, which is a community of users. Community blogging can play an important role in a user group, or a news website. We also learned how to manage the different levels of privileges for users in a community.

In the next chapter, we'll walk through the process of creating a complete non-blog website from scratch.

10
Creating a Non-Blog Website

As you have seen while reading this book, WordPress comes fully equipped to power a blog with all of its particular requirements of post handling, categorization, chronological display, and so on. However, powering blogs is not WordPress's only purpose. In fact, there are millions of websites out there right now running WordPress where blogging is not the primary focus of the website. I myself have built many such sites.

A non-blog website is likely to primarily be a brochure website or an informational website. It may have an area (like Announcements or Recent News) that utilizes some of WordPress's blog functionality, but is primarily composed of hierarchical pages and perhaps even some other information.

In this chapter, we will create a theme and a complete non-blog website from scratch. We will focus on creating a design appropriate to the purposes of the website, implementing it into a functional theme, and we will even discover how to make a new type of information object using WordPress 3.0's new **custom post type** functionality.

Our client is a bookstore

For the purposes of this chapter, we are a website development company with a new client. Our new client is a bookstore named True to the Book, located in a fictional town (Speciality) in a fictional state in the US (HQ). They are a small, independent bookstore that focuses on books for children. They want to have a website where people can learn about:

- Announcements about events going on at the store
- Books the store owners recommend
- The store's history, location, and philosophy

They've asked for a design that is relatively clean and non-intrusive, easy to navigate, and not cluttered with too much stuff. They'd especially like to be able to update the website themselves, as they do not have the revenue to pay someone every time they need to add an announcement or a book or change their phone number.

The Design

In consultation with the store owners, we come up with a brand-new design for their website. Let's look at the screen types we've designed:

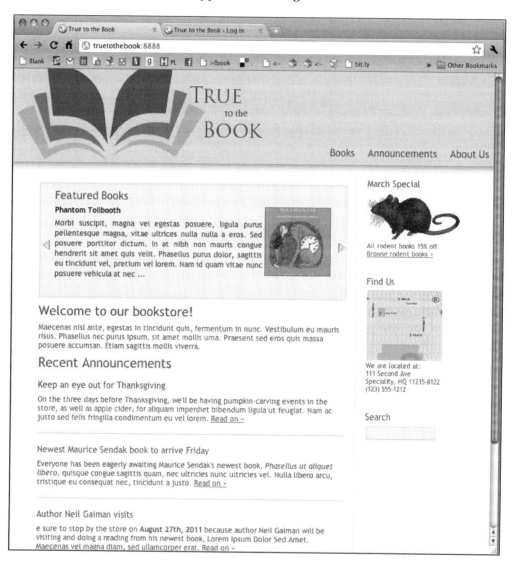

The homepage fulfils a few of the bookstore's requirements:

- A slideshow where the owners can specify a few books to feature, to catch people's attention and keep the site fresh.

- An introductory paragraph about the store.

- A list of the 5 most recent announcements.

- A sidebar with the monthly special, store location, and search. Right from the homepage, the visitor will have access to the information they are most likely to want.

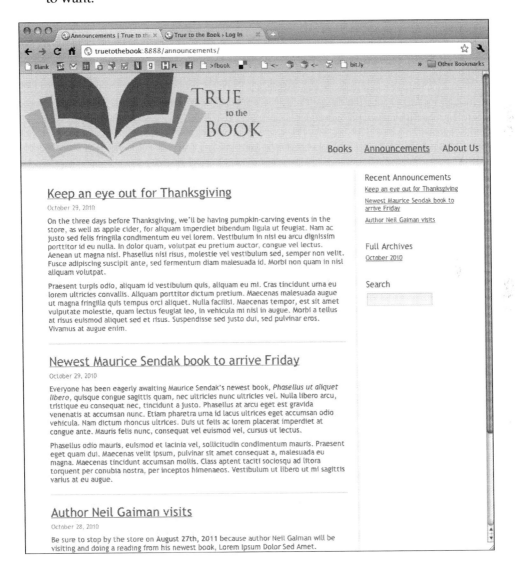

The announcements page has the following features:

- Announcements listed in reverse chronological order (like a blog)
- An RSS link to subscribe to announcements
- Recent archives in the sidebar, as well as the global search box

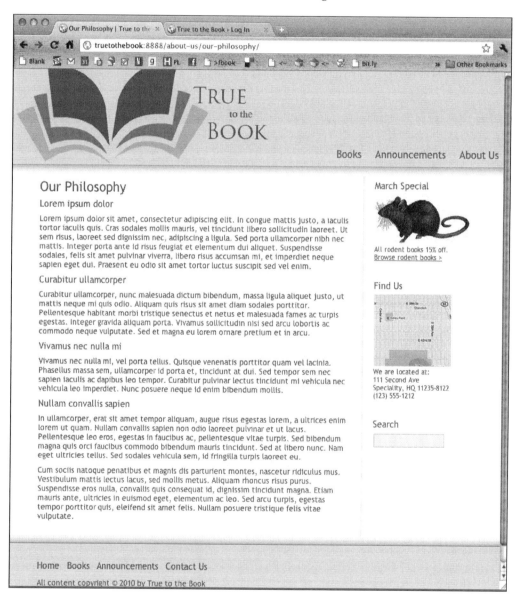

Every regular page on the site will have the same sidebar as the homepage, as well as the title of the page and its content; clean and simple.

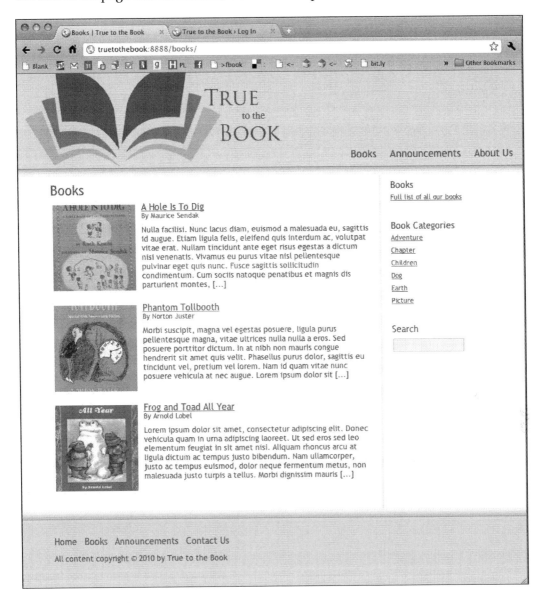

There will be book pages, one for each book category that lists the books, showing, for each, a thumbnail image of the cover, the book title and author, and an excerpt of the book summary. Clicking on either the cover or the title should take the visitor to the book page itself.

The sidebar, shared by both book pages and book category pages, needs to have a list of book categories to make browsing easier in addition to the global search.

The book page itself should show a larger version of the book cover, the author and title, the complete book summary, and also the categories to which that book belongs.

New features covered in this chapter

This chapter will involve making a new theme from scratch. Many of the features this new theme needs have already been covered in previous chapters (enabling a sidebar, common template tags, adding a custom menu to a widget, and so on). We will gloss over these briefly here.

However, there are a number of new pieces of functionality we have not explored in previous chapters, and this is on what we will be focusing. These include:

- Designating a template page to be the front page of the website
- Creating multiple sidebars
- Creating a custom post type with a custom taxonomy
- Altering custom post type display in the WP Admin
- Creating theme files for a custom post type

Before getting started, I strongly recommend that you get the code packet for this chapter. Included in the code packet, you will find:

- Initial theme
- Final theme
- Content export
- Book images for the three books
- Plugins recommended in this chapter

Let's get started!

Introducing the initial theme

We're not going to go over every step of creating the initial starter theme, because we've covered much of that functionality in previous chapters. I've included the initial theme in the content download for this book. Let's take a look at what we're starting with.

What we are starting with

In the previous chapters, we already learned the basics of creating a theme, starting with the stylesheet, index.php, and screenshot.png, and moving on to create the basic theme files (header.php, footer.php, functions.php, and so on). For the purposes of getting started with this chapter, I'm going to assume you can create those files on your own. In the code download for this book, the basic files have been provided, so you can download that, and follow along as we add the new stuff.

Initial theme files and functionality

The basic theme with which we are starting, which you can create yourself using skills from earlier chapters or download, has the following files:

- functions.php
- footer.php
- header.php
- index.php
- page.php
- style.css

as well as images required by the design and the screenshot.png. Except for page.php and style.css, which have nothing new about them, let's look at each file, and look at the areas with bits of code that expand on what we learned earlier in the book.

functions.php

In addition to adding theme support for custom thumbnails and automatic feed links, we've got code in the functions.php file, specifying navigation menu areas. These are like sidebar areas, in that they designate a spot where users can insert a particular menu they create. This code looks like this:

```
register_nav_menus( array(
   'main' => 'Main Navigation',
   'foot' => 'Footer Navigation',
) );
```

Our theme has two menu areas, one in the header and one in the footer. This code will put these two areas on the Menus page in the WP Admin so users can choose which menu goes in which spot. We'll see how to designate a particular spot in the theme when we look at header.php and footer.php.

The other important thing in our `functions.php` file is the code specifying three sidebar areas. In *Chapter 6*, we learned how to register a single sidebar. The `register_sidebar()` function actually takes parameters, like so many other WordPress functions. If you specify different names for your sidebars, you can have multiple sidebars. So our sidebar code in `functions.php` looks like this:

```
register_sidebar( array(
    'name' => 'Pages Widget Area',
) );

register_sidebar( array(
    'name' => 'Blog Widget Area',
) );

register_sidebar( array(
    'name' => 'Books Widget Area',
) );
```

(For this particular theme, I added some CSS-related code to the sidebars as well, which you'll see in the downloaded code. For our purposes here, however, it's not important).

header.php

The `header.php` file is mostly just HTML, though of course it has the WordPress functions `bloginfo('stylesheet_url')`, `wp_head()`, `body_class()`, and other standard ones we saw in earlier chapters. The only new thing I'd like to point out here is the `wp_nav_menu()` function, which looks like this:

```
<?php wp_nav_menu('theme_location=main&depth=2') ?>
```

We've passed it two pieces of information. The first is `theme_location`. This matches one of the two navigation menus we registered in `functions.php`, in this case the one we called `main`. The second argument is `depth`. I've set up the son of suckerfish mouseover CSS for this menu, but it's only configured to handle two levels of items. If a user puts in more than 2, the menu would look bad. `depth=2` tells WordPress to ignore third and above-level menu items.

footer.php

The `footer.php` file is pretty simple, being only 20 lines long, and most of that is HTML. One item in there is the second nav menu:

```php
<?php wp_nav_menu('theme_location=foot&depth=1') ?>
```

Almost identical to the one in the header, except for the different theme location and the depth of 1.

If you look at the CSS, you'll see that the website's sidebar is right here in the footer. I didn't bother to separate it out into `sidebar.php` because it will be included on all pages along with the footer anyway. In the sidebar is some conditional code that will tell WordPress which widget area to display depending on if the user is visiting a page or a blog-related page:

```php
<?php
if (is_page() || is_search()) dynamic_sidebar('Pages Widget Area');
else dynamic_sidebar('Blog Widget Area');
?>
```

The argument passed to `dynamic_sidebar()` tells it which widgetized area to show, depending on if the user is looking at a page or search results, or if the user is looking at an announcement or announcement archive. We'll be adding another condition to this area when we add our custom post type.

index.php

Remember that `index.php` is the file WordPress will look at by default for everything. This website will have only a few types of views, namely, pages, blog archive (the announcements), search results, books, and book archives. I'll be creating special templates for pages and books, so `index.php` will actually only be handling the blog archive and search results. It will therefore need next and previous page links, some code to handle 404 (not found) errors, and the loop.

There's a bit of conditional code I included in `index.php` so that it can handle search and archives just a little differently from single posts. This is simpler than creating `archive.php`, `search.php`, and `single.php` in addition to `index.php` when they are all nearly identical. Within the loop, instead of simply putting `the_content()`, we've got the following:

```php
<?php
    if ( is_archive() || is_search() ) {

    if (has_post_thumbnail($post->ID))
```

```
        echo '<a href="'.get_permalink().'" rel="bookmark">'.get_the_
post_thumbnail($post->ID, array(75,75), array('class'=>"alignleft")).
'</a>';
        the_excerpt();

    } else the_content('Continue reading &rarr;');
?>
```

This code says "If it's an archive or search results, display the excerpt" and "otherwise, show the full content". There's another bit of new code in the code block above, which references has_post_thumbnail() and looks like this:

```
if (has_post_thumbnail($post->ID))
echo '<a href="'.get_permalink().'" rel="bookmark">'.get_the_post_
thumbnail($post->ID, array(75,75), array('class'=>"alignleft")).'</
a>';
```

This code says "if there is a featured image specified for this item, print an HTML image tag for it at 75x75 pixels, with class alignleft". As we are planning to use featured images for our books, this will make them stand out in the search results.

Setting up the starter content

In order to be able to see our content conforming to the theme, let's start with some initial content and settings.

1. **Initial settings**. There are some basic settings that make sense for a non-blog website. After you've gotten a name and tagline figured out and set up your local time on the main **Settings** page, navigate to **Settings | Discussion**. The bookstore doesn't want to have to manage comments, so uncheck the box next to **Allow people to post comments on new articles**. You may want to change other settings on this page as well to discourage pingbacks, and so on.

2. **Sample post**. Delete the sample post and comment WordPress created when it was installed.

3. **Default category**. Change the category **Uncategorized** to **Announcements**; as the bookstore doesn't plan to have multiple categories, this should be the default.

4. **Create content.** Create a few pages and posts. Here are mine:

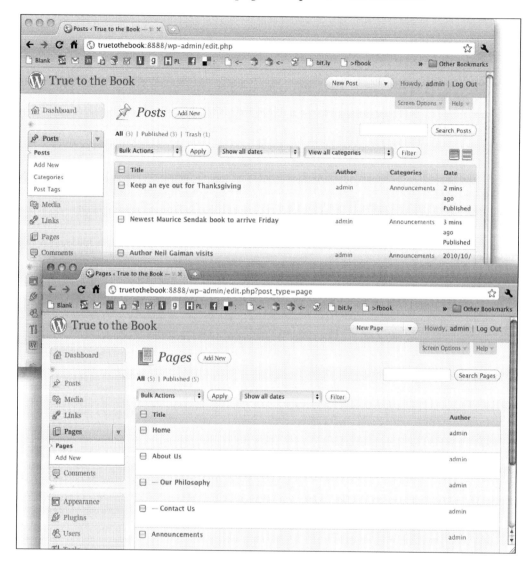

5. Under **Settings | Reading**, set the default page to **Home** and the default **Blog** page to **Announcements**. This way, people will see a page, the homepage, when they first come to the site, and not the latest blog posts. To see the latest blog posts, what WordPress thinks of as the blog main page, they'll go to a separate page in the hierarchy, the page you've named Announcements.

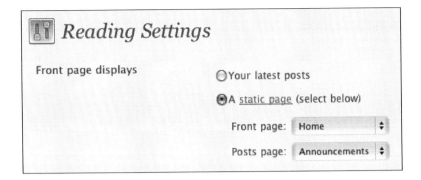

6. Under **Appearance | Menus**, create two menus, one for the header, and one for the footer, and give them to their assigned places. I named my two menus **Header** and **Footer**:

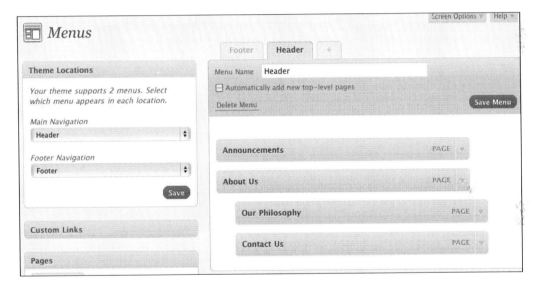

7. Under **Appearance | Widgets**, create a few widgets, and assign them to the two sidebars we are using. I've created three each for the **Pages** and **Blog** sidebars:

Checking out the frontend

With the initial theme and some start content installed, this is what our website looks like.

Homepage:

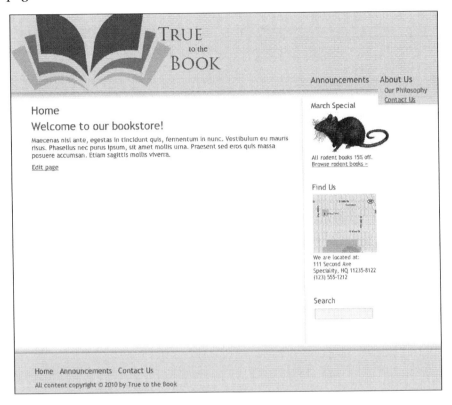

Announcements page:

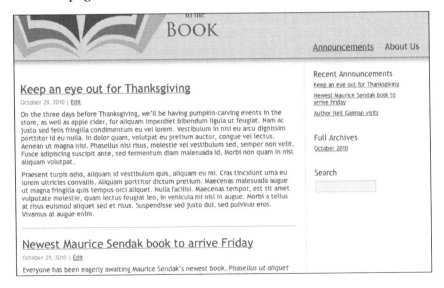

Search results:

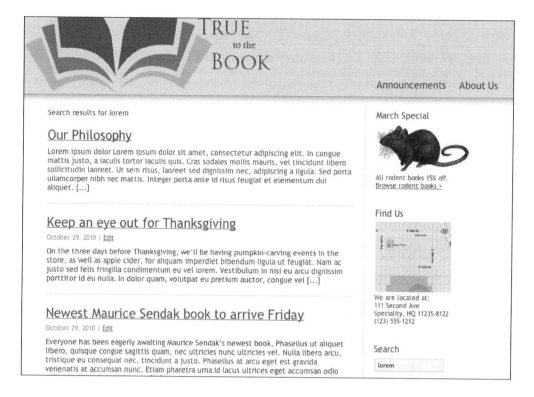

Adding plugins

Let's add some useful plugins to the bookstore website. The store owners don't want people to be able to comment on posts or pages, but they do want people to be able to e-mail them. They also want to show the most recent 5 announcements on the homepage, and they'd like a featured item slider as well. Let's take care of these one at a time.

Contact Form 7

There are many plugins that will add a contact form to your WordPress site, some of them very powerful. We are going to use **Contact Form 7** for this website, because it's relatively straightforward and easy to install. Download this plugin here: `http://wordpress.org/extend/plugins/contact-form-7/`.

Once you've installed and activated the plugin, navigate to its settings page:

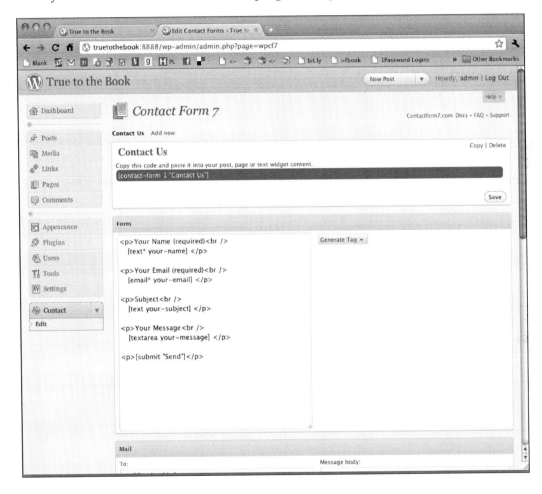

All of the default settings here will work just fine, though you may want to scroll down a bit and change the e-mail address if it's wrong. All you need to do initially is copy the shortcode at the top of the page (in brown), and paste it into your **Contact** page:

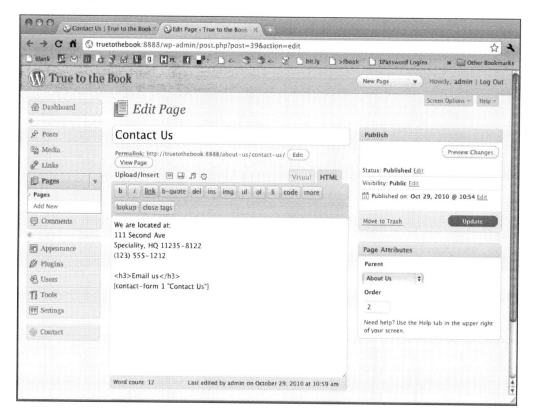

Update the page, and take a look at the contact page with the functioning form:

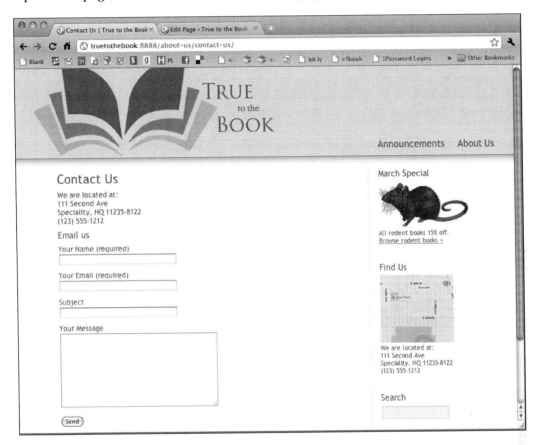

April's Call Posts

April's Call Posts is a plugin I wrote, because I found that a lot of my clients wanted to be able to include a list of posts on pages other than archive pages. This powerful plugin provides a shortcode that enables you to do just that. As the bookstore wants to be able to show its most recent 5 announcements on the homepage, it will find this shortcode useful. Download it here: `http://wordpress.org/extend/plugins/aprils-call-posts/`.

Once you've installed and activated the plugin, insert the shortcode into the **Home** page:

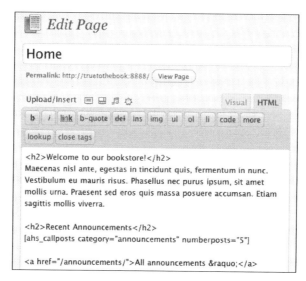

When you update the page, and revisit the main page of your site, you'll see the call posts' shortcode at work:

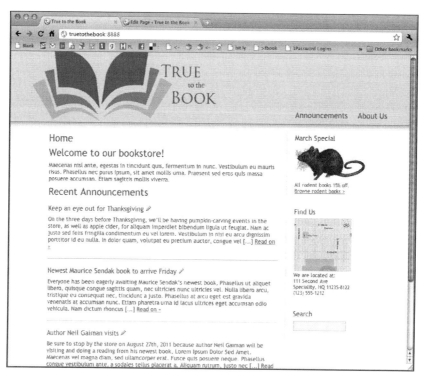

The little pencils are direct links to edit the posts; don't worry, they only show up if you're logged in.

Smooth Slider

The last plugin we'll be adding is named Smooth Slider. We'll primarily be using it for books, which we'll be creating later in the chapter, but let's go ahead and install it now.

Installing the plugin

Get the plugin here: `http://wordpress.org/extend/plugins/smooth-slider/`.

Once you've got it installed and activated, take a look at the settings page:

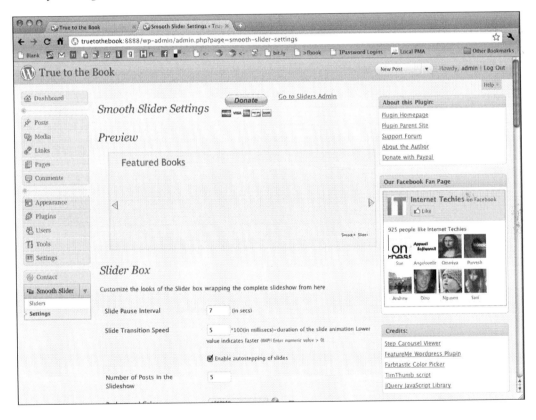

I've already changed a few things about the display like some colors, and the title of the box, and so on. You can leave the default settings or change the display as well.

This plugin adds a box to every Add/Edit screen in the WP Admin, allowing you to feature posts or pages. Just to get started, let's add a page to the slider.

Adding content to the plugin

Find the page you want included in the slider, and edit it. When editing the page, you'll see a new box below the content area:

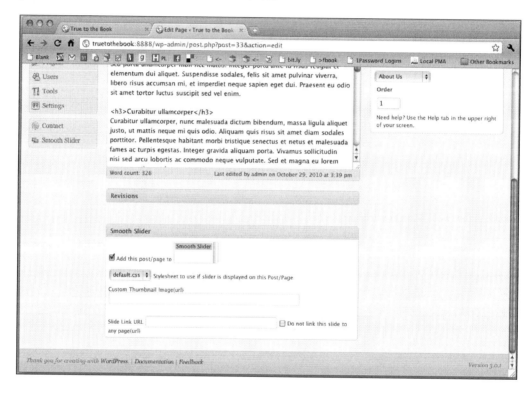

I've checked the **Add this post/page to** box and also selected **Smooth slider** in the menu next to it, and then updated the page. Do this for a few other pages or posts as well. When you revisit the Smooth Slider management page, you'll see the items you selected in the list:

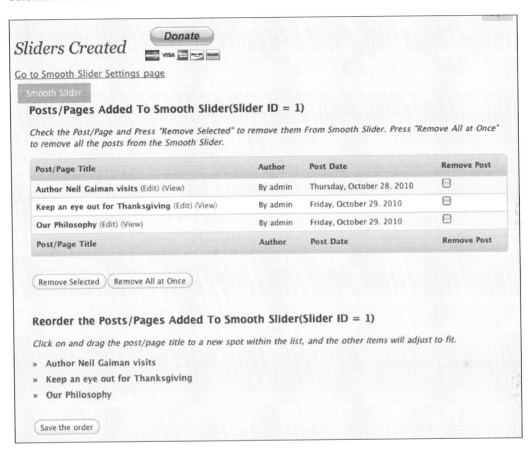

Adding the plugin to your theme

We'd like to show the slider only on the homepage. To do that, we just add some conditional code to `page.php`, telling it to detect if we are on the homepage, and if so, and if the plugin function exists, display the slider. Find your `page.php` file and right above the loop (`while()`) add this:

```php
<?php
if (is_front_page())
```

```
   if (function_exists('get_smooth_slider'))
      get_smooth_slider();
?>
```

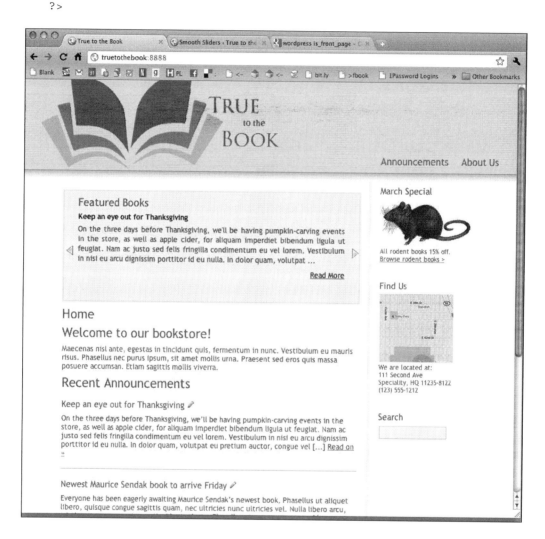

We've got a great non-blog website. It has pages and announcements and a customized homepage and two sidebars with different sets of widgets and two menus. Now let's move on to the really exciting page—creating **custom post types**.

Creating a custom post type: book

The custom post type functionality was added to WordPress in version 3.0 because people wanted to be able to specify new objects. The most commonly known objects are posts and pages, but there are actually already three other custom types in the WordPress backend: attachments, revisions, and nav menus.

We're going to create a custom post type named **book**.

To specify that you'd like to have a custom post type in your theme, you can add some code to your theme's functions.php file. This is what we'll be doing. However, keep in mind that you can also attach the custom post type to a plugin or a widget if you don't want it to be tied to a particular theme.

Registering a new post type

To register a new post type, all you have to do is add some simple code to your functions.php file. It's good practice to tie the creation of the new type to the init of the theme, so that it gets called a at good point in the booting process, so we'll use the hook for init. Your initial custom post type code looks like this:

```
add_action('init', 'book_init');
function book_init() {
    register_post_type('book');
}
```

The register_post_type() function takes an array as its second parameter, and in that array you can specify whether the object is public, whether it should be involved in rewriting the URL, what elements it supports on its editing page, and so on. Let's set up an array of all the arguments and then pass it to the function. Now our code looks like this:

```
add_action('init', 'book_init');
function book_init() {
  $args = array(
    'public' => true,
    'publicly_queryable' => true,
    'query_var' => true,
    'rewrite' => array('slug' => 'books'),
    'capability_type' => 'post',
    'hierarchical' => false,
    'menu_position' => null,
    'supports' => array('title','editor','custom-fields','thumbnail'),
  );
  register_post_type('book',$args);
}
```

I've chosen each of these parameters because they make sense for the book custom post type. Let's take a look at them:

- `public`. This means that the post type is available publicly, like posts and pages are, rather than hidden behind the scenes. It'll get a UI, it can be shown in navigation menus, and so on.

- `publicly_queryable`. This defaults to the same value as public, but I've restated it anyway.

- `query_var`. Allows queries to be made for this particular post type.

- `rewrite`: Specifies that the post type can be used in the rewrite rules for pretty permalinks.

- `capability_type`: On which of the existing object types will this object be based? In this case, it's posts.

- `Hierarchical`: Whether each item can have a parent item, like pages do.

- `menu_position`: This refers to the location in the WP Admin's main navigation menu. The default is "below comments"

- `supports`: This an array of the capabilities users see when creating or editing an item. For books, we're including four of ten possible items.

 These are just some of the arguments you can pass. Read about the others in the Codex: `http://codex.wordpress.org/Function_Reference/register_post_type`.

Now that we've got the basic post type set up, let's add some labels.

Adding labels

You can add labels to your custom post type so that WordPress knows what to say when talking about it. First, let's simply create an array of all the labels. Put this as the first thing inside the `book_init()` function:

```
$labels = array(
    'name' => _x('Books', 'post type general name'),
    'singular_name' => _x('Book', 'post type singular name'),
    'add_new' => _x('Add New', 'book'),
    'add_new_item' => __('Add New Book'),
    'edit_item' => __('Edit Book'),
    'new_item' => __('New Book'),
    'view_item' => __('View Book'),
    'search_items' => __('Search Books'),
    'not_found' => __('No books found'),
    'not_found_in_trash' => __('No books found in Trash'),
);
```

Then add a single line of code to the `args` array, telling it to use the labels.

```
$args = array(
    'labels' => $labels,
    'public' => true,
    ...
```

The next step is to add messages, which is what WordPress tells the user when they are doing stuff with books.

Adding messages

Whenever a user updates, previews, or does anything with a book, you'll want them to see an accurate message. All we need to do is create an array of messages, and then hook them in to WordPress. Here's the code:

```
add_filter('post_updated_messages', 'book_updated_messages');
function book_updated_messages( $messages ) {
    $messages['book'] = array(
        0 => '', // Unused. Messages start at index 1.
        1 => sprintf( __('Book updated. <a href="%s">View book</a>'),
esc_url( get_permalink($post_ID) ) ),
        2 => __('Custom field updated.'),
        3 => __('Custom field deleted.'),
        4 => __('Book updated.'),
        5 => isset($_GET['revision']) ? sprintf( __('Book restored to
revision from %s'), wp_post_revision_title( (int) $_GET['revision'],
false ) ) : false,
        6 => sprintf( __('Book published. <a href="%s">View book</a>'),
esc_url( get_permalink($post_ID) ) ),
        7 => __('Book saved.'),
        8 => sprintf( __('Book submitted. <a target="_blank"
href="%s">Preview book</a>'), esc_url( add_query_arg( 'preview',
'true', get_permalink($post_ID) ) ) ),
        9 => sprintf( __('Book scheduled for: <strong>%1$s</strong>. <a
target="_blank" href="%2$s">Preview book</a>"),
          // translators: Publish box date format, see http://php.net/
date
          date_i18n( __( 'M j, Y @ G:i' ), strtotime( $post->post_date )
), esc_url( get_permalink($post_ID) ) ),
        10 => sprintf( __('Book draft updated. <a target="_blank"
href="%s">Preview book</a>'), esc_url( add_query_arg( 'preview',
'true', get_permalink($post_ID) ) ) ),
    );

    return $messages;
}
```

This code creates a function named `book_updated_messages()` that sets up an array of messages and returns it. We call this using the filter for `post_updated_messages`.

Now, our custom post type is ready to use! Go to your WP Admin, and reload it. You'll see a new menu has appeared under **Comments**. It's called **Books**. Let's add a book:

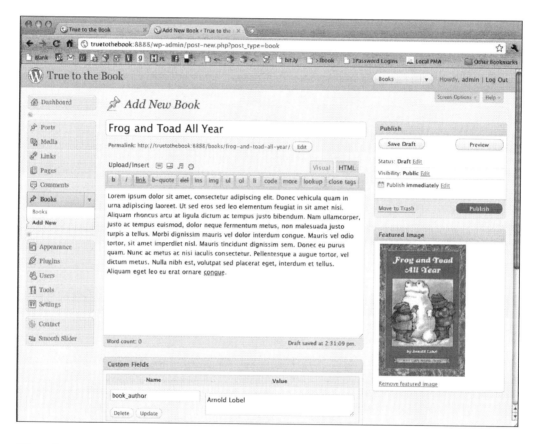

Note that I've given it a custom field named `book_author`, and I've also uploaded a featured image for the book cover.

I'll also add a couple more. Now, when you go to the main Books page, you'll see your books listed:

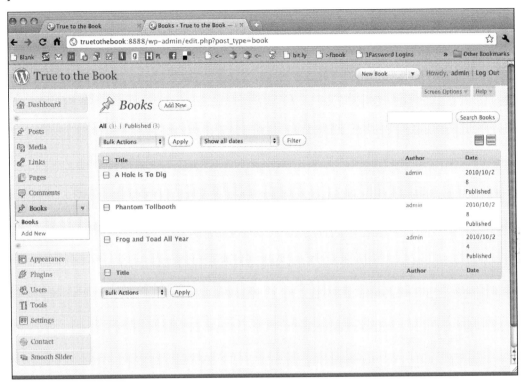

If you click on **View** for one of these books, you'll see the book displayed using the `index.php` theme template.

Let's make some new template files to display our books.

Creating book template files

WordPress needs to know how to display your new post type. We have to create a template for a single book and one for the list of books.

First we'll make a book version of single.php. It must be named single-post type name.php, which in our case is single-book.php. Using page.php as your starting point (as it's already the closest to what we'd like our book page to look like), let's add display of the custom field book_author and display the featured image automatically. The loop now looks like this:

```php
<?php get_header() ?>

<?php if (have_posts()) : ?>

    <?php while (have_posts()) : the_post(); ?>

        <div <?php post_class() ?> id="post-<?php the_ID(); ?>">
            <h2><?php the_title(); ?></h2>

            <div class="entry">
                <b>By <?php echo get_post_meta($post->ID, 'book_author',
true); ?></b>
                <?php if (has_post_thumbnail($post->ID)) echo get_the_
post_thumbnail($post->ID, 'medium', array('class'=>"alignleft")); ?>
                <?php the_content(); ?>
            </div>
            <div class="clr"> </div>
        </div>

    <?php endwhile; endif; ?>

<?php get_footer() ?>
```

Now, when you visit a single book page, the author's name is displayed and the book's cover shows up automatically:

Our next task is a page that will show a listing of the books, like `index.php` does. There's a problem, however. If you go to the domain /books, you get a 404 error. There are trac tickets for this, so it may be fixed soon. In the meantime, C. Murray Consulting has provided a great plugin that fixes this problem. You can get it here: `http://wordpress.org/extend/plugins/simple-custom-post-type-archives/`.

Once you've installed and activated this plugin, you can create a template file named `type-book.php` that will function as your listing of books. This will look very similar to `index.php`, except that you probably want to include a thumbnail of the book cover, the book author, and always just an excerpt of the summary. You can see the full code I settled on if you look at the code download for this chapter. In the meantime, here is the important part:

```php
<?php if (has_post_thumbnail($post->ID)) echo get_the_post_
thumbnail($post->ID, 'thumbnail', array('class'=>"alignleft")); ?>

<h3><a href="<?php the_permalink() ?>" rel="bookmark"><?php the_
title(); ?></a></h3>
    <small>By <?php echo get_post_meta($post->ID, 'book_author',
true); ?></small>

<?php echo the_excerpt(); ?>
```

Now, when I navigate to the main books page, I'll see them listed:

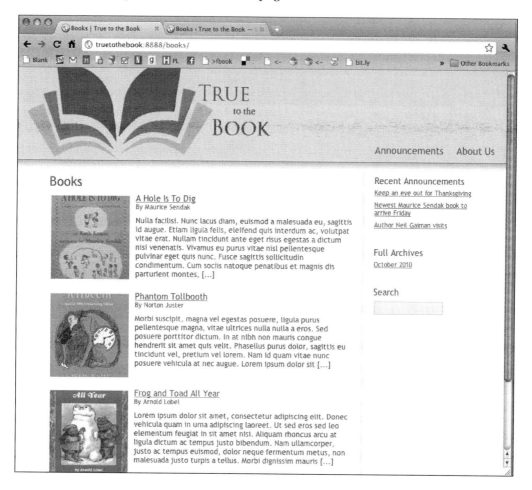

One thing that I'd like to change about both of these pages is to instruct them to display a book-specific sidebar instead of the blog sidebar. The first step is to add a function to `functions.php` that checks to see if we are looking at a book page. Following is the function:

```
function is_book() {
    global $wp_query;
    if ('book' == $wp_query->query_vars['post_type']) return true;
    else return false;
}
```

Now let's open `footer.php` and add some new conditional code. Add an `if` statement and an `else` to the conditional sidebar area, and now you'll have this:

```php
<?php
if (is_book()) dynamic_sidebar('Books Widget Area');
else
if (is_page() || is_search()) dynamic_sidebar('Pages Widget Area');
else dynamic_sidebar('Blog Widget Area');
?>
```

I'm also going to make some other changes now:

1. Add a **Books** item to the main navigation menu and the footer navigation menu.

2. Add a **Books** item to the **Books Widget Area**.

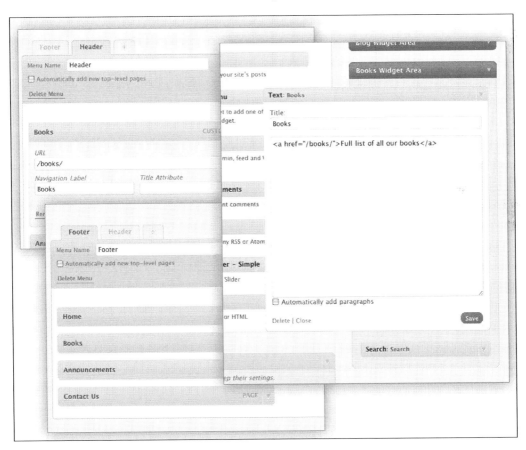

Registering and using a custom taxonomy

The bookstore wants to be able to categorize their books, and they don't want to mix book categories and post categories. Even though they are using just one post category for now (Announcements), they may need the flexibility in the future to add additional categories. So, we are going to create a custom taxonomy named **Book Categories**.

Add the following code to your `functions.php` file:

```php
add_action( 'init', 'build_taxonomies', 0 );
function build_taxonomies() {
    register_taxonomy(
        'book_category',
        'book',
        array(
            'hierarchical' => true,
            'label' => 'Book Category',
            'query_var' => true,
            'rewrite' => true,
        )
    );
}
```

Like the `register_post_type()` function, the `register_taxonomy()` function allows you to register a new taxonomy within WordPress. You can read up on the details of all of the parameters you can add in the codex (`http://codex.wordpress.org/Function_Reference/register_taxonomy`). For now, you can see we're calling it a `book_category`; it belongs to the object type `book`, it's `hierarchical`, you can `query` it, and it needs to be included in the `rewrite` of URLs.

Next, we need to make this taxonomy available to books. Simply find the `$args` array we used when registering the book post type, and add this item to the array:

```php
'taxonomies' => array('book_category'),
```

When you return to the WP Admin and edit a book, you'll see the Book categories have appeared on the right, and they are also in the main navigation on the left.

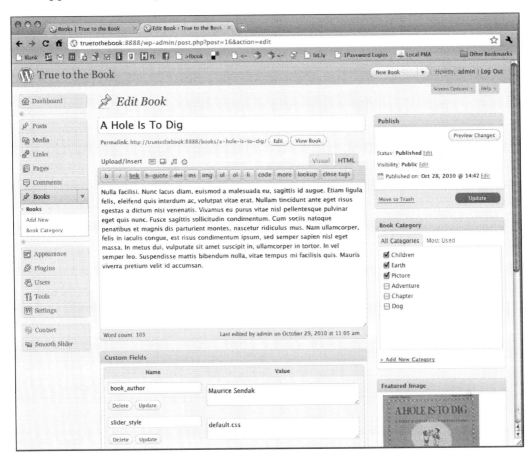

After you've added some categories and assigned them to the books, let's take a look at displaying those categories on the front of the website. First, we'll add them to the single book display. Open `single-book.php`, and add this code in an appropriate place within the loop, for example, after `the_content()`:

```php
<?php echo get_the_term_list($post->ID,'book_category','<b>Categories:
</b> ',', ',',','') ?>
```

You're using the function `get_the_term_list()`, which takes the following arguments:

- ID of the post (`$post->ID`)
- Name of the taxonomy (`book_category`)
- Print before the list (`<b>Categories:</b>`)
- Separate items in the list with (`,`)
- Print after the list ()

Also, now that you've got categories, you can visit **Appearance | Menus**, and add links to those categories to your header menu, and you can also create a custom menu with all the categories and add it to the **Books Sidebar**.

> Note that if, at any point during the creation of your custom post type and custom taxonomy, you get a 404 from WordPress when you don't think you should, then visit **Settings | Permalinks**. Sometimes WordPress needs to refresh the permalinks to make the new links work correctly.

Customizing the admin display

The final thing we can do to realize our new Book custom post type fully is to change its display in the admin. Books don't need to be displayed in the admin in order of post publication date. We don't need to know the WordPress user who created it, and we do want to see the book categories and the thumbnail. Let's go back to `functions.php`.

First, we'll change the default sort order to be `post_title`:

```
add_filter('posts_orderby', 'ahs_orderby');
function ahs_orderby($sql) {
    global $wpdb, $wp_query;
    if ( is_admin() && is_book() ) {
        return $wpdb->prefix . "posts.post_title ASC";
    }
    return $sql;
}
```

What this snippet of code does is create a new function, `ahs_orderby()`, that says "if the user is in the WP Admin, and if he or she is working with a book object, then add some SQL to the query for ordering by `post_title`". Then, this function is hooked into the `posts_orderby` hook WordPress provides.

Next, we'll change the columns that are displayed:

```
add_filter('manage_posts_columns', 'ahs_custom_columns');
function ahs_custom_columns($defaults) {
    global $wp_query;
  if (is_book()) {
        unset($defaults['comments']);
        unset($defaults['author']);
        unset($defaults['categories']);
        unset($defaults['date']);
        $defaults['book_category'] = 'Categories';
        $defaults['thumbnail'] = 'Image';
    }
    return $defaults;
}


add_action('manage_posts_custom_column',  'ahs_show_columns');
function ahs_show_columns($name) {
    global $post;
    switch ($name) {
        case 'book_category':
            echo get_the_term_list($post->ID,'book_category','','
','');
            break;
        case 'thumbnail':
            if (has_post_thumbnail($post->ID)) echo get_the_post_
thumbnail($post->ID, array('50','50'));
            break;
    }
}
```

The first bit says "don't show comments, author, date, and categories, but do show book categories and thumbnail", and the second bit says "for the book categories column, print the list of categories and for the thumbnail column, print the `get_post_thumbnail()` function".

Revisit the Books page in the WP Admin, and it now looks like the
following screenshot:

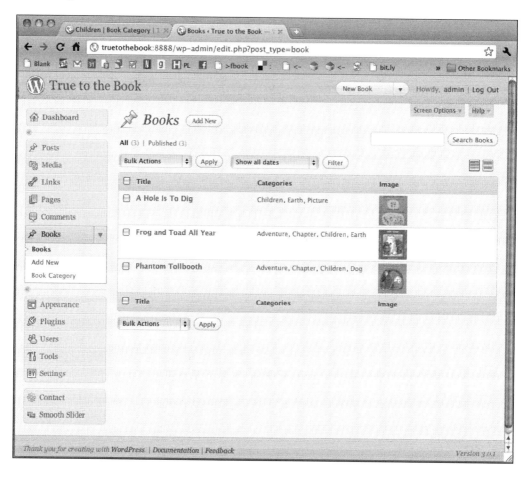

Finalizing the bookstore website

All of the coding for our custom bookstore is complete. The last step we should do
at this point is change the three items in the Smooth Slider from posts and pages
to books instead. Once that's done, the site is ready to hand over to the client.

Summary

We covered a lot of excellent material in this chapter. In addition to designing and building a basic theme that focuses primarily on non-blog content, we also created multiple widget areas, multiple menu areas, added a smooth slider to the homepage, used April's Call Posts to display a few recent posts on the homepage, created a custom post type and custom taxonomy, specified which sidebars should display under which types of conditions, and even modified the display of the WP Admin's books page. We created a complete, new, powerful, non-blog website. Be proud!

In the next and final chapter of this book, we'll cover some general maintenance and troubleshooting for WordPress administrators, as well as provide a list of useful functions, CSS, and template files.

11
Administrator's Reference

This chapter will provide information to help you with the WordPress administrative tasks. A few topics that have been covered elsewhere in the book are explained in greater detail here.

I'll review the essentials, and then give you some important links that you can visit for more details. This chapter is a kind of a 'cheat sheet' to which you can refer for quick answers to common administrative issues.

System requirements

The minimum system requirement for WordPress is a web server with the following software installed:

- PHP Version 4.3 or greater
- MySQL Version 4.1.2 or greater

Although Apache and Nginx are highly recommended by the WordPress developers, any server running PHP and MySQL will do.

 Learn more about system requirements at: http://wordpress.org/about/requirements/.

Your system will also need to be set up in a particular way if you want to use pretty permalinks, which give you nice-looking URLs throughout your site.

Enabling permalinks

If you want to be able to use the built-in WordPress permalinks, you must have an Apache web server with `mod_rewrite` enabled.

If you are using Windows IIS, there are still ways to implement permalinks; the most straightforward being to buy Helicon's ISAPI_Rewrite (`http://www.helicontech.com/isapi_rewrite/`), though you'd need cooperation from your hosting company. There are other ways as well; start at the following codex link. This topic is too extensive to be explored in depth in this book, but I encourage you to search the Internet for other people's solutions.

 Learn more about permalinks at: `http://codex.wordpress.org/Using_Permalinks`.

The importance of backing up

You never know when there could be a glitch in your server or a lightning strike, so it's a good idea to make regular backups of your site. There are a couple of approaches, which I will outline in the following sections.

Easy, quick, frequent content backups

The most important part of your site, and also the part that you will never be able to re-create is the content contained in the database. You should back up your database frequently. Exactly how often, will depend on the number of times you change your content.

If you're running a blog, do a backup whenever you've posted 2 or 3 new posts. If you're running a non-blog website, backup every time you make significant changes to your content or add new pages.

The question you should ask yourself is, "If my server or host completely fizzles out today, how much time would it take me to re-create what's not already backed up?"

Luckily, your website content is pretty easy to back up. You can directly export the content of your database using phpMyAdmin or any other database tools provided by your host. Even easier, install the **WordPress Database Backup** plugin. It's small, uncomplicated, reliable, and easy to use. You can download it at: `http://wordpress.org/extend/plugins/wp-db-backup/`.

Once it's installed and activated, you can navigate to **Tools | Backup**, and download a backup file to your computer. This plugin also allows you to schedule backups daily, weekly, or monthly. It is much easier to schedule a backup to take place once a month or week automatically, even if you update only sporadically. It is a good rule of thumb to have a regularly scheduled backup running no matter how rarely the site is updated.

Backing up everything

In addition to your database, there are other irreplaceable files that make up your WordPress website. These include:

- The theme you are using
- The plugins you've installed and activated
- The files you've uploaded

WordPress stores all of these things in the same folder named `wp-content/`. Every time you change your theme and install a new plugin, you should make sure that you have a backup of these things on your home computer. After that, you don't need to back these two things up regularly because they won't change.

However, the files you upload are a collection that changes over time as you add more files. If you add a photo with each blog post, then that collection changes as frequently as you post. You should be sure to create a backup of the `wp-content/uploads/` folder pretty regularly, which you can easily do via FTP. If you have an FTP program with a **synchronize** feature, then you won't have to constantly re-download older files, or do a lot of hunting and pecking for new ones.

If the thought of getting going with FTP is too intimidating, you can try out the BackupWordPress plugin. It will create archive backups of your WordPress files, as well as an SQL backup. However, I recommend this plugin with caveats only, since the plugin is still a) officially in beta, b) has not been updated since November 2007, and c) is officially only compatible up to WordPress 2.3.1. People with newer versions have had mixed success. On a bright note, as of this writing, I have been in contact with the developer and hope to look into helping get this plugin up-to-date.

Verifying your backups

Be sure to verify your backups! Every time you download a database export or use FTP to download files, make sure to take a close look at the downloaded files. Sometimes backups get interrupted or there are glitches in the system. It's better to find that out right in the beginning, rather than when you need to rely on your backups later.

Upgrading WordPress

In *Chapter 2*, we briefly discussed upgrading your existing WordPress version to the latest available version. In this section, we will take a closer look at the upgrade process.

What about the built-in upgrader?

As of WordPress 2.6, you can upgrade in one click from within WordPress. You can use the built-in upgrade to replace steps 3 to 7 in the following list, but you should still carry out the other steps. Also, the built-in upgrade does not work on all servers.

Do it gradually for a big jump

Something to keep in mind is that if you're upgrading from a very early version of WordPress to a very recent version, you should do it in steps. That is, if you find yourself in a situation where you have to upgrade across a large span of version numbers, for example from 2.2 to 3.0.3, I highly recommend doing it in stages. Do the complete upgrade from 2.2 to 2.3.3, then from 2.3.3 to 2.5, then from 2.5 to 2.7, and finally from 2.7 to 3.0.3. When doing this, you can usually do the full content and database backup just once, but verify in between versions that the gradual upgrades are going well before you move onto the next one.

You can download the previous stable versions of WordPress from this page: http://wordpress.org/download/release-archive/.

Of course, another option would be to simply do a new installation of the latest version of WordPress and then move your previous content into it, and I encourage you to consider this course of action. However, sometimes contents are harder to move than it is to do the upgrades; this will be up to you to decide your specific server situation and your comfort level with the choices.

Steps for upgrading

The steps involved in upgrading WordPress are as follows:

1. Back up your database.
2. Back up your WordPress files.
3. Put WordPress in Maintenance Mode.
4. Deactivate all your plugins.
5. Download and extract WordPress.
6. Delete old files.

7. Upload the new files.
8. Run the WordPress upgrade program.
9. Update permalinks and `.htaccess`.
10. Install updated plugins and themes.

Backing up your database

Before upgrading WordPress, you should always back up the database. If anything goes horribly wrong with your upgrade, you won't lose everything. We reviewed how to back up your WordPress website earlier in this chapter, so you can refer back for specific instructions.

Backing up your WordPress files

Remember, the complete content of what creates your site is contained not only in the database, but also in certain files on the server. Always back up all of your files as well, just in case something goes wrong with the upgrade.

Again, refer back to the backup instructions above if you need to review the steps.

Put WordPress in Maintenance Mode

If you think that visitors or other users will want to visit a WordPress site during the time you're upgrading it, you might want to consider putting the site into Maintenance Mode. This can be done relatively easily with a plugin like the following one: `http://wordpress.org/extend/plugins/maintenance-mode/`. It will show a splash page to non-administrative users while you're working on the site, and you can even set it to be active for only a specific period of time. If you don't want to use a plugin, there are other ways as well.

Deactivating all your plugins

The plugins that you have installed with your current version of WordPress may not work with the newest version of WordPress. Also, if you leave them active while upgrading, your new WordPress installation may break. So, before upgrading WordPress, you should play it safe and deactivate all the active plugins. If you're using the built-in upgrader, you don't have to worry about this step because the upgrader does it for you.

To deactivate plugins, log into your WP Admin and navigate to **Plugins**. Deactivate everything at once by clicking the master checkbox at the top of the table, choosing **Deactivate** from the **Bulk Actions** menu, and clicking on **Apply**.

Downloading and extracting WordPress

Now, download the WordPress ZIP file onto your computer from `http://wordpress.org/download/`.

After downloading WordPress, extract all of the files in a new folder named `wordpress`.

Deleting old files

Now delete all the files and folders of your previous WordPress installation except these:

- `wp-config.php`
- `wp-content/`
- `wp-includes/languages/` (if you have used a specific language pack)
- `.htaccess` (if you have used custom permalinks)

The easiest way to delete the files and folders that you will be replacing is to access your server via FTP.

Uploading the new files

If you're not already connected via FTP, connect now. Select all of the files in the `wordpress` folder on your computer, except for the `wp-content` folder, and upload them to your server.

Running the WordPress upgrade program

WordPress takes care of the next step for you: running the upgrade. This script usually takes a look at your database and makes alterations to it, so that it is compatible with the new version of WordPress.

To access it, just point your browser to your WordPress website, and you'll be prompted to do the upgrade. Alternatively, you can take a shortcut by going directly to `http://yourwordpresssite.com/wp-admin/upgrade.php`.

Click on the **Upgrade WordPress** link.

Updating permalinks and .htaccess

You may have to update the permalink settings so that they match the previous installation. Your permalink settings dictate what the .htaccess file should look like. If WordPress cannot access your .htaccess file because of permissions problems, then the permalinks page will display a message letting you know about it. That message will also tell you what text needs to be in the .htaccess file, so that you can create or update it yourself.

Installing updated plugins and themes

In your WP Admin, visit the plugins page again. If there are new versions of any of your installed but now inactive plugins, there'll be a note telling you so. If you have any plugins that are not part of the WordPress **Plugin Directory**, this is a good time to check the websites for those plugins to see if there's an upgrade available.

You can also take a look at the **Plugin Compatibility** lists on this page: http://codex.wordpress.org/Plugins/Plugin_Compatibility.

Once you're sure that the plugins you want to use are up-to-date, activate them one at a time so that there are no problems.

This is also a good time to check for updates for the theme you are using. In the wp-content folder on your computer (which you did not upload, remember?) there is an updated version of the default theme **twentyten**, which I always like to have around even if I'm not using it. You can simply replace the entire wp-content/themes/twentyten folder with the new one.

You can check for a new version of the theme you are using on the developer's website, or in the WordPress **Theme Directory**. Of course, you have to be sure you haven't made any theme customizations directly to the theme you're using. If you have, they will be overwritten when you run the theme upgrade. If you want to customize an existing theme, be sure to make a child theme (covered in an earlier chapter of this book).

Migrating or restoring a WordPress site

Sometimes you may find yourself in a situation where you need to move your WordPress website from one server to another or from one URL to another. Alternatively, if something gets fried on your server and is restored, you need to recreate your damaged WordPress site. Here you'll essentially need to do the same things as you would in a migration.

I highly recommend that you check out this page in the WordPress codex, which has detailed step-by-step instructions to migrate your WordPress website under a variety of different circumstances: `http://codex.wordpress.org/Moving_WordPress`.

This page will be kept up-to-date as time moves on. If you need to do a migration and don't have access to the codex right now, you can follow these steps for migration:

1. Download a backup of your database (as described earlier in this chapter, in the section on backing up). If your URL is going to change, you may want to use a different plugin to download your database. It's called WP Migrate DB: `http://wordpress.org/extend/plugins/wp-migrate-db/`. This plugin will change URLs for you (or you can do so manually, as described in step 4 below).

2. Download all of your files (as described earlier in this chapter, in the section on backing up).

3. Look in your downloaded files for `wp-config.php`. Find the lines that define the connection to the database.

   Edit these lines so that they now have the database name, database username, database password, and database hostname for your new database.

4. If your URL is going to change, and you did not use the WP Migrate DB plugin, do this: Open the SQL file that you downloaded in a text editor, and do a global search for your old URL to replace it with the new one. Save the changes.

5. Upload all of your files to your new server.

6. Implement your SQL file in your new database.

7. Change the permissions of your `wp-content` folder if necessary, so that you'll be able to upload files without any problems.

8. Change the absolute path of your WordPress folder in the database. You can do this by running a PHP file inside your WordPress `wp-content` folder. The code of this PHP file is `<? echo getcwd() ?>`. Now, execute this file using your browser and grab the result. Then, run the following SQL command by replacing the old path with the new path on your own server, on your database:

   ```
   update wp_options set option_value='/new/path' where
       option_name='fileupload_realpath'
   ```

9. Log in to your new WP Admin, and check the permalinks. You may have to reset them if your `.htaccess` didn't come over properly.

You're done!

If you're restoring your site on the same server, with no changes in the location or the database, then you can skip steps 3, 4, and 8. Steps 1 and 2 (to back up) should be done before the meltdown!

Setting file permissions

To install and maintain WordPress properly, you may need to change permissions to different files and folders in the WordPress folder so that uploads and built-in updates will work from within WordPress. Usually, this affects people on Unix servers, though it affects some Windows servers as well.

What are file permissions?

File permissions are settings that indicate who is allowed to do what. That is, some users may have permission to alter the contents of a file, some may have permission to only read it, and some may not even have read/write access. In addition to read/write permissions, there are also "execute" permissions. If a file is executable, then this permission indicates who can execute that file.

For Unix file permissions at a glance, look at the following chart:

File/Folder	Owner permission	Group permission	User permission	Total	Numerical equivalent
/	rwx	rw	rw	rwxrw-rw-	766
/.htaccess	rwx	rw	rw	rwxrw-rw-	766
/wp-admin	rwx	r--	r--	rwxr--r--	744
/wp-includes	rwx	r--	r--	rwxr--r--	744
/wp-content	rwx	rwx	rw-	rwxrwxrw-	776
/wp-content/ themes	rwx	rwx	rw-	rwxrwxrw-	776
/wp-content/ plugins	rwx	rw-	rw-	rwxrw-rw-	766

Permissions for WordPress

The best permission scheme for a WordPress installation is for all of the files to be owned by your user (your server's user, not your WordPress user), and be writable by your user. On top of that, any file that WordPress will need to modify (such as just about anything in wp-content) should be group-owned by both your user and the webserver's user (often called dhapache or nobody).

If you've installed your own WordPress website yourself, then you shouldn't need to modify any permissions for all WordPress functionality to work.

If you're having trouble using the built-in upgrader or plugin installer, do not chmod everything to 777 (world-writable). Instead, check with the hosting provider or people who run your server, and ask what they recommend.

How to set permissions

You can change permissions to files and folders using any FTP client. If you have shell access, you can use shell commands to change file permissions. If you're using an FTP client, select the files you want to change permissions for and look for menus like **Get Info**, **File Attributes**, or **Change Permissions**. There will be a GUI, often with checkboxes, that lets you choose permissions for different files. Some hosting control panels, such as Fantastico for example, allow you to change permissions through the control panel itself.

If you are using shell, change the file permissions with the chmod command. For example, the wp-admin folder should be set as rwxr--r-- or 744; and to change the permissions for the wp-admin/ folder, run the following command:

```
chmod -R wp-admin 744
```

 Learn more about WordPress and file permissions at: http://codex.wordpress.org/Changing_File_Permissions.

Troubleshooting

In this section, we will discuss problems that may arise during installation and execution of WordPress, and provide solutions for troubleshooting them.

Troubleshooting during installation

Most of the problems discussed here have been taken from the WordPress installation **FAQs (Frequently Asked Questions)** and **Troubleshooting FAQs**.

Headers already sent

Problem : When you point your browser at your website, you may get an error that displays a **headers already sent** message on your page. The whole page may look scrambled, and it will not function.

Cause: WordPress uses PHP session functions. If anything is sent by the server to the browser before these session functions, even if just a blank space, then the session functions will not work properly.

Solution: You have to figure out where the error lies. Usually, it is a file that you have edited manually. If you remember, you edited the `wp-config.php` file while installing WordPress. Open the file with your text editor, and make sure that there is nothing before `<?php` in the first line or after `?>` in the last line.

Page comes with only PHP code

Problem: When you point your browser at your website it displays the PHP code instead of its contents.

Cause: This happens when your server is not parsing PHP, but is instead treating it the same as any text or HTML file. This is a server configuration problem; either PHP is not installed on your server or it is not configured to function properly.

Solution: To solve this problem, contact the system administrator for your server or try installing PHP.

Cannot connect to MySQL database

Problem: WordPress cannot connect to the MySQL database, and is displaying an error.

Cause: This might happen if:

- The database parameters are incorrect
- The daemon/service is not running properly
- In MySQL Version 4.1 and later, the password encryption settings have been changed a bit, as a result of which PHP cannot connect to some versions of MySQL

Solution: To solve this problem, you can try the following:

1. Open your `wp-config.php` file, and check that the database parameters are correct.

2. If you are sure that these settings are correct, check if the MySQL daemon/service is running properly. If MySQL is not running, run this service. If MySQL is already running, try restarting the service. If you are not running your own server, check in with your hosting company's support people.

3. If you are sure that your database parameters are fine, and MySQL is also running, then connect to MySQL using your MySQL command-line tool and run these commands:

    ```
    set password = OLD_PASSWORD('your_current_password');
    flush privileges;
    ```

    This will use the old encryption of passwords so that PHP can connect to MySQL.

Basic troubleshooting

As you have probably already figured out, the best place to look for troubleshooting tips is the WordPress.org website, both the codex and the support forum. The codex even has a page devoted to basic troubleshooting: http://codex.wordpress.org/Troubleshooting.

If you're more technically inclined, take a look at this handy article on using the build in Debugging Mode in WordPress: http://fuelyourcoding.com/simple-debugging-with-wordpress/.

Below are some of the most common problems people encounter when setting up WordPress; if you don't see yours here, I encourage you to visit the codex.

Cannot see posts

Problem: Posts are not seen, and the message "search doesn't meet criteria" is displayed.

Cause: This can happen because of caching. For example, you have searched once, and WordPress stored the search result inside its cache; so every time you visit the page, you see the old result.

Solution: You can solve this problem by clearing the cache and cookies from your browser.

Making a site totally private

Need: If you are running your blog for a personal and private group (or for your own official department) so that only members of your group can see it, then you would want to secure it with some kind of authentication.

Solution: WordPress has no built-in facility to do this, but there are many plugins (such as **Members Only**) that will force visitors to log in as a WordPress user before they can see the site at all.

I don't receive the e-mailed passwords

Problem: You don't receive the e-mailed passwords.

Cause: This problem may happen if your web server has no **SMTP (Simple Mail Transfer Protocol)** server installed, or if the mail function is explicitly disabled.

Solution: Please contact your system administrator, or try installing Sendmail (or any other mail server) properly.

Tips for theme development

In *Chapter 6*, we covered theme development pretty thoroughly, though you can get a much more in-depth tutorial in theme development from the excellent book *"WordPress Theme Design"*, Packt Publishing, ISBN 9781847193094.

This section lists the top template tags and stylesheet classes that you'll want to have if you're going to be developing themes. These are the most essential (with some of my personal favorites thrown in).

Template tags

Following is a partial list of WordPress template tags. For a complete list, visit the Codex. This is a good place to start: http://codex.wordpress.org/Template_Tags.

In the list that follows, I do not cover the parameters that can be passed to these functions. You'll want to visit the Codex to find out about the default settings for each tag and how to override them.

The **header and informational tags** are as follows:

The tag	What it does
wp_title()	Prints an appropriate title for your blog (the post title, the archives title, the page title, or whatever is appropriate for the current page)
bloginfo('name')	Prints out the name of your blog, as specified on the main options page in your WP Admin
wp_head()	An essential part of the <head></head> tag, because a variety of things get printed out by this tag, depending on the details of the blog
bloginfo('stylesheet_url')	Prints out the path to the stylesheet of the current theme

The tag	What it does
bloginfo('rss2_url')	Prints out the RSS 2.0 feed URL for your blog
body_class()	Prints out a list of appropriate class names in the body tag. It should be used to replace <body> like this: `<body <?php body_class(); ?>>`

The following tags can be used **inside the loop**:

The tag	What it does
the_title()	Prints out the title of the current post or page
the_time()	Prints out the date and time of the post or page
the_content()	Prints out the formatted post or page content
the_category()	Prints out a list of the categories that belong to this post
the_tags()	Prints out a list of the tags associated with this post
the_author()	Prints out the name of the post or page author
edit_post_link()	If the person viewing the blog is a logged-in blog user, this tag will print out a link for editing the post (very handy!)
the_permalink()	Prints out the URL of the post or page itself (must be used within a `<a href=""></a>` tag)

The tag	What it does
comments_popup_link()	If comments_popup_script is not used, this displays a normal link to the comments for the post or page

post_class()	If you put this tag inside the `<div>` for your posts, it will generate a list of classes for the categories and tags that belong to this post. For example, if you put this in your template:
	
	`<div <?php post_class(); ?>>`
	
	WordPress will print something like this:
	
	`<div class="post category-recipes category-locavore tag-holiday tag-pasta tag-recipe tag-spinach">`

get_post_meta()	Use this function to get the value stored in a custom field. Just pass this function the current post id, the name of the custom field you want, and true to get the value of that custom field
get_the_post_thumbnail()	Prints out a complete img tag for the featured image

The following tags can be used for **lists and navigation**:

The tag	What it does
prev_post_link()	When viewing a single post, this prints a link to the previous post (the one with the next newest timestamp)
next_post_link()	When viewing a single post, this prints a link to the next post (the one with the next newer timestamp)
wp_list_pages()	Prints a list of all the pages in your WordPress site
wp_get_archives()	Prints a list of archives (by post, by month, and so on)

The following tags can be used to **include** PHP files:

The tag	What it does
get_header()	Includes header.php from the current theme folder
get_footer()	Includes footer.php from the current theme folder
get_sidebar()	Includes sidebar.php from the current theme folder
comments_template()	Prints the standard list of comments and comment-submission forms, unless there is a file in the theme folder named comments.php, in which case that is included instead
get_search_form()	Prints the standard search form
include(TEMPLATEPATH. '/filename.php')	Includes filename.php from the current theme folder

The following are some of the most useful conditional tags. Note that some of them *can* take a parameter, so be sure to look them up in the codex for details.

The tag	What it does
is_front_page()	Returns true if user is viewing the front page of the site, regardless of whether it's the most recent blog post or a page
is_home()	Returns true if user is viewing the main page of your blog, which can either be the front page of your site or the page you designated as the **Posts page** in **Settings	Reading**
is_page()	Returns true if user is viewing a page
is_single	Returns true if user is viewing a single post
is_archive()	Returns true if user is viewing an archive page of blog posts (monthly, yearly, category, tag, and so on)
is_search()	Returns true if user is viewing search results
has_post_thumbnail()	Returns true if the post (only parameter is a post ID) has a featured image or designated thumbnail assigned to it

Learn more about conditional tags at: `http://codex.wordpress.org/Conditional_Tags`.

Class styles generated by WordPress

WordPress helpfully applies classes to just about everything it generates, thus making it easy for you to style WordPress-generated elements on your page. Here is a starter list of those styles. If you want to know what the other styles are, create a templates and view the source of the page it creates.

Class or ID	Where to find it
`.page_item`	On the `<li>` of every page in the generated page list
`.current_page_item`	On the `<li>` of the current page in the generated page list
`.current_page_parent`	On the `<li>` of the parent of the current page in the generated page list
`.page-item-23`	On the `<li>` of the page with `ID=23` (there is one of these for each page) in the generated page list
`.menu-item`	On the `<li>` of every item in the generated nav list. As with pages, `menu-item-parent`, `current-menu-item`, etc are also generated for appropriate items.
`.widget`	On the `<li>` of every widget
`.cat-item`	On the `<li>` of every category in the generated category list
`.current-cat`	On the `<li>` of the current category in the generated category list
`.cat-item-13`	On the `<li>` of the category with `ID=13` (there is one of these for each category) in the generated category list
`#searchform`	On the `<form>` for the generated search form

Learning more

If you want a complete list of template tags, refer to the WordPress Codex at `http://codex.wordpress.org/Template_Tags`.

Summary

In this chapter, we covered many of the common administrative tasks you may face when you're managing a WordPress-driven website. This includes backing up your database and files, moving your WordPress installation from one server or folder to another, and doing general problem-solving and troubleshooting.

We also covered some of the most basic and useful template tags that you'll need when creating your own WordPress themes.

You should now feel well-equipped to address all of the more and less usual administrative tasks for your website or blog.

WordPress is a top-notch CMS, which has matured tremendously over the years. The WordPress Admin panel is designed to be user-friendly, and is continually being improved. The code that underlies WordPress is robust, and is the creation of a large community of dedicated developers. Additionally, WordPress's functionality can be extended through the use of plugins.

I hope you have enjoyed this book, and have gotten a strong start with administering and using WordPress for your own site, whatever it may be. Be sure to stay connected to the WordPress open source community!

Index

Thank you for buying
WordPress 3 Complete

About Packt Publishing

Packt, pronounced 'packed', published its first book "*Mastering phpMyAdmin for Effective MySQL Management*" in April 2004 and subsequently continued to specialize in publishing highly focused books on specific technologies and solutions.

Our books and publications share the experiences of your fellow IT professionals in adapting and customizing today's systems, applications, and frameworks. Our solution based books give you the knowledge and power to customize the software and technologies you're using to get the job done. Packt books are more specific and less general than the IT books you have seen in the past. Our unique business model allows us to bring you more focused information, giving you more of what you need to know, and less of what you don't.

Packt is a modern, yet unique publishing company, which focuses on producing quality, cutting-edge books for communities of developers, administrators, and newbies alike. For more information, please visit our website: www.packtpub.com.

About Packt Open Source

In 2010, Packt launched two new brands, Packt Open Source and Packt Enterprise, in order to continue its focus on specialization. This book is part of the Packt Open Source brand, home to books published on software built around Open Source licences, and offering information to anybody from advanced developers to budding web designers. The Open Source brand also runs Packt's Open Source Royalty Scheme, by which Packt gives a royalty to each Open Source project about whose software a book is sold.

Writing for Packt

We welcome all inquiries from people who are interested in authoring. Book proposals should be sent to author@packtpub.com. If your book idea is still at an early stage and you would like to discuss it first before writing a formal book proposal, contact us; one of our commissioning editors will get in touch with you.

We're not just looking for published authors; if you have strong technical skills but no writing experience, our experienced editors can help you develop a writing career, or simply get some additional reward for your expertise.

WordPress 3 Site Blueprints

ISBN: 978-1-847199-36-2   Paperback: 230 pages

Ready-made plans for 9 different professional WordPress sites

1. Everything you need to build a varied collection of feature-rich customized WordPress websites for yourself

2. Transform a static website into a dynamic WordPress blog

3. In-depth coverage of several WordPress themes and plugins

4. Packed with screenshots and step-by-step instructions to help you complete each site

WordPress and Flash 10x Cookbook

ISBN: 978-1-847198-82-2   Paperback: 268 pages

Over 50 simple but incredibly effective recipes to take control of dynamic Flash content in Wordpress

1. Learn how to make your WordPress blog or website stand out with Flash

2. Embed, encode, and distribute your video content in your Wordpress site or blog

3. Build your own .swf files using various plugins

4. Develop your own Flash audio player using audio and podcasting plugins

Please check **www.PacktPub.com** for information on our titles

WordPress 2.8 Theme Design

ISBN: 978-1-849510-08-0   Paperback: 292 pages

Create flexible, powerful, and professional themes for your WordPress blogs and web sites

1. Take control of the look and feel of your WordPress site by creating fully functional unique themes that cover the latest WordPress features

2. Add interactivity to your themes using Flash and AJAX techniques

3. Expert guidance with practical step-by-step instructions for custom theme design

4. Includes design tips, tricks, and troubleshooting ideas

WordPress 3.0 jQuery

ISBN: 978-1-849511-74-2   Paperback: 316 pages

Enhance your WordPress website with the captivating effects of jQuery

1. Enhance the usability and increase visual interest in your WordPress 3.0 site with easy-to-implement jQuery techniques

2. Create advanced animations, use the UI plugin to your advantage within WordPress, and create custom jQuery plugins for your site

3. Turn your jQuery plugins into WordPress plugins and share with the world

4. Implement all of the above jQuery enhancements without ever having to make a WordPress content editor switch over into HTML view

Please check **www.PacktPub.com** for information on our titles

WordPress 2.8 Themes Cookbook

ISBN: 978-1-847198-44-0   Paperback: 312 pages

Over 100 simple but incredibly effective recipes for creating powerful, custom WordPress themes

1. Take control of the look and feel of your WordPress site

2. Quick recipes to get started and successfully build advanced themes

3. Step-by-step instructions and useful screenshots for easy learning

4. Give a professional look to your web site with popular JavaScript libraries

WordPress MU 2.8: Beginner's Guide

ISBN: 978-1-847196-54-5   Paperback: 268 pages

Build your own blog network with unlimited users and blogs, forums, photo galleries, and more!

1. Design, develop, secure, and optimize a blog network with a single installation of WordPress

2. Add unlimited users and blogs, and give different permissions on different blogs

3. Add social networking features to your blogs using BuddyPress

4. Create a bbPress forum for your users to communicate with each other

Please check **www.PacktPub.com** for information on our titles

Made in the USA
Lexington, KY
25 October 2011